The Gusii of Kenya

Social, Economic, Cultural, Political & Judicial

Perspectives

John S. Akama

Nsemia

Copyright © 2017 John S. Akama

All rights reserved.

First Edition: March 2017

Published by Nsemia Inc. Publishers (www.nsemia.com)

Cover Concept Illustration: Abel Murumba

Cover Design: Danielle Pitt

Layout Design: Linda Kiboma

Production Consultant: Matunda Nyanchama

Note for Librarians:
A cataloguing record for this book is available from Library and Archives Canada.

ISBN: 978-1-926906-55-3

DEDICATION

To the memory of Prof. Joseph Nyasani

ABOUT THE AUTHOR

John S. Akama is the Vice Chancellor of Kisii University. He is the founding Principal of the then Kisii University College which he led to formally acquiring a Charter in 2013 to become a full-fledged university.

Prof. Akama did his undergraduate studies in education at the University of Nairobi. He then proceeded to the USA where he undertook Masters and PhD studies at Ohio State University and Southern Illinois University, respectively. On returning to Kenya he joined Moi University as a Lecturer and rose to the rank of Professor, teaching at both undergraduate and postgraduate levels.

Over the years, Prof. Akama has conducted extensive research and has published widely in diverse areas such culture, sociology, and tourism and wildlife conservation. His keen interest and research in the evolution, culture and history of the Gusii is reflected in this book.

COVER PICTURE

This is an artist's rendition of a traditional Kisii homestead.

TABLE OF CONTENTS

LIST OF FIGURES

ACKNOWLEDGEMENTS

Writing a book dealing with the history and culture of an indigenous African Community cannot be an effort of one person. There are many people, with shared oral and written knowledge of the Gusii community, whom I relied upon to develop this book. In this regard, there are many unsung heroes and heroines, especially the distinguished Gusii elders who were the depository and custodians of the Gusii history and culture, and managed to sustain the rich Gusii Cultural heritage, from generation to generation. I acknowledge, in a special way, that this oral history and culture forms the basis of the book.

I owe a lot of gratitude to members of the Gusii Council of Elders. Over the years, these senior Gusii elders have provided forums through which various aspects of the Gusii history and culture are enunciated. The many ideas on Gusii culture presented in the book originated from some of those cultural forums.

In addition, deserving special mention are the many scholars of African history and Gusii culture who are based at Moi University, Eldoret, whose initial efforts of developing a book on Gusii ethnography and culture are reflected in this publication. Similarly, warranting special mention is Robert Maxon, a distinguished Professor of African History at West Virginia University and one of the leading scholars of Gusii history and culture. Many of his wonderful ideas on the Gusii people are reflected in this book. Special acknowledgement also goes to Matunda Nyanchama for his role in tying the loose ends of this work.

I thank Margaret Barasa of Kisii University for having time to read the manuscript and eliminate typographical errors. I also most sincerely thank Jemimah Nyamweya, Edinah Maobe, Teresa Ntabo and Dennis Okinyi, and all the staff at Kisii University, Vice Chancellor's Office, for their tireless efforts in typing the many rough drafts of the book and providing efficient photocopying and bindery services.

Last but not least, I would not forget to thank members of my immediate family, particularly my loving wife Mallion Kwamboka, my two sons, Bruce Orang'o and Larry Otwori and my daughter Teresia Nyakoinani. These special people in my life have, over the years, tolerated my imperfections. They have always showered me with love and special words of encouragement, especially when the going gets tough.

FOREWORD

A people's culture and history provide the foundation upon which a society builds its unique identity. This gives a distinct bearing, which the people use to develop systems as they move forward from the present into the future and hence assure their survival, growth and prosperity. Consequently, it cannot be gainsaid that without proper understanding of one's past, lessons that can be learnt (both failures and successes) cannot be useful in building a better society. This understanding pertains to individuals, communities, even as a country, and relates to critical past events, cultural heritage, socio-economic and political governance.

As a Kenyan citizen, and a long serving public servant, I must concede that I have been shaped by a myriad of past critical events, cultural values and social attributes shared by the Gusii community (the subject of this book) wherein I was born and raised. These historical events were juxtaposed within the broader context of the Kenyan society and indeed, within the wider milieu of the forces of modernity and globalization.

It is some of these rich historical events, unique cultural values and social attributes that are captured in this book. Reading through the narration in this landmark work, one gets a clear understanding of various aspects of the Gusii way of life, how the people interacted and socialized amongst themselves and their neighbours, and how the people managed their natural environment.

However, it should also be stated that many of the Gusii social attributes and cultural heritage have, over the years, undergone rapid transformation as the Gusii people become part of the so-called 'global village'. As enunciated in this book, from the onset of the British colonial rule, the Gusii, as is the case with other indigenous African communities, were coerced, sometimes with the use of blunt military force, to shun indigenous social norms and cultural values. Furthermore, with the entrenchment of Western capitalistic principles, philosophical values and cultural orientation, many of the Gusii social systems and cultural values have been obliterated. Some have been wiped out while many others are fast disappearing.

In this regard, *The Gusii of Kenya,* serves as a depository containing the description, analysis and contextual explanation of diverse aspects of Gusii historical processes, social-cultural values and ethnographical trends that are fast disappearing without documentation for posterity.

It is an invaluable repository of knowledge, some of which could shape the present and future society. The work also underlines the need for the Kenyan people, especially the youth, to be inculcated with the diverse and rich histories and cultures of the various Kenyan communities. These form a mosaic of diverse histories, cultural values and social systems that collectively define our unique identity as Kenyan.

One should, however, avoid any tendency to romantize past social norms and cultural values as were practised by our forefathers and foremothers. There is a need to be pragmatic about identifying what from the past is of value today: that which advances the cause of humanity. We must understand that a people's cultural values and social-economic systems are not static. They continually evolve and adapt to emerging social, cultural and economic trends as society matches into the future. Clearly, there were and still are various aspects of Gusii cultural practices that may be seen as retrogressive and/or are at variance with contemporary ways of life and have to be abandoned.

However, wholesale abandonment of people's cultural values, and social norms and blind aping of alien cultural values, can have far reaching negative consequences as currently witnessed in many parts of Africa. As the Kiswahili saying goes, *'mwacha mila ni mtumwa"*. (i.e., one who abandons his/her culture/heritage becomes a slave of other people's cultures). It is in this spirit and foresight that I recommend this book to the broader Kenyan and global audience, and other readers who have an interest in understanding of the unique indigenous culture and rich history of the African people such as represented by the Gusii of Kenya.

HON. (DR.) SIMEON NYACHAE, E.G.H.

PREFACE

Kenya has 42 ethnic communities that range from the relatively expansive Kikuyu, Luo and Kalenjin communities, to the medium size ones such as the Gusii, Meru, and Kamba, and the relatively small size ones such as the Ilmoro, Orkiek and Rendille. The amalgamation of this mosaic of diverse indigenous communities currently forms the rainbow state of Kenya.

The promulgation of Kenya as a state was, however, not arrived at by a deliberate internal act of political agreement based on the free will of the Kenyan people. Kenya came to be through an external act promulgated by the European colonizers during the period of the so-called "scramble for spheres of influence" in the African continent in the late 19th century. Further, these processes of external economic control and socio-political dominance continue up to the present, albeit in a different and more subtle manner.

In their overarching imperial urge to subdue and eventually control the perceived virulent African communities, the British colonial government applied various methods and administrative strategies that included, but were not limited to the use of brute military force. They were aided by agents of imperialism, including the missionaries, pioneer traders and adventure seekers. Consequently, indigenous African communities were coerced and made to abandon their age-old and time-tested indigenous political, social, cultural, and economic institutions of governance. In the process they came under the colonial system of governance that was superimposed over the indigenous communities. In this regard, indigenous institutions of governance were at best perceived to be inferior systems that were to be urgently replaced with the 'superior' Western systems of governance. At their worst, indigenous systems were perceived as barbaric punctuated by retrogressive practices that were to be eliminated at all costs.

However, it should be stated that these political, social, cultural and economic processes of colonial dominance and eventual control were not always monolithic in nature. In many instances, indigenous African communities resisted the imposition of colonial systems of governance as they struggled to preserve their indigenous cultures. This sometimes involved whole communities rising up in arms to fight the colonial aggressors.

In this regard, many African communities were only subdued through brutal use of superior gun power that caused huge losses of property. This is in addition to fatalities that sometimes ran into hundreds (if not thousands) of African lives. This is what happened to the Gusii community when they rose up in arms to resist colonial rule in the early twentieth century. Thus, it is important to note that many indigenous African communities resisted colonial control and tried to preserve elements of their indigenous cultures against all odds.

It is within these persistence processes of perpetuating elements of African culture that this book has been written by an indigenous African scholar who, over the years, has traversed diverse ways of life that incorporate Western-based formal education and elements of indigenous Gusii enculturation that have been acquired through informal processes of interaction with Gusii elders and other members of the broader community.

It should, however, be noted that this book provides only a brief elucidation of complex political, social, cultural and economic processes of indigenous Gusii governance systems. It is within these cultural and historical perspectives that this book has been written. More so, it should be stated from the onset that most of the Gusii cultural attributes and ethnographic traits that are presented in this book are fast disappearing or have disappeared altogether. Thus, the book will serve as a depository containing the description, analysis and explanation of various aspects of Gusii culture and ethnography that is fast disappearing without being documented for posterity. In this regard, this book has been written with a broad understanding that a systematic presentation of the various historical and cultural elements of the various Kenyan communities such as the Gusii can play a critical role in promoting cross-cultural awareness and harmonious co-existence of Kenyan people who come from diverse ethnic communities.

This book has been authored for a broader readership by Kenyans and other people of goodwill who have got a critical understanding that it is through purposeful and positive engagement of people from diverse cultures that this world can be made a better place for people from all walks of life and cultures to live in a peaceful and harmonious environment. Thus, the critical questions that we should engage in include but are not limited to: What are the various ethnic communities that form the current Kenyan state? Where have these ethnic communities come from and what are their various experiences and cultural practices? Finally, how can we harness these diverse cultural practices and historical experiences of the various Kenyan ethnic communities to build a prosperous and harmonious nation-state? Of course, a book of this nature may not have ready-made answers to these critical questions.

On the other hand, notwithstanding existing problems and challenges that are common in any society, the Kenyan people should continue working together with a clear understanding that cultural diversity is not a weakness in itself but is a strength, particularly, if it is properly harnessed. Perhaps, it is in this indigenous cultural understanding and the urge to promote common Kenyan destiny that the framers of the Constitution of Kenya, 2010 have elegantly stated that: "This Constitution recognizes culture as the foundation of the nation and as the cumulative civilization of the Kenyan people and nation."

CHAPTER ONE

INTRODUCTION

The Gusii, as is the case with most African communities in different parts of the continent, currently, face a myriad of diverse problems and challenges. These challenges include (but not limited to): high levels of poverty and youth unemployment or underemployment, increasing levels of crime and general insecurity, social and cultural decadence and many other vices that are associated with modernity and Western capitalism. These social and economic problems are clearly visible to any casual observer conversant with what is currently happening in most African societies throughout the continent. Over the years, many scholars, particularly those with Eurocentric persuasion, have extensively elucidated on the sorry state of African affairs. Their general conclusion is that these problems and challenges have origins in the inherent inability of Africans to positively manage their own affairs and chart a sustainable way forward. It is, however, important to note that, whether these Eurocentric assertions are true or not, is not the subject of this book. This book uses the study of the Gusii people to illuminate various life attributes of indigenous African communities.

The Gusii community currently inhabits Kenya's south-western highland region, not far from the Tanzanian border and approximately 60 kilometres to the southeast of Lake Victoria. The study provides a systematic encapsulation of the Gusii indigenous social, economic, cultural, judicial and political institutions mainly covering a period of about 400 years.

Perhaps, more importantly, it should be noted that it had taken the Gusii people and other African communities, many years to develop and initiate various social, cultural and political institutions that they used to manage their lives in a sustainable manner. Consequently, it is clear that these indigenous institutions, over the years, served their various needs and demands relatively well. Furthermore, these indigenous institutions were time-tested and were not haphazard in nature, as many colonial and post-colonial scholars may want to belief. Thus, they were well thought out governance and resource management systems and strategies that had gone through various processes of evolution and development. These evolutionary processes had, perhaps, taken hundreds if not thousands of years to evolve, and were passed on from one generation to the other using various methods and/or processes of learning and enculturation.

1

These indigenous institutions were, however, not necessarily static as they went through various transformational changes depending on existing circumstances, such as changing environmental conditions, peoples' ingenuity, innovativeness, and various forms of individual and societal imaginations. In addition, the Gusii as was the case with most other African communities did not live an insular life, nor were they isolated from other neighbouring African societies. Instead, over the years, there were continuous socio-cultural and economic interactions, and exchange of new ideas and products between the Gusii people and neighbouring communities such as the Luo, Kipsigis and Maasai, who were predominantly non-Bantu. The various forms of social and cultural interactions were either based on long-term symbiotic co-existence between the Gusii people and their neighbours, or were sometimes based on existing short-term adversarial exigencies and/or both depending on the prevailing circumstances. In addition, through various processes of assimilation, adoption, and enculturation, there were always re-alignments and development of new socio-economic, political, and cultural systems and structures.

For instance, the Gusii people had long-term symbiotic relationships with the Luo and Kipsigis. From the time the Gusii first encountered the Luo in the early 17th century, at a place called *Yimbo* (present day Siaya County), the two communities started a long-term symbiotic economic relationships and social interactions that have lasted to this day. It is particularly interesting to note that in the more than 400 years that the Gusii have lived adjacent to their Luo neighbours, they have never had any form of long-term altercations and/or fighting. Instead, over the years there has been a positive cultural, economic, and political exchange between the two communities. A good example pertains to the language and the many Dholuo words found in the Ekegusii language and vice-versa. This is notwithstanding the fact that one group is Bantu and the other is Nilotic.

From the time of early European penetration into the Gusii region in the late nineteenth century, the Gusii were coerced and/or were unduly influenced by powerful external forces of modernity and capitalism (forces that originate and are conceived in the Western World) to shun their indigenous cultural values and social norms. In the process, they were inculcated into the Western cultural values and materialism. The Gusii, like many African people on the continent, were especially made to believe that their indigenous cultural heritage and practices were primitive and/or inferior vis-à-vis those of Western societies. In the process, they were made to adopt these Western socio-cultural values, in most instances wholesale.

Consequently, most of the socio-economic and political policies and institutions that were superimposed on African communities (including the Gusii) have over the years tended to recognize and reward people based on their acceptance of "advanced culture" (i.e., the Western way of life and material production). Furthermore, indigenous modes of production and technologies were rendered obsolete by colonial policies and institutions that sought to transform indigenous economies and link them to the global capitalistic economic structures that are mainly driven by market forces. In line with Western thinking, the large-scale production and mass consumption of goods and services was encouraged as indigenous people in the Third World societies adopted Western socio-cultural values and became dependant on Western modes of technological production. Thus, what the African people valued in their respective cultures was left to die as people shifted their perceptual preferences and socio- cultural orientation to Western modes of material production and cultural practices.

When reconstructing the Gusii history and culture, what is really interesting is the fact that although the Gusii were a Bantu community, they were surrounded by predominantly Nilotic communities, namely the Luo, Kipsigis and Maasai. It is also noted that over the years, the Gusii closely interacted with these non-Bantu communities involving economic, social and cultural exchanges. However, notwithstanding this intense social and economic interaction, the Gusii managed to retain their cultural and social orientation as a distinct Bantu community. These Nilotic neighbours, particularly the Maasai, were numerically and sometimes militarily superior to the Gusii. Notwithstanding those factors, the Gusii managed to hold themselves together and survived as a distinct Bantu community against all the odds that were stacked against them.

In view of the above, one critical question that can be asked is: what really made the Gusii Bantu culture survive for so long amidst all these threats of annihilation? Also, and perhaps more interestingly, in recent years, the Gusii have experienced exponential growth in their numbers. For instance, in the last 70 years, Gusii population has increased from a paltry 200,000 people in the 1940s to the current population of over 3.5 million people. This massive growth of population is unprecedented anywhere in the face of the earth. Consequently, it can also be asked: what are the main factors that have propelled the recent exponential growth of the Gusii population?

Another major contention of this study is the argument that many, if not most, of the current social, economic, cultural and political problems witnessed in Gusii land and, indeed in other many parts of the Africa, can be traced to the period of the conquest and eventual establishment of colonial rule over the African people in the late 19th century. However, in recent years, many social scientists and other researchers, mostly with Eurocentric orientation, have dismissed this assertion as being simplistic and/or naive. They argue that the binary approach to issues only manages to gloss over complex problems and challenges that confront many African communities, including the Gusii. For instance, they contend that as intelligent human beings, there is no way the Africans became mere passive objects or victims in the face of powerful forces of European colonisation. Instead, they argue, Africans were active and /or willing participants in the emerging colonial drama and, in one way or the other, they managed to define their own destinies within the various forms of colonial entanglements.

These forms of Eurocentric conception, however, lose the main point: that the establishment of European rule over African communities, including the Gusii, unleashed major and unprecedented forces of European imperialism over the African people. Indeed, the reverberations of these powerful transformational forces are being witnessed up to the present time. It is worth noting that, in most instances, the African people were coerced, through the brutal use of gun power, to abandon their time tested indigenous institutions, and were forced, in most instances, to accept the European modes of governance and capitalist systems of development. The effects of these powerful colonial forces are still being felt today in post-independence Africa, with the attendant contemporary forces of globalization and adoption of extreme individualistic-oriented lifestyles undergirded by wanton materialism.

Nevertheless, it should not be construed that the author is romanticizing or advocating for the total return to the by-gone indigenous socio-economic systems and cultural practices. In view of this, the main point of departure is that the Gusii and other African communities should rediscover themselves by identifying main elements of the overarching indigenous socio-economic, cultural and political practices as shown in the study of the Gusii. In particular, the people should make a concerted effort to discover and apply relevant positive aspects of indigenous institutions and socio-cultural values, and adapt them to their personal and communal lives. The ideal situation would be that, as much as the Gusii and other African people apply Western technology and scientific knowledge and skills to enhance their socio-economic well-being, they should also endeavour to understand and adopt their indigenous socio-economic systems and cultural orientation that can give the people unique social and cultural identity and promote a sense of pride and common destiny.

CHAPTER TWO

HISTORICAL EVOLUTION AND EVENTUAL SETTLEMENT IN GUSII LAND

Introduction

This chapter provides an anthropological and historical analysis concerning the evolution of the Gusii as a distinct Bantu community. It shows that the Gusii form part of the larger Bantu people whose original cradle land has been traced as far west as the current Niger-Cameron region of Western Africa. In this chapter, it is further postulated that it was from this original cradle land where several proto-Bantu groups evolved and gradually dispersed to broader areas of sub-Saharan Africa, occupying more than one third of the African continent. It was within this broad historical orientation and cultural milieu that the Gusii and other closely related Bantu groups such as the Maragoli, Kuria and Zanaki gradually dispersed and eventually settled in their current homelands in Western Kenya and North-western Tanzania, respectively. In addition, this Chapter provides a brief description of the location and geographical features of Gusii land, particularly, showing that Gusii land physiography is relatively mountainous and has got divergent and unique geographical landscapes. Finally, the chapter presents the original Gusii clans and the emergence of core Gusii clans.

Evolution of the Bantu: A Brief Overview

For a clear understanding of the evolution of the Gusii, their origin should be put in broader perspective of the evolution of the African people, in Africa in general and Eastern Africa in particular. The Gusii are part of the Bantu speakers, one of the major linguistic classifications of the African people. Linguistics has demonstrated that the ancestral Bantu language, proto-Bantu, originated in the grassland area of Cameroon and the adjacent Benue region of Nigeria in West Africa. These researchers base their argument on the fact that, linguistically, the current Tiv, Efik, and Duala languages of this region are the closest relatives to proto-Bantu. This provides evidence that this area was the cradle land of all Bantu speakers. It was from this region that the ancestors of the Bantu speakers dispersed and spread to wider areas of Africa (i.e. Western, Southern and Eastern Africa).

Ethno-linguistics has provided a relative chronology for the dispersal of Bantu speakers from their West African origin. Sometime after 3000

B.C., the first stage of the expansion began. The proto-Bantu speakers had knowledge of root crop cultivation and pottery making and thus were able to move south toward the wetter Congo basin. This Bantu expansion eventually became established on the savannah fringe north of the Congo River by about 500 B.C. During the second millennium B.C., the first differentiation of Bantu into eight sub-groups took place. One of the groups to emerge was the proto-Eastern (or Mashariki) Bantu. This group of Bantu speakers pushed into the tropical forest in the Congo basin. The group further differentiated and some moved into the great lakes region during the first millennium B.C. Some communities speaking Eastern Bantu reached the Kivu Rift Valley by 1000 B.C. (Shoenbron, 1998).

The spread of Bantu speakers to East Africa was aided by the domestication of plants and animals and the use of iron technology. The use of iron tools greatly increased agricultural production and encouraged the opening up of more virgin land for agricultural production and establishment of new settlements. It is important to note that the movement and eventual settlement of various Bantu groups in Eastern, Central and Southern Africa was a slow and gradual process that took many centuries. Anthropological and linguistic evidence indicate that by about 2500 years ago, various groups of Bantu speakers had taken residence in the Lake Victoria region. These came to form part of what is known as the Great Lakes Bantu. The earliest dates for the settlement of Great Lakes Bantu in the region to the West of Lake Victoria, provided by archaeology, range from 600 B.C. to 200 A.D. Subsequently, Great Lakes Bantu divided into several sub-groups including Greater Luhya and Eastern Nyanza. These Bantu speakers moved to the East, following a route North of Lake Victoria to the Mount Elgon area during the period ranging from 200 to 800 A.D. Although oral tradition suggests a close connection between the history of the Luhya and the Gusii, current linguistic classification places Gusii within the Mara sub-group of East Nyanza. The Gusii language has closest affinity with the Kuria, Zanaki and Ngoreme (Schoenbron, 1998).

It is important to also recognize that these Bantu-speaking ancestors of the Gusii did not move in a vacuum. People speaking languages quite distinct from Bantu also inhabited the Great Lakes region of East Africa. The Great Lakes Bantu languages contain loan words from Central Sudanic, Southern Cushitic, and Eastern Sahelian languages. This word borrowing formed part of the process by which Bantu speech came to predominate in the region. Bantu languages acted "like sponges and soaked up or retained the knowledge of preceding and neighbouring communities" (Schoenbron, 1998).

The process was, no doubt, complicated. It is not easy to say precisely whether the Bantu pushed aside earlier residents, absorbed those residents, or if the earlier residents adopted Bantu speech. Nevertheless, the interaction between people speaking different languages and following different cultural traditions played a part in the emergence of the Gusii and other Bantu-speaking groups of the Lake Victoria region as distinct language and ethnic entities.

****

Turning now to the traditional history of the Gusii, about 1000 years ago, the ancestors of the Gusii, Kuria, Suba and Logoli were living at a place called Goye, in the current Yimbo-Kadimo area. It can therefore be postulated that it was from the Yimbo-Kadimo area that the ancestors of the Gusii, Kuria, Suba and Logoli gradually spread and eventually settled in scattered areas in Urima, Ulowa, Sare and the Got Ramogi area in present-day Siaya County. It can also be argued that, due to many years of social interaction and acculturation, some of the pioneer Bantu groups were eventually assimilated by the Luo. According to Luo folk history, their ancestors had their first encounter with ancestors of the Samia, Bunyala, Gusii and Logoli in the Yimbo-Kadimo area over 800 years ago. Probably, it was in this particular region that the current Suba evolved into a distinct ethnic community from that of the Gusii and Logoli who remained together.

The ancestors of the Suba were the first group of people to disperse from the Goye area, taking a South-westerly direction, and they eventually settled in their current homeland in South Nyanza. Based on the reconstruction of existing folk history, the ancestors of the Gusii and Logoli for many years had close cultural and social interaction with the pioneer Luo ancestors, such as the joka-Jok group. Luo elders in the Ramogi area refer to the Bantu families that they found already settled along the Yimbo-Kadimo Hills as the *kombekombe* people. According to folk history, the settlements of the *kombekombe* stretched from the Yimbo-Kadimo Hills to the Usenge Hills in the South and to the slopes of the Samia Hills in the North. Interestingly, the current Kanyibule clan in Yimbo traces its ancestry to a subgroup of the *kombekombe* people who were assimilated into the Luo culture (Ochieng', 1974).

Apart from existing folk history, there is scant information on the forms of social and cultural interaction that existed between the ancestors of the Luo and those of the Gusii and Logoli and other Bantu families that had settled in this region. However, the contention that various Bantu families were dislodged and eventually driven out of the Yimbo-Kadimo region by the arrival of the joka-Jok group of the Luo should be treated with caution. Of course, situations of increasing human population pressure on available resources (as appears to have happened in the Yimbo-Kadimo area during this period) may have led to localized conflicts and skirmishes between the Luo and their Bantu neighbours. Each community struggled to replenish the supply of livelihood resources such as land, livestock and agricultural produce upon which each community depended for sustenance. In fact, these forms of resource use conflicts are documented in the existing folk history of the Yimbo and other Luo clans in Siaya. In this regard, it is appropriate to state that the long-term relationship that existed between the Luo and their Bantu neighbours was more of mutual and symbiotic co-existence than outright enmity.

Thus, it can be postulated that by 1500 A.D., the region around Yimbo-Kadimo and the Got Ramogi area was experiencing population pressure relative to available sustenance resources. As a consequence, various Bantu and Luo families decided to disperse to adjacent lands in Sakwa, Asembo and Seme in search of virgin lands for agricultural production and human settlement. It was in this process of gradual dispersal that the ancestors of the Gusii and Logoli moved from Yimbo-Kadimo and, eventually, settled in areas adjacent to present day Kisumu in the late 16th Century. However, due to unavoidable circumstances, the settlement of the Gusii and Logoli ancestors at Kisumu was relatively brief.

Gusii Elders' Narrative

According to existing mythology, as narrated by elders, the Gusii originated from a mystical place called "Misiri". However, the exact spatial location of this place is not known. When asked to indicate the exact location of "Misiri", Gusii elders simply state that "this was a far-off place that was situated in a north-westerly direction from the current Gusii homeland". Gusii elders further contend that their ancestors moved from "Misiri" over eight hundred years ago, taking an easterly direction. The Gusii ancestors eventually settled near the Mt. Elgon region in Western Uganda. Gusii mythology goes further to state that at the time the ancestors of the Kuria, Luhya, Meru, Kikuyu and Kamba ethnic communities whom the Gusii elders fondly refer to as, *abanto baminto* (our people) were together. Interestingly, existing mythology among other Kenyan Bantu communities also trace their origins to this mystical place. The mythologies are also, generally, in agreement with the Gusii contention that when their ancestors moved from the cradle land, they all belonged to the same Bantu family.

Based on these Bantu mythologies, one school of thought contends that "Misiri" is the same place as biblical Egypt in North Africa. This, however, appears to be very unlikely as there is no existing collaborative linguistic, archaeological or ethnographical evidence to support this theory. Consequently, it can be argued that although, in all likelihood, this mystical place did indeed exist, there is no collaborative evidence to support the theory that it is the same place as contemporary Egypt. Furthermore, researchers who have written on the history of the Kenyan ethnic communities have tended to create an erroneous impression of uni-lineal movement of people from one spatial location to another within a very short time frame. Consequently, the overall picture that emerges on the evolution of contemporary Kenyan ethnic communities, such as the Gusii, is one of the people were always on the move, migrating from one geographical location to another in a uni-lineal pattern and within a very short timeframe. Perhaps the underlying reason that has brought about this historical conception is the fact that most of the pre-colonial history of contemporary African communities has mainly been reconstructed using oral narrations, folk history and mythology. It should be stated that one of the main characteristics of folk history and mythology is that, although the overall information they contain may have elements of historical truth, in most instances, these oral narratives lack in detail and accuracy of explanation and presentation of historical facts and events.

It is quite common, for instance, that events which might have happened over 1000 years ago may be presented as if they took place the other day. This is mainly due to the fact that folk history and other forms of oral narration are usually based on word of mouth that is passed down from one generation to another. With time, however, human memory fades, and as a consequence, the exact detail and the chronology of events may be forgotten and/or inadvertently distorted. Thus existing oral narrations of the Gusii and other Kenyan communities that assert that it only took a limited timeframe of less than 1000 years for their ancestors to migrate from the mystical land, "Misiri" and settle in the Mt. Elgon region should be treated with a lot of caution. It can therefore be argued that the processes of migration and settlement of various African communities in Kenya, and indeed the whole of Africa, should be perceived as complex and slow processes of gradual dispersal, social interaction and cultural assimilation. These complex evolutionary processes took place over hundreds and perhaps thousands of years. Unfortunately, their detail and magnitude may never be known.

The Gusii as a Distinct Ethnic Community

The settlement of the Gusii and Logoli ancestors at Kisumu was short-lived. It probably did not last more than 30 years (one generation). The region around Kisumu (as it is still at present) was characterized by unreliable rainfall distribution and such environmental conditions were not suitable for animal husbandry and the growing of subsistence crops that formed the basis of Gusii and Logoli sustenance. Worse still, around the time the Gusii and Logoli ancestors settled at Kisumu, the middle of the sixteenth century, this region was hit by a severe and prolonged drought that lasted for over six years. This led to the demise of large numbers of cattle and extensive crop failure, resulting in severe famine and starvation. This widespread ecological disaster and social calamity led to the parting of ways of the Gusii and their Logoli relatives. Due to the severe famine, the dispersal of Gusii and Logoli ancestors from Kisumu was characterized by the abrupt movement of small groups of people, comprising closely-knit family members who searched for food and other sustenance resources.

It was within this social and ecological context that small clusters of closely knit families that eventually became the current Logoli/Maragoli people dispersed from Kisumu, taking a north-westerly direction. These family members first settled in the higher altitudes of Seme and Maseno, before moving further North and eventually settling in the cooler and wetter regions in the current Maragoli Hills. As the Logoli ancestors moved northwards, other small clusters of families that eventually became the current Gusii people took a south-easterly direction and eventually settled in the Kano plains in the late 16th century.

It should, therefore, be emphasized that the settlement of clusters of families in the Kano Plains marked the start of the final stage of the Gusii evolution into a distinct ethnic community. According to Gusii folk history, however, families that eventually settled in the Kano Plains were initially on hunting expeditions in search of wild game and fish.

Gusii mythology goes further to state that these initial Gusii families were led by people who were experienced hunters capable of supplying their respective families with sufficient game meat for immediate sustenance. During this period (over 300 years ago), the Kano Plains are said to have been a "Park-Like Country" that was made up of tall savannah grasslands and acacia trees. These plains also teemed with a diverse array of tropical savannah game such as the gazelle, hartebeest, buffalo, bushbuck and wildebeest. Consequently, the Kano Plains provided an ideal hunting ground for the Gusii hunters. In addition, fish was quite plentiful in the many rivers and streamlets that crisscrossed the Kano Plains. Although their initial intention was probably not to make permanent settlements in this area, these initial Gusii families decided to settle in this area permanently.

A clear indication that shows that the Gusii families that settled in the Kano Plains were on hunting expeditions is the fact that most of these family units adopted specific wild animals as their totems that acted as symbols of communal identity and unity. It can be said that totems are used by people who believe that they belong to a common ancestry to, symbolically at least, bind them together, having common responsibilities towards one another. The people are therefore united together by their common faith and reverence to the family totem that was highly revered and had a lot of magical religious value.

Original Gusii Clans

Gusii folk tales contend that the leaders of the initial Gusii family units that settled in the Kano Plains were sons of a great family patriarch called Mogusii; the name Abagusii translates, literally, as "the people of the family patriarch called Mogusii". Mogusii is said to have been a brother of Moragoli, the founder of Logoli/Maragoli community. Both Mogusii and Moragoli died in Kisumu. The names of the sons of Mogusii were Mosweta, Mochorwa, Mobasi, Mogisero and Monchari (also known as Machabe). It is the names of these Gusii patriarchs that have been passed down in Gusii genealogy; hence, the main Gusii Clans derive their names from these patriarchs.

Clan	Founder	Totem
Abasweta	Mosweta	*Engoge/Ngoge (Baboon)*
Abagirango	Mochorwa	*Engo (Leopard)*
Ababasi	Mobasi	*Enchage (Zebra)*
Abanchari	Monchari	*Engubo (Hippopotamus)*
Abagisero	Mogisero	*Engoge/Ngoge* (Baboon)

Furthermore, all the main Gusii clans are referred to (at least by Gusii elders) using their respective totem names as a sign of veneration to the totems and the respective clan founders. Whenever, referring to the origins of the main Gusii clans, Gusii elders always use both the names of the founders in conjunction with their respective totem names as a sign of reverence to Gusii ancestors, the community and spiritual well-being of the Gusii people at large. Thus, the clan totems are usually perceived as harbingers of good omens and prosperity.

The Abasweta whose totem is *engoge* (baboon) constitute the largest Gusii clan. The sons of Mosweta include: Ntindi, Oibabe, Mosigisa, Osiango, Mosamaro and Morangi. It should be noted that from the descendants of Mosweta have evolved the current Gusii groups including Kitutu, Nyaribari and Machoge.

The second largest Gusii clan is that of Abagirango. According to the Gusii mythology, name (Abagirango) is derivative of the clan totem *engo* (Leopard) or Abagirango that literally translates as "people who refused to kill a leopard".

The third largest Gusii clan is the Ababasi or Basi whose totem is *enchage* (zebra). According to Gusii mythology, Mobasi was a nickname that was given to one of the sons of Mogusii as recognition of his expertise in slaughtering animals. It is this nickname that eventually took root as the name of the clan, perhaps because of the satirical strength of this terminology.

The fourth main Gusii clan is the Abanchari whose totem is *engubo* (hippo). The Abanchari elders fondly refer to themselves as *Monchari o'mache chindiba chiobokendu* (the people who originated from the deep sea) – probably referring to their mythical origins in Lake Victoria – among the Luo of Nyakach. Both existing Gusii and Luo folk histories trace the origins of the Abanchari to the Luo clan of Karachuonyo in South Nyanza. According to this mythology, Monchari, who is also referred to as Machabe, is said to have been one of the sons of a famous Luo elder Chieni, who was the founder of the current Karachuonyo clan in Luo land.

Most of the Gusii and Luo elders concur that Machabe, son of Chieni, was ostracized by his clansmen after committing an abominable act or breaking a taboo, i.e., spilling the blood of a fellow kinsman. It is said that after being ostracized from his Karachuonyo clan, Machabe sought refuge among the Gusii clan of Abagisero where he eventually married one of the daughters of Mogisero called Monchari. For easy acceptance and adoption into the Gusii community, the descendants of Machabe may have decided to adopt the name of their mother as their clan name.

Finally, the Abagisero form the smallest Gusii clan; it appears that they are a breakaway group from the original Abasweta clan. This is probably an indication that the two groups originally belonged to the same clan. Interestingly, the Abagisero also appear to have linkage with the Karachuonyo Luo clan. This is one of those important aspects of Gusii origins that require further research and investigation to uncover the historical truth surrounding this mystical socio-cultural relation that has existed between the Gusii and the Luo.

It is important to note that while the Gusii clans that have clear information that links them to the original Gusii patriarch "Mogusii" are the Abasweta, Abagirango and Ababasi, the remaining Gusii clans do not appear to have a clear linkage to the patriarch. It can therefore be postulated that these clans might have originated from elsewhere (i.e., from Luo land). It may also be posited that the other smallest Gusii clans (i.e., the Abanchari and Abagisero) might have emerged as a result of long-term interaction and enculturation between the Gusii and their Luo neighbours. Overall, it can be estimated that the various Gusii clans lived in the Kano Plains for about 150 years (1600 – 1750).

Consequently, by the middle of the 18th Century, Gusii settlements extended to parts of Nyakach in the west and stretched further East to the Kabondo area. The settlements also extended further north to the slopes of the current Kipsigis Hills. Also during this period, the population of the Gusii people was relatively limited, probably not exceeding 5,000 inhabitants scattered in the expansive Kano Plains.

The Gusii practiced mixed farming, keeping livestock and growing subsistence crops such as millet, sorghum, pumpkins and sweet potatoes. Thus, it can be hypothesized further that throughout their stay in Kano, the Gusii had abundant supplies of various sustenance resources.

Finally, it can also be posited, based on existing historical and anthropological information, that the Gusii and some Luo ancestors had a lot of social interactions and cultural exchange, especially in the Kano Plains. Indeed, the two communities had a long-term symbiotic relationship. Thus, whereas the Gusii supplied their Luo neighbours with agricultural produce such as finger millet, sorghum, sweet potatoes and pumpkins, they in return received iron tools including spears, beads and hoes; in addition, they received clay pots and baskets from the Luo. Additionally, there was also a lot of cultural exchange and inter-marriages between the two groups, especially between the Gusii and the Luo clans of the Kabondo and Karachuonyo.

Current Location and Settlement

The current land inhabited by the Gusii in Western Kenya (the term Gusii is an ethnographic convention formed by dropping the plural marker in the Ekegusii language; Abagusii is the term the people use to refer to themselves) covers a total land mass of approximately 800 square miles, and is situated between longitude 35 30' and latitude 0 30' South. Throughout the book, this region is referred to as Gusii land or the Gusii highlands. Administratively, Gusii land currently is made up of Kisii and

Nyamira counties. It borders Kericho County in the North, Bomet County in the East and Narok County in the South. Gusii land also borders Homa Bay County in the West and Migori County in the South West (Figure 1).

Figure 1: A Map showing the location of Gusii Land (Kisii & Nyamira) and other Counties.

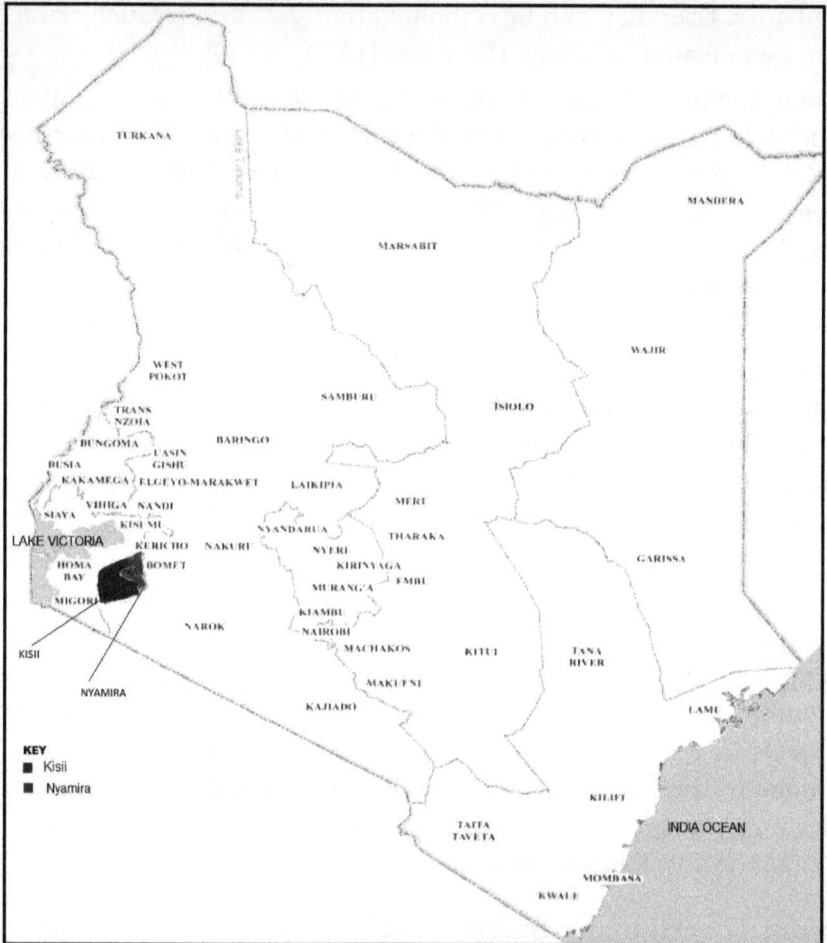

Source: Adapted from Kenyan Government, 2013

Gusii land is relatively hilly and the terrain rises in the south east direction to an altitude of 7,000 feet (2,134 meters) and slopes westwards (in the direction of Lake Victoria) reaching an altitude of 4,500 feet (1,372 meters) at its lowest point. The physiographic of this region is quite diverse, ranging from flat-bottomed valleys that are the source to many streams, rivers and riparian landforms. It also consists of several escarpments, hills and mountains that make most of the landscape. In the south west of the Gusii highlands is the Vinyo Escarpment that consists of stiff cliffs rising to over 1,000 feet above the adjacent Kamagambo Plains. The Vinyo Escarpment is bisected by a large gorge through which River Gucha flows on its way to Lake Victoria. Another prominent feature in Gusii land is the Manga Escarpment in the North West. The Manga Escarpment consists of an imposing stretch of cliffs that run in a north-westerly direction in the present Central Kitutu and West Mugirango locations.

The most prominent rivers that drain Gusii land are Gucha and the Sondu respectively, and their several tributaries and streamlets. The Gucha originates in North Mugirango and traverses Kitutu, Nyaribari, Bobasi, Machoge and South Mugirango locations onwards to Migori District in South Nyanza where it drains into Lake Victoria. The Sondu starts from the Borabu/Sotik area, and flows in the northern parts of Gusii land, along the boundary with Kericho County.

The river enters Nyakach in Kisumu District before draining into Lake Victoria (see Figure 2). Gusii land also possesses many swamps and riparian vegetation in the valley bottoms such as Sironga, Riamoni, Nyanturago and Chirichiro. Most of these riparian landforms are situated within the Keroka erosional surface that is composed of pleistocene rock deposits. These formations include black clay, alluvium and silt clay soils that have been eroded from surrounding highland areas. However, due to increased human settlement and cultivation, most of these riparian wetlands have been reclaimed. Relief, drainage and existing rock formations have thus influenced the soil formation in Gusii land. The high altitude areas in the east have dark alluvium soil, whereas the lower lying areas in the West consist mainly of a mixture of light coloured clay soil.

On the whole, Gusii land has extremely fertile soils that are suitable for various agricultural activities. In addition, the climate of Gusii land is ideal for growing of diverse crops that support an extremely high density of human settlement. It should also be noted that despite the region's closeness to the equator, Gusii land is generally characterized by relatively moderate to cool and pleasant temperate-like climatic conditions. On average, maximum temperatures range from 83° F (28.4° C) at the lowest altitudes to73°F (22.8°C) at high elevations. On the lower side, minimum temperatures range between 61.5°F (16.4°C) and 50°F (9.8° C).

Rainfall in the region is generally plentiful, capable of supporting diverse agricultural activities and animal husbandry. It ranges from an annual average of over 2000 mm in the east to about 1600 mm in the west. The region has a bimodal rainfall pattern; the long rains start towards the end of February and usually continue to May, whereas the short rains fall from August to December.

The vegetation of Gusii land is mainly influenced by rainfall distribution patterns and the area's physiography. Prior to the settlement of the Gusii people in the early Nineteenth Century, most of the natural vegetation in the region was mostly montane forest (Ojany, 1988). By the beginning of the twentieth century, however, the intense clearing of the forests to make room for much needed human settlement and agricultural production had converted most of the Gusii land to open savannah woodlands characterized by small scattered trees and tall grasses. Most of the grass is mainly of "Kikuyu and Star type". The Kikuyu grass is mainly found in areas with altitude 6,000 ft. and higher in the east whereas the Star grass is mostly found in lower-lying areas in the west.

This vegetation pattern distinguishes the two main ecological zones of Gusii land. As Maxon (2003) puts it, the two ecological zones have, on the whole, provided Gusii land with favourable opportunities for the development of a diversified and productive agrarian economy. It is also important to note that the ecological differences of the two zones have, over the years, been recognized by the Gusii people who refer to the lower ecological zone in the west as Chache, and the higher ecological zone in the East as Masaba. Following these ecological differences, land use patterns and population distribution differences have also characterized the two zones.

Current Gusii Clans

At the beginning of the twentieth century, the Gusii people had managed to expand and realign themselves into several clans that form the current main grouping of the Gusii (Figure, 2)

Figure 2: A Map showing the land occupied by major Gusii Clans

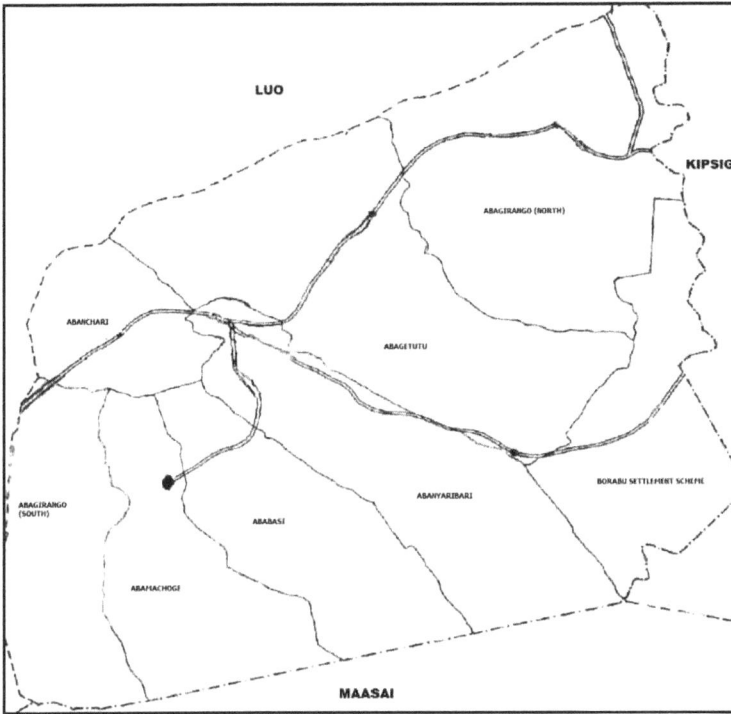

Source: Adapted from Kenya Government, 1989

Abagetutu (Kitutu)

After leaving Transmara, most Abasweta sub-clans including Abagetutu, Abanyaribari, Abasamaro, Abarangi, Abanyaikoma, Abageka and Abanyagatanyi settled in the central part of Manga Escarpment. Due to the urge to unite and confront external aggression, most of these Abasweta sub-clans eventually joined together and became part of the bigger Abagetutu Clan. The Abagetutu were the descendants of Oisera (the Sweta military leader who had led the Gusii sub-clans from Transmara area). After the death of Oisera, his son Nyakundi took over the leadership of the Sweta people. Nyakundi was a highly gifted leader, and during his time the Abagetutu clan prospered and became the most prominent Gusii group. Nyakundi encouraged all the Abasweta people in Manga to establish *ebisarate* in order to defend themselves effectively against external aggression. Later on, Nyakundi was able to persuade a

17

number of other non-Sweta sub-clans including Abatabori, Abatondo, Ababasi, Abambaba, Abakeira and Abagisero to become part of the larger Abagetutu Clan. It is this recognition that Abagetutu are made up of people from different Gusii clans that the Abagetutu/Kitutu clan is referred to in Gusii parlance as *Enda y'Enchogu* (the stomach of an elephant).

Abanyaribari (Nyaribari)

When the Sweta leader, Oisera, died around 1830, Onyangore, a half-brother to Nyakundi, staked claim to inherit the Sweta leadership by virtue of being the eldest son of Oisera. However, most of the Abasweta elders felt that Nyakundi had better leadership qualities than his half-brother Onyangore who was accused of being arrogant and aloof. Consequently, the Sweta elders decided to anoint Nyakundi as the new Sweta leader. Feeling let down, Onyangore, with his supporters, mainly from the Nyaribari sub-clan, revolted against the leadership of Nyakundi. In the open hostility and feud that ensued, Onyangore with his followers broke away from the rest of the Kitutu clan and moved away to form the Abanyaribari clan. The Abanyaribari first settled in the Nyanchwa Hills near Kisii Town from where they eventually spread to the Nyaura and Kiogoro area. Onyangore, the leader of the Abanyaribari, died at Kiogoro and was succeeded by one of his followers by the name Nyamwamu who remained the ruler until the arrival of the British in Gusii land. By 1850, the Abanyaribari had evolved into several sub-clans including the Abanyamasicho, Mwamoriango, Abamobea, Abaguche, Ababuria, Abatondo, Abakimotwe, and Abasigisa, among others.

Abagirango (Mogirango)

In their movement from Ngarora, a section of the Abagirango people had moved southwards and settled in South Nyanza. They currently form part of the Kuria people. However, the majority of the Abagirango joined the Abasweta people and retraced their way back to their original settlement in Isecha in the Northwest of the Manga Escarpment. This is the group that eventually came to be referred to as the people of North Mogirango. Some of the sub-clans that currently form part of North Mogirango include the Abagichora, Abanyaiguba, Abanyamatuta, Abakimori, Abakurati, Abanyakoni, Abanyamorita, Abamabacho, Abaisanga and Abakiambori.

In later years, members of the Abagirango moved from Isecha and spread to the Rangenyo-Nyabite area and other parts of their current settlements in North Mugirango and West Mugirango. However, in their movement from Ngarora, a smaller group of the Abagirango people opted not to move to Isecha. They instead joined the Ababasi and Abamachoge sub-groups and eventually settled in the Nyagoe forest[1]. In the 1840s, they moved from the Nyagoe area and spread to the Nsaria, Mesesi and Ntamocha areas. These are the people who are currently referred to as the South Mugirango. At present, the main sub-groups of the South Mogirango people include: Abagetenga, Abatabori, Abasinange, Abaige, Abamware, Abanyaramba and Abaisanga.

Ababasi (Basi/Bassi)

Similar to the Abagirango clan, when the Ababasi dispersed from Ngarora area in Transmara, a smaller section of the people moved south, crossed the Migori River, and settled in South Nyanza. They eventually became part of the present Kuria people of South Nyanza. However, a large section of the Ababasi moved together with other Gusii clans and eventually retraced their way back to the Nyagoe forest. From the Nyagoe area, the Basi people eventually dispersed to the Nyang'iti Hills South of Kisii Town. It was from this region that the Basi eventually spread to the Sameta area; by around 1870, the Basi had spread further East to the Nyamache and Kiongongi areas. Currently, the Ababasi clan have 3 union sub-clans where others fit into as follows: **Abagetaorio, Abaitang'are and Abamasige.**

1. *Abagetaorio (Union Clan)*

- Abagichoncho   - Abandonya
- Abamesichi   - Abakinami
- Abaigesa   - Abanyangama
- Abagesumi

2. *Abaitang'are (Union clan)*

- Abasansa   - Abatang'are
- Abakimweri   - Abasingi
- Abanyangande

3. *Abamasige (Union clan)*

- Abagesaka   - Abagetorora
- Abanyameuru   - Abamorasi
- Abamogacho   - Abagisoywa
- Abamooku

(Source: Abai. J .Ochoi. *Mwanyagetinge* 2013, Metro Graphics Inc.USA).

---

1   See next chapter on the movement of the
     Gusii on leaving the Kano Plains

Abamachoge (Machoge)

The Abamachoge are descended from Ntindi who was one of the sons of Mosweta Ngoge. In their movement from Ngarora, the Abamachoge broke away from the other Sweta subgroups and joined the Ababasi people with whom they moved to Nyagoe forest. Later, the Abamachoge together with the Ababasi moved from the Nyagoe forest and eventually settled at the Nyang'iti area. It was from here that the Abamachoge eventually moved southwards into the Magenche area in 1900. Currently, the main sub-clans that form the Machoge clan include: the Abambaba, Abakione, Abaochi and Abamachoge.

Abanchari (Nchari)

In the movement from Ngarora, the Abanchari were the first people to retrace their way back to the Nyagoe forest before being joined later by the Ababasi and Abamachoge. Later on, the Abanchari never, in fact, moved away from Nyagoe. They only expanded to nearby areas such as Matongo, Keboye, and Nyamatuta. The current main sub-clans of the Abanchari include: the Abagiakumu, Abamariba, Abagenda, Abanyando and Abamachabe.

Conclusion

This chapter has explicated the evolution of the Gusii with a view to a better understanding of the current core clans. The concept was approached from the mythological, anthropological and ethnolinguistic perspectives. Based on this, the original Gusii clans and the emergence of core Gusii clans (Kitutu, Nyaribari, Mogirango, Bassi, Machoge and Abanchari) are historically juxtaposed to show the expansion and realignments of the clans in the twentieth century. Further, it has been elucidated that the location and settlement of the Gusii was strategically placed in relation to warfare and supplies of various sustenance resources. It is important to point out that the settlement and clan realignments, in particular, are evidence of the struggle and survival of the Gusii clan in the midst of belligerent neighbouring communities as will be explained in the following chapter.

CHAPTER THREE

STRUGGLE AND SURVIVAL STRATEGIES

Introduction

This chapter encapsulates various elements of the recent Gusii history, particularly their struggles and survival strategies amidst threats of hostility and possible assimilation by their larger non-Bantu neighbours. The chapter covers a period that forms the defining moment of the Gusii community. Their movement and settlement can be considered as one of the great Gusii epics. It is elucidated that for their long-term survival, the Gusii had to adopt various defensive strategies of fending off perceived internal and existing external aggressors.

An Epic Journey: Brief Overview

By the mid-18th century, the population of both the Gusii and the Luo living in the Kano Plains had increased substantially and in the process put stress on available resources. As a consequence, there was need for dispersal to surrounding virgin areas in the current Eastern and Southern Nyanza region. Because of pressure on sustenance resources, family and/or inter-clan rivalry among the Gusii increased, and inter-ethnic conflicts between the Gusii and their Luo neighbours intensified, as each group attempted to acquire an adequate supply of existing sustenance resources. It was within this broad socio-economic context that the Gusii clans started to send harbingers to scout the possibility of establishing new frontier settlements in the highlands region situated to the southeast of Kano. The Gusii, however, were initially dissuaded from moving to the high altitude areas. This was due to the fact that the area was thickly forested and had extremely cold climatic conditions compared to the park-like Kano Plains where the Gusii people had led a leisurely lifestyle for a long period of time.

It can, however, be argued that the urgency to disperse to the adjacent high altitude areas was accentuated when the Gusii, for the first time, came into direct contact with the aggressive Isiria Maasai raiders coming from the Kamagambo lowlands to the Southeast (Figure 2). It should be emphasized that the arrival of the Maasai in the Kano Plains completely destabilized existing socio-cultural harmony between the Gusii and their Luo neighbours. Unlike the low-level inter-clan rivalry that existed amongst the various Gusii clans, and the occasional inter-ethnic skirmishes with their Luo neighbours, the belligerent Maasai raiders were a different ball game altogether. Driven by their strong cultural belief that all cattle wherever they were (i.e., including those that were in the possession of other people) were their birthright, the Maasai started launching fierce nocturnal raids on Gusii and Luo villages to capture livestock.

The Gusii, particularly, found themselves vulnerable to the Maasai raids that were mainly executed during the wee hours of the night since they were not used to those forms of warfare. Thus, in most instances, the nocturnal raids usually caught Gusii people by surprise. The Maasai raiders could make swift nocturnal attacks, surrounding the whole Gusii villages, burning down houses and granaries, and killing anybody who dared to challenge them. In the widespread confusion that ensued, the Maasai drove away large herds of Gusii livestock. If the Gusii warriors attempted to make counter-attacks to repulse the enemy, they found their cumbersome long spears to be no match for the Maasai bows and arrows that they manipulated and used at a distance.

***Figure 3: A Map showing location of Gusii Land and parts of Luo,
Kipsigis and Maasai Land***

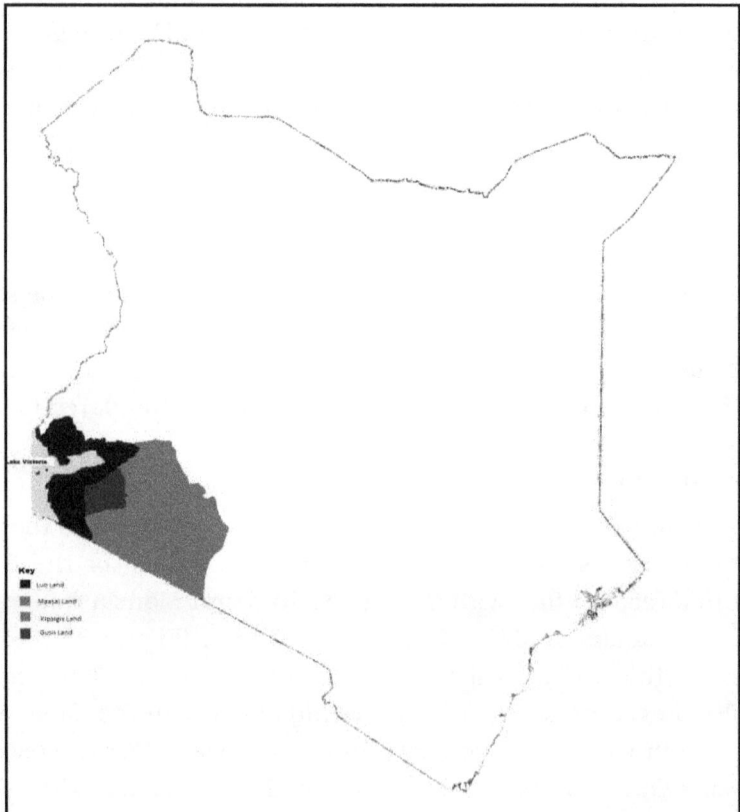

Source: Author, 2014

Consequently, for the sake of self-preservation, the Gusii had no option but to seek refuge in the rugged Manga Escarpment and the adjacent hills. However, it can also be postulated that another important "push-factor" that might have contributed to the urgency of their movement from the open grassland areas of Kano was that they were now being sandwiched by two dominant non-Bantu communities, namely the Luo and the Maasai. The Gusii thus faced the eminent danger of socio-economic annihilation and cultural assimilation. The marauding Maasai raiders relentlessly attacked and killed the Gusii people, capturing livestock and destroying property (i.e., burning down houses and granaries) in the process. On the other hand, Luo neighbours, who were numerically superior to the Gusii, were increasingly impacting on Gusii culture and lifestyle. Thus, it can be posited that there was an increased overall realization, among the Gusii, of the over-bearing influence of Luo culture coupled with an incessant urge for self-preservation that added to the urgency of Gusii movement from the Kano Plains.

Settlement in the Manga Hills

Realizing that the odds were against them as a community, members of the various Gusii clans therefore decided to migrate to the secluded high altitude areas of the Manga Hills (Figure 3). Due to the prevailing hostile circumstances, the Gusii people moved together in distinct family units that were made up of closely knit kinsmen led by a distinguished family patriarch who provided urgent leadership and security. This was mainly for security reasons; furthermore, members of the same lineage could easily turn to one another for assistance in times of emergency (e.g., when being attacked by Maasai cattle raiders).

The first Gusii group to move from the Kano Plains consisted of members of the Abagirango clan who were under the leadership of their renowned Girango warrior whose name was Tabichi. At first, the group settled in the current North Mugirango location in Nyamira District before moving and eventually settling at Isecha in the Manga Hills. The Abagirango were followed by members of the Abasweta clan who moved past North Mugirango and eventually settled in the central parts of the Manga Hills near Ikuruma. Manyatta led the Abasweta. Later, some Sweta families, consisting mainly of the Abasiango and Abasigisa lineage, moved further South to Tabaka plateau in the current Gucha District in Kisii County.

Figure 4: A Map showing major Gusii Physiographical and Historical Areas

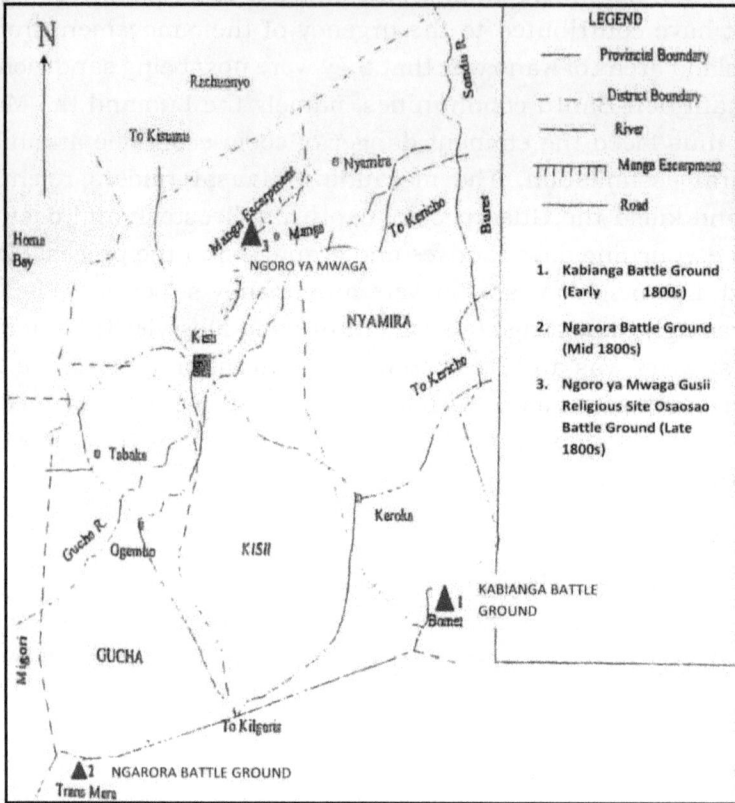

Source: Author, 2014

Unfortunately, while in Tabaka, these families were discovered by the Maasai who once again started raiding their villages. As a consequence, they made a hasty retreat, retraced their way back north, and eventually settled in Nyagoe forest, south of the Manga Hills. Later on, people from other Gusii clans also moved from the Kano Plains and settled in high altitude areas adjacent to the Manga Hills. They included family from the Ababasi and Abanchari clans who were led by Ogichoncho and Oisukia, respectively. Members of the Ababasi clan led by their leader Ogichoncho moved and settled in the Nyagoe forest, near present Kisii Town, while members of the Abanchari clan led by Oisukia settled in the Marani area also close to the Manga Hills.

It should also be stated that some of the Gusii people remained behind in Kano Plains, and, over time, most of these people were assimilated and became part of the Luo. However, most of the Gusii families that eventually adopted Luo culture maintained their original Gusii clan names such as Abagusero, Abanchari and Abasweta.

Movement into the Kabianga Region

As already stated above, most of the Gusii clans who had moved from Kano Plains had settled in Manga Escarpment and the adjacent areas of Isecha Hills and Nyagoe forest. These settlement patterns (i.e. various Gusii clans staying in close proximity with one another) were probably necessitated by security considerations. Due to their initial experience with ferocious Maasai raids, it can be stated that the Gusii immigrants were basically looking for areas that were strategically situated that could facilitate easy defence. Thus, the Manga Escarpment and the adjacent high altitude and forested areas may have appeared to be quite ideal. Furthermore, the steep cliffs, raised escarpments and flat-topped hills could enable Gusii warriors to scout approaching Maasai raiders. This would give them adequate time to position themselves in strategic sites along the steep escarpments to confront the approaching enemy. However, over time, the closely linked and concentrated Gusii settlements started to experience increased population pressure relative to the available resources.

As a consequence, several segments of the Gusii started dispersing adjacent virgin habitats in search of new places to settle. Particularly, several Gusii families from Manga-Isecha-Nyagoe triangle decided to move eastwards and eventually settled in Kipkelion area, along the present Bomet/Kericho border. Due to unforeseeable circumstances, Gusii settlement in the Kipkelion area did not last long. First, the Gusii found out that the place was extremely cold and was thus not suitable for human habitation and the growth of their staple food crop, finger millet (*obori*). Consequently, soon there was persistent crop failure leading to severe famine and starvation. Secondly, the area appeared to be disease prone, as many people were affected by weather elements and started to die from pneumonia and other related respiratory ailments. Probably, what finally broke the camel's back, however, was the arrival of the Kipsigis raiders in the Kipkelion area.

At this point, it is important to mention that since famine and other forms of pestilence had already weakened the Gusii, the raiders easily overran Gusii villages and captured most of their livestock, women and the youth. These chains of calamities led the Gusii people to become expiated and distraught to the extent of naming the place "Kabianga", which literally translates to "the place where nothing flourished". It is interesting to note that this place has retained the Gusii name up to the present time, despite the fact that it is currently inhabited by people who are predominantly Kalenjin-speakers.

As a result of this chain of calamities, various Gusii families started to retreat from the Kabianga area, most of them taking a south westerly direction. They passed through the present Sotik, Gelegele and Ikorongo locations before eventually settling in present Transmara, at a place called Nyangarora, named after a famous Gusii military leader Ngarora who was killed by Maasai raiders in the vicinity. However, some Gusii families, mainly from the Tabori, Gusero and Basi clans, decided to remain in the Litein-Sotik area, and they were eventually assimilated into the predominant Kipsigis culture.

However, soon after their settlement in the Transmara area, the Gusii once more started to experience vicious Maasai raids. In a constant spirit of make or break, Gusii warriors led by Ngarora made a last ditch effort to fend off the Maasai. But when their gifted military leader Ngarora was felled in one of the battles, the Gusii once again opted to make a hasty retreat from Transmara, retracing their way back to their original settlements in the Manga Hills. It was in this hasty retreat that some families from the Abasweta, Abanchari, Ababasi and Abagirango clans lost track of their main Gusii families. These stray families eventually moved and settled in parts of present day South Nyanza. These are the people who currently form part of the Kuria people of South Nyanza and Northern Tanzania.

However, most of the Gusii families, under the leadership of Oisera (who took over the military leadership from his father, Ngarora), retraced their way back into their original settlements in the Manga- Nyagoe-Isecha Triangle. By the early nineteenth century, most of the Gusii families were once again clustered around the Manga Escarpment to the East, the Nyagoe forest to the South, and the Isecha- Rangenyo area to the North.

Similarly, it is important to note that when the Gusii returned to their original settlements, they became quite conscious of their vulnerability to attacks from their belligerent neighbours. It did not take long before they once again started experiencing attacks from the Kipsigis and Maasai raiders who made daring incursions into Gusii villages that were situated in the frontier areas of Isecha to the North of the Manga Hills, while the Maasai cattle raiders started attacking outlying Gusii villages in Nyagoe forest. In many instances, the Gusii had to make spirited counter attacks to repulse the enemy who appeared hell- bound to overrun them. It was in this socio-cultural milieu that the Gusii undertook various defence mechanisms to defend themselves against the enemy.

Adopting a New Military Strategy

First, the Gusii developed a strategy whereby young men were always posted in strategic frontier posts that were situated on hilltops. Whenever signs of approaching raiders were detected, the scouts blew war horns to alert people in the adjacent villages of the approaching enemy. In such instances, Gusii warriors would leave whatever they were doing, swiftly arm themselves, hide themselves and take a position in strategic locations ready to confront the approaching enemy.

Second, since in most instances the Maasai and Kipsigis raiders were mainly after Gusii livestock, various Gusii clans identified specific locations, such as reclusive caves, escarpments and sheltered valley bottoms. The locations were surrounded by steep slopes; they could temporarily hide their cattle from probable raiders, especially during night time when most of the people were asleep.

Third, in order to protect themselves against nocturnal Maasai raids, the Gusii started constructing defensive systems that involved the digging of deep trenches around enclosed homesteads (allowing only one main entrance to the village). These defensive systems were called *chiburi* (sing. *eburi*). In other instances, the Gusii constructed *chindwaki* (sing. *orwaki*); *chindwaki* were forts built around their homesteads. Each *orwaki* one had a single entrance and was surrounded by deep trenches with spikes. Eventually, the people realized that a combination of the two defensive systems (i.e. construction of the walls (*chindwaki*) combined with the building of trenches around villages) was most effective in fending off the enemy.

Fourth, various Gusii clans established military encampments, *ebisarate* (sing. *egesarate*), on the outskirts of the adjoining villages where all able-bodied Gusii young men (typically from the age of 16 to late 20s) were required to stay for a prolonged period of time. While living in the encampment (*egesarate*), they received training on various fighting and defensive skills, and it was here that they were called upon to provide protection for the community against external aggressors and/or cattle rustlers, whenever the need arose. Furthermore, livestock kraals were constructed around the *ebisarate* where all Gusii livestock was supposed to be kept, especially during the night (the most probable time when raiders could attack outlying villages). Young Gusii warriors kept constant vigil: guarding their families and cattle against possible raids from the Maasai and Kipsigis raiders.

Fifth, the Gusii adopted the use of bows and arrows in fighting the enemy. The use of bows and arrows was more effective compared to the cumbersome shields and spears, especially during times of extensive and drawn out confrontation with the enemy. Thus, in case of drawn-out confrontations, Gusii warriors could face the enemy with bows and arrows, which were easy to manoeuvre and could be carried for long distances. These defensive initiatives appear to have been effective against Maasai and Kipsigis raiders. Consequently, with the increase in human population in the original settlement areas of Manga-Isecha-Nyagoe, the Gusii people started feeling safe enough to spread and establish new settlements in other areas of the Gusii highlands region.

Other defence weapons/means used by Abagusii include the following:

1. **SLINGS (*chinduruche*):** This was a skill taught to boys from boyhood when herding animals in the field. The boys perfected this art over the years. In every locality there were gifted youths, especially the left handed ones, who could precisely aim and knock the target at an instant. Unlike bows and arrows, which required skills to make, slings required pebbles, which were readily available.

2. **POISONED STICKS (*chimbambo*):** This was a kind of chemical weapons which worked very well on the paths to cattle *bomas*. Sharpened bamboos, and slender sticks were dipped into some 'poisonous' paste (usually from snake venom) and everybody was advised to keep off. The enemies were terribly inflicted once they ventured there. Early in the morning, those who set the weapons could remove the poisoned sticks and return them in the night, just like the police remove spikes at road block.

3. **CURSES (*ebiranya*):** There were prophets/seers (*ababani*, sing. *omobani*) who cursed with accuracy when called upon. It is claimed that this was the case with the battle of Mogori/Osaosao. Gusii prophets cursed that the Gusii would no longer be beaten by the Kipisigis following earlier predictable defeats. It is believed in some quarters that it is the curse that led the Kipsigis warriors to over confidence into the battle and hence the heavy losses they suffered. Note that *Omobani* Sakawa Ng'iti is believed to have had such powers.

Finally, various Gusii sub-clans realized the importance of being united in temporary cooperative efforts, *risaga*, in order to effectively confront massive external raids by the enemy. Particularly, after being vanquished by the Kipsigis at Kabianga and the Maasai at Nyangarora, many smaller Gusii sub-groups decided to join the larger Abasweta clan for defensive purposes. In prevailing circumstances, there was an urgent need for the Gusii to be united in order to be able to effectively confront external aggression and protect the resources, especially livestock, from plunder. It was within this context that smaller Gusii sub-groups turned to the Abasweta clan for military leadership.

The Osaosao/Mogori Battle as the Turning Point of Gusii History

The outbreak of Osaosao Battle (also known by Kipsigis elders as the Mogori War) was perhaps a definitive moment for the Gusii and their survival as a distinct ethnic community. In the mid-1890s, there was a severe outbreak of cattle pestilence (rinderpest) in the Kipsigis community. By 1895, the Kipsigis had lost almost all of their animals to the pandemic. Thus, with an aim of replenishing their stock, Kipsigis warriors started making regular cattle raids in the Manga-Isecha-Nyagoe region. These daring incursions, initially, caught the Gusii unawares.

With increased determination and confidence, Kipsigis warriors started raiding villages beyond the frontier territory of Northern Mogirango. By 1896, the raiders were penetrating into the heart of Gusii community, spreading into the West and South Mogirango, Kitutu, Bonchari and Bomachoge. As was customary, when the Gusii were confronted with an external aggressor, Nyakundi, who was the senior most *omokumi* (pl. *abakumi*) of Kitutu sent emissaries to summon other leading Gusii clan elders, *abakumi* or *abanguru*, to a meeting at Isecha in Central Kitutu. Being informed by the urgency of the meeting, all the *abakumi* converged at Kitutu to discuss the enormity of the danger that was confronting the Gusii people as a whole. After serious consultation, the *abakumi* reached a consensus that all Gusii people were confronted with possible annihilation as a result of the attacks the Kipsigis were regularly making on the Gusii community. The raiders attacked whole villages, burning houses and granaries and massacring Gusii warriors before driving away Gusii herds.

After the discussions, Nyakundi led the gathering of *abakumi* in making a solemn agreement/oath (*emuma;* pl. *chimuma*) to wage total war against the aggressors should they strike. He made the standard proclamation: *mwanchire twensi tochake esegi naababisa baito Abasigisi* (have you all agreed that we declare an all-out war against our enemies the Kipsigis?) All the *abakumi* responded in agreement by uttering the standard proclamation: *eee twanchire* (yes we have all agreed). To bind all the *abakumi* to this common course, Nyakundi, assisted by a famous Gusii prophet-leader, Sakawa, led the elders to the holy site, *Ngoro ya Mwaga*, in the Manga hills (Figure 3). After performing the ritual of throwing pieces of firewood to the hole to appease the ancestral spirits, the elders made a joint oath committing their people to go to war with the

Kipsigis. Then Sakawa gave sacrifices to bless the Gusii warriors who were soon to confront the formidable enemy.

Immediately following this ceremony, the *abakumi* returned to their specific clans. Each of them then urgently summoned their clan councils, *chitureti* (sing. *etureti*), meetings to relay the message of the impending war against the Kipsigis aggressors. Afterwards, the war horns were blown all over Gusii community to inform warriors to arm themselves in readiness for an epic battle against a common enemy. In 1896, Kipsigis cattle raiders were seen in the vicinity of the Manga Hills in Central Kitutu. Coincidentally, this place was adjacent to *Ngoro ya Mwaga*. Both Gusii and Kipsigis elders concur that a pitched battle took place. It raged along the Manga Escarpment and adjacent lands. In the battle, Kipsigis warriors were totally vanquished by a joint Gusii force. Furthermore, according to both Gusii and Kipsigis folk history, a whole generation of Kipsigis warriors was wiped out. The pitched battle was so intense that the water of the adjacent Mogori and Charachani rivers turned red due to human blood oozing out of the bodies of the butchered Kipsigis warriors whose bodies were thrown in the river.

Afterwards, the Gusii warriors followed the retreating Kipsigis and slaughtered them almost to a man. They later took the war to the Kipsigis territory in the Sotik-Belgut-Kabianga area. Kipsigis elders concur that during this war, their community lost most of their young men. Due to the unprecedented catastrophe, a young generation of Kipsigis boys was hurriedly initiated into adulthood to inherit the many widows whose husbands had been massacred during the Mogori war. The war has also gone into Gusii folk history as one of those defining moments when the future of the Gusii as a distinct community was brought into focus. After vanquishing the enemy, Gusii people started systematic movement and settlement in frontier territories of North and West Mugirango approaching the Sondu-Sotik area.

The Osaosao battle is so engrained in the minds of Gusii elders that they still remember some of the victory songs the Gusii warriors sang on their way home after vanquishing the enemy. One of the victory songs went as follows:

Ekegusii	English Translation
Ee sanyera abanto x3	Unite all the Gusii warriors x 3
Ee sanyera x3	Yes, unite x 3
Tokaga Mogori nero Ngarora[1]	Don't think Mogori battle is the same as
	Ngarora
Ee sanyera	Yes, unite
Ee sanyera abanto x3	Unite all the Gusii warriors
Ee sanyera x3	Yes, unite

Conclusion

This chapter has elucidated that the Gusii were a small Bantu community that was sandwiched between relatively larger non-Bantu communities such as the Luo, Maasai, and the Kipsigis. Further, it has been indicated that the Manga Escarpment and adjacent hills were of strategic importance, especially in terms of serving as natural defence areas against external aggression, particularly from the belligerent and highly militarized pastoral Maasai community. An interesting historical phenomenon that comes out is that the Gusii were not an insular community. Through this period which lasted for more than 300 years, the Gusii interacted closely with their non-Bantu neighbours either during periods of trade and other cross-cultural exchange or during unavoidable times of wars. Through this inter-ethnic interaction, new sub-clans emerged whose biological roots were not necessarily Gusii. Based on this, it can therefore be argued that many sub-clans that are founded dotted in borderline areas such as the Abagisero, Abanchari and Abatabori are historically an aerial group of mixed Kisii, Luo, Kipsigis and Maasai.

CHAPTER FOUR

SOCIO-CULTURAL AND POLITICAL ORGANIZATION

Introduction

This Chapter gives an elucidation of some Gusii socio-cultural structures and governance systems. It is shown that the Gusii lineage system was based on patrilineal principles and that the smallest unit of Gusii social structure was the homestead, *omochie* (pl. *emechie*), which was headed by the family patriarch, *omogaka bw'omochie*. This was followed by village social structure, *riiga/enyomba* (pl. *amaiga/chinyomba*), which consisted of descendants from the same grandfather or great grandfather. In the chapter, it is presented that it was a combination of the various *riiga (amaiga)* social organizations that formed the next most significant Gusii social and political organization (i.e., the clan, *egesaku*). Finally, it is presented that it was a combination of the various Gusii clans situated in different parts of Gusii land that formed the Gusii ethnic community.

Socio-Cultural Evolution: Brief Overview

By around 1700, the Gusii had evolved into a distinct ethnic community with a population of approximately 5,000 people. In addition, the Gusii had undergone systematic processes of cultural and social evolution and had managed to adjust to the environmental conditions of the Kano plains. The Gusii people moved, in the mid-eighteenth century, from the Kano plains to their current homeland in the Gusii highland region. This region has wet and cold climatic conditions and a rugged mountainous physiography. This confronted the Gusii with new challenges which necessitated the emergence of new forms of socio-economic and political organization. These enabled the people to adjust and adopt to the new ecological and climatic conditions that were quite different from those of the low lying and warmer Kano plains.

Apart from what appeared to be an inhospitable natural environment, the Gusii had to contend with hostile and threatening non-Bantu neighbouring communities, particularly the Maasai and Kipsigis. With the passage of time, however, the Gusii eventually managed to adjust to the new environment and were able to harness the existing natural resources for their sustenance. As they adjusted, they also developed survival techniques to fend off external aggression. As a consequence, they evolved various defensive strategies, social and political systems that led to relatively long time political stability and social tranquility. Due to these favourable conditions, there was a rapid increase of Gusii population and relative economic prosperity that was based on mixed farming that involved livestock husbandry and the growing of subsistence crops.

Living in a distinct ecological environment, holding similar cultural values and the recognition that they belonged to a common ancestry made the Gusii people feel that they were one and the same people, *abanto abamo*. The Gusii, therefore, perceived themselves as being distinctly different from the neighbouring ethnic communities. The people were bound together by their common language, same cultural values and social practices. However, it should be stated that, politically, the Gusii people were divided into various self-sustaining and autonomous clans. These clans (e*bisaku*, sing. *egesaku*), borne out of patriarchal lineage, formed the basis the Gusii social and political organization, starting from the smallest socio-political unit, the homestead, *omochie*, to the sub-clan or clan level. It was the conglomeration of these various self-governing and autonomous clans that formed the broader Gusii community.

Gusii Lineage System

The Gusii lineage system followed patrilineal principles that entailed tracing one's descent on the male side. Once a woman was married, and the requisite customary marriage rites were performed, she transferred her allegiance to the husband's lineage, *egesaku*. In this lineage system, the basic social organization was the homestead that was headed by a family patriarch, *omogaka bw'omochie*. An ideal Gusii homestead consisted of the family patriarch, his wives, his married sons and the other unmarried children in the family. The homestead formed the basis of Gusii lineage ties that extended to sub-clan and clan level and, eventually, encompassed the whole Gusii community. As a matter of tradition, the Gusii trace(d) their lineage starting from the homestead, sub-clan, clan, and eventually extending to the broader Gusii community.

A Gusii homestead (*omochie*) formed a distinct self-sustaining socio-political and economic entity that generated its own sustenance resources and carried out most of its socio-economic activities independently. In the homestead, the wife and her children could cultivate specific pieces of land that were adjacent to the homestead. By clearing and cultivating the land, the wife and her children (specifically sons), in most instances, established a legal claim of ownership over that piece of land. The family also owned cattle and other livestock. Typically, the male members of the homestead claimed legal ownership of these cattle and the rest of the

34

livestock. Cattle were highly valued in the whole Gusii community as a source of bride wealth, and symbols of family wealth and prestige.

All the children of the same father, whether coming from different wives, considered one another as belonging to the same family. Although at face value there always appeared to be social and economic harmony in the homestead, in most polygamous families, there were always petty incidents of jealousy and rivalry typically between the sons of different wives. These were commensurate to the available family resources (land and cattle) and the ability of the family patriarch to maintain social harmony and tranquility in his homestead. On the whole, heads of homesteads had a lot of authority and influence over their wives and children; and they were presumed to have magical-religious powers to curse those members of their homesteads who failed to show loyalty and obedience to them.

Apart from maintaining family harmony and smooth running of all the homestead's social and economic activities, the head of the homestead also ensured family obedience and observance of various Gusii customs, norms, traditions and religious rituals. By virtue of his roles and functions, a family patriarch commanded immense respect and authority that was commensurate to his social status and control of family resources.

The Gusii lineage system was, however, based on egalitarian principles of social equity and natural justice. The homestead head was therefore supposed to treat all his wives and sons equally. He was also expected to share all the available family resources, such as land and livestock, equitably amongst all his progeny, without any form of favouritism.

After the homestead, the next level of the kinship-lineage chain consisted people who traced their descent to the same grandfather. The decendants of the same grandfather formed a social unit that was referred to as *riiga*. However, in terms of socio-political functions and economic activities, *riiga* did not play any significant role. It was a combination of all the homesteads belonging to other related *riiga* groups that formed the second most significant socio-economic political grouping of the Gusii people, the clan. As already stated, the clan was virtually an autonomous socio-political and economic entity. Usually, people belonging to the same clan occupied a specific geographical location that was exclusively owned by the clan. All male members of a particular clan were always prepared to defend their socio- economic and political integrity against any form of encroachment by people belonging to other clans, including defending themselves against any form of aggression from other clans.

It is important to note that the formation of various distinct Gusii clans started during the time of initial settlement of the Gusii people in the Kano plains approximately 300 years ago. In most of their dispersal and settlement patterns, the Gusii people belonging to closely knit family groups usually moved and settled in close proximity with one another mainly due to security considerations. When the various Gusii families dispersed from the Kano to their current homeland in the Gusii highlands region, they followed the pattern of movement and eventual settlement. Closely knit families belonging to the same kinship group settled on specific ridges and on the cascading hill were usually separated by valley bottoms and rivers or streams. With the passage of time, there was an increase in population, and members of various kinship groups that had settled on particular ridges eventually evolved into the various Gusii clans that have existed up to the present.

Consequently, various Gusii clans still occupy specific geographical locations. However, it should also be stated that the clans were always dynamic economic and political entities. As population increased, over time, and land and other types of resources became scarce, people belonging to the same clan became divided due to conflicts over the sharing and utilization of available resources. These forms of intra-clan divisions and disagreements led to serious conflicts among people belonging to the same clan. In this kind of situation, some family/kinship groups decided to move away and occupy land in adjacent frontier territories.

This eventually led to the formation of new sub-clans that eventually evolved into full-fledged distinct clans. However, in most instances there were strong kinship ties and shared solidarity among people belonging to the same clan. All clan members, especially the men, were supposed to be always ready and prepared to protect their resources, such as land and livestock, as a united group.

Furthermore, there was supposed to be no prolonged animosity, conflict or physical confrontation among people belonging to the same clan. The injuring or shedding of blood of people belonging to the same clan was considered a taboo and could result in serious consequences to the supposed offenders, including the payment of a big fine in the form of cattle. In cases involving the murder of a person belonging to the same clan, for example, the offender could be banished from the clan. But in most cases involving any form of any disagreements and conflicts between people of the same clan, friendship was supposed to be re-established as soon as possible through a cleansing ceremony known as *ogosonsorana*. If the existing conflicts continued to persist, however, then one of the affected family/kinship unit might decide to move out of the clan land all together and settle in the adjacent frontier territory, away from their former clan; thus they eventually severed all kinship links with that clan.

More importantly, perhaps, people belonging to the same clan usually undertook various social and economic tasks together. In certain times of the year, when need arose for instance, members of the same clan could form temporary cooperative groups that were called *amasaga* (sing. *risaga*). These performed specific tasks such as the clearing of virgin forestland for cultivation and the construction of new homes for fellow members of the clan.

Usually, people in a specific clan performed various functions, roles and obligations based on age and gender. The elderly men or homestead heads were for instance, responsible for providing leadership and guidance to people in respective homesteads and sometimes to the whole clan, as situations demanded. Young men, on the other hand, were supposed to look after family and clan cattle and provide military defence against any form of external aggression. As for women they were supposed to cultivate the land, tend crops (e.g. weeding), and perform most household chores.

Although there were no clearly defined centralized political organizations and institutions that brought all the clans together, the Gusii people were made to feel and act as one social entity through their common culture and beliefs. Consequently, there were strong cultural ties that united the Gusii people together and made them perceive themselves as a distinct ethnic community that was different from the neighbouring communities such as the Luo, Maasai and Kipsigis.

In order to maintain their distinct institutions, important Gusii cultural values and socio-economic practices were sustained and passed down from one generation to another. Given that, above the clan level, there was no formal political and administrative structure that bound the various Gusii clans together, various clans acted as self-contained independent units. Beyond the clan level, therefore, what made the Gusii people perceive each other as a distinct cultural and social entity was the language, culture and various social practices. This was based on the fact people recognized the important historical factor that they had a common patrilineal founder called Mogusii.

Core Principles and Values Governing Gusii Life

A key component that defined the Gusii as a distinct ethnic community was the manner in which they defined their social behaviour and group interactions. The Gusii social system that governed individual behaviour was anchored in a moral code of conduct, *chinsoni*, which stipulated various ways in which people of different generations related to one another in any social setting, starting from the homestead or clan level and extending to the whole Gusii community. The application of this code of social conduct started from the basic Gusii social unit, the homestead, where the concept of *chinsoni* was strictly adhered to by every member of the family. The *chinsoni* concept was a clearly defined code of conduct that governed the behaviour of the family in the homestead. As an example, young women were not allowed to have face to face encounters with their fathers and other male relatives in their fathers' level, e.g. uncles. As well, fathers, were not allowed to enter houses of their married sons nor were sons allowed into places where their parents slept.

This set of rules, roles and functions guided people's daily way of life and provided motivation to undertake accepted practices and behavioural restraint that was crucial in maintaining appropriate moral and social order at the homestead level and other intermediate social groupings extending to the whole of the Gusii community. Consequently, Gusii children were born and brought up in a physical and social environment that was rich in moral norms and social values that governed the people's way of conduct during their lifetime within the community.

Figure 5: The Physical Layout of Traditional Gusii Homestead as Governed by the Chinsoni Concept.

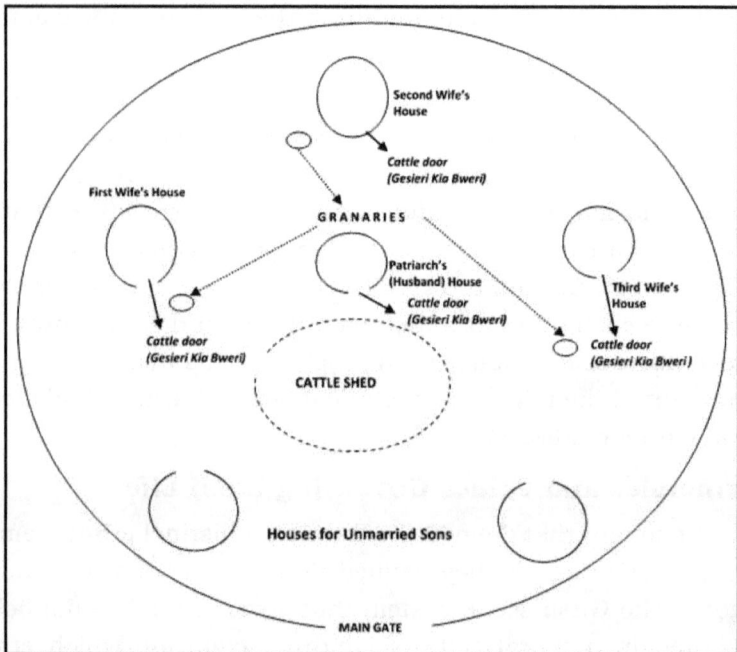

Source: Author, 2014

As started previously, a Gusii homestead consisted of *omogaka bw'omochie*, the patriarch of the homestead, his wives, married sons and their wives and children, and the other unmarried children. In most instances, the elder had his own distinct house within the homestead, *etureti*, where he constantly held council with his adult sons to deliberate on important issues affecting their homestead. It was also at the *etureti* where the family patriarch met and entertained important visitors and friends, and people who paid him homage for advice or discussion on issues that affected the whole kinship unit, *egesaku*. Each wife in the homestead owned her own house that had an expansive yard. Most of the cultivated land for each wife was usually located adjacent to her house.

The family patriarch was supposed to rotate his stay in the different houses of his wives as situations demanded. Within the homesteads there were also houses for the initiated sons, *chisaiga* (Figure, 5). However, most of the able-bodied unmarried young men from different homesteads within a particular kinship unit, *egesaku or riiga*, were supposed to spend most of their time in military encampments, *ebisarate*, where they assembled their family livestock and grazed them together for security reasons.

The main purpose for the unmarried young men staying together in the military encampments was to provide requisite defence against cattle raids and also to provide protection against any other form of internal or external aggression. At the encampments, they also shared a lot of cultural education passed down from older men to the younger ones.

The concept of *chinsoni* was strictly adhered to in the design and construction of houses and other structures in the homestead and even in the interior design of Gusii traditional houses. In addition, the *chinsoni* code of conduct involving issues such as inter-generational interaction, individual avoidance behaviour and recognition of ritual sites closely adhered to when building houses in a homestead. As LeVine (1996) succinctly puts it:

> ....the interior spaces and external placement of Gusii houses conformed to a design in which every detail was endowed with significance for social interaction and ritual. Each role, each stage and transition in life was defined by assigned and forbidden spaces and by customary actions performed in those spaces using traditional objects. The domestic organization of life constituted a heavily prescribed and proscribed world for residents of the homestead and or their guests as well, which were treated according to equally detailed normative prescriptions [as was contained in the *chinsoni* code of conduct].

As stated elsewhere, each homestead formed a distinct and autonomous entity. It was a self-contained entity that produced its own food and managed its internal affairs of governance and administration of justice and the sharing of resources independently. Adjacent homesteads of the same lineage sometimes undertook certain assignments together, including activities such as the clearing of fallow land, cultivation, livestock herding, fencing and construction of houses, carrying out rituals and providing common defence. This was, however, strictly based on a voluntary basis and the norms of kinship reciprocity as various family and communal needs arose which required concerted effort beyond the homestead level.

The strict observance of the *chinsoni* code of conduct at the homestead level served as the prototype for moral conduct and social behaviour at other levels of social organization such as the sub-clan, clan and indeed the whole Gusii community. At the homestead level, family members were classified into different generational groupings and there were clear sets of moral norms of avoidance that governed the behaviour of people belonging to different generational groupings. For instance, a child was supposed to act in a restrained manner and to follow a prescribed avoidance behaviour when dealing with his/her parents and siblings. Avoidance behaviour was strictly enforced, particularly between parents and their children. However, there appeared to be certain levels of relaxation of avoidance behaviour between age-mates, siblings and grandparents and their grandchildren.

Consequently, it was a common practice among the Gusii people that when they met with people within their kinship and clan group, the first thing they were supposed to do was to inquire about the generation to which each person belonged and if there existed any form of family relationship. After establishing their generational classification and clan relationships, then the people knew how they should relate to one another depending on appropriate behavioural norms of restraint and familiarity. Appropriate generational and familial relationship terminologies that were applied at the homestead level were also extended to broader social groups such as clans and the Gusii society at large. The various forms of conduct such as behavioural avoidance, restraint and familiarity were accordingly applied.

Further, the concept of *chinsoni* provided a detailed code of conduct based on extreme modesty and restrained conduct, for instance, between parents and their children. Examples of these restrained behaviours included not touching one another, not seeing each other undress or in a state of being naked, and not being involved in explicit discussion of sexual matters. More importantly, as stated previously, a father was prohibited from entering the houses of his married sons under any circumstance. In addition, there was supposed to be minimal interaction between a father and his daughters-in-law. This kind of avoidance behaviour made sure that there was no chance of incest in the homestead.

Furthermore, the use of explicit euphemistic words referring to sexual and reproductive matters was strictly forbidden when people to whom the rules of avoidance and restraint applied were present, e.g. father, son and daughter or mother and son. For the Gusii these rules of avoidance and restraint between people of different generations and family or kinship relationships provided an ideal social model or moral governance starting from the domestic or homestead level. It extended to external settings such as the sub-clan or clan level. This promoted specific behavioural patterns and enhanced the maintenance of social distance between people belonging to different generational categories and kinship relationships.

Consequently, the *chinsoni* code of conduct provided the Gusii people with an ideal social model that guided behaviour and gave meaning and purpose to people's lives. Since the Gusii had no written records to enshrine their code of conduct, the Gusii model on ideal behavioural norms and social interactions was to a large extent implicit in nature. For instance, it was considered obvious to always show customary respect and obedience to various members of the homestead and the other extended family members based on hierarchical pattern where those people in high social status, such as heads of homestead, made decisions and gave orders that were supposed to be obediently adhered to by those below them. The head of the homestead, to take a specific example, gave orders to his wives and children and he expected obedience from them.

This chain of command from the top-down continued to various levels of relationships; for instance, the wives gave orders to their children, and the married sons to their wives and children. They in turn expected obedience from them. It was a serious offence to challenge a specific command coming from someone who was higher in the hierarchy. Usually, any form of disobedience would lead to severe punishment, particularly disobedience from a child to his or her parent. However, it should be stated that there were built-in checks and balances that governed the manner in which hierarchical power was exercised. Sometimes there was a lot of consultation among various members of the homestead before important decisions such as use of family land, giving consent to a son who had reached the required age to marry and the payment of bride wealth were made. This was done within the autonomy of each homestead.

Consequently, an ideal Gusii social model was one in which the people took pride in their unique social conduct which promoted restraint and modesty as were contained in the concept of *chinsoni* that had a lot of prohibitions concerning accepted social behaviour and the manner in which people interacted and related to one another.

Furthermore, avoidance was applied among the Gusii as a programmatic way of maintaining appropriate physical and social distance to prevent any form of socio-economic and cultural conflicts, particularly at the homestead level. It can therefore be stated that this social model of moral behaviour assisted in minimizing aggressive and sexual misconduct, and it fostered moral order and social harmony among the Gusii people.

The *chinsoni* code was a main factor that defined the Gusii as a distinct ethnic community. It prescribed the manner in which the Gusii defined their social behaviour and group interactions among themselves. The moral code of conduct, *chinsoni*, stipulated various ways in which people behaved and related with one another in any social setting either in the homestead or clan level; and it defined social interactions and behavioural conduct of the Gusii people as a whole.

One can ask what would have happened to those that broke the code. It worth stating that violating the code was considered taboo and attracted sanctions. At the homestead level, for instance, such violation would attract the wrath of the patriarch whose powers were wide and sweeping. In its worst form, violation of the code could prompt the pronouncement of a curse which could lead to the culprit being ostracized. In such situations, a curse could only be lifted following a systematic process such as *ogosonsorana* mentioned earlier. It is worth noting that only certain individuals in the society had powers to cleanse those that were cursed.

In general, *chinsoni* code sanctions were serious enough and acted as deterrence to any errant persons that may violate the code. Consequently, most community members followed the code without question, a situation that resulted in social-cultural mores that ensured order and peace in the society.

Conclusion

From the foregoing discussion, a conclusion can be drawn that the social structure regulated the interactions among members of the Gusii community. It provided the guidelines within the cultural norms for achieving the goals defined by the Gusii cultural values. Further, it is also presented that the social relations among the Gusii were governed by rules of kinship which were anchored in the *chisoni* code of conduct. The *chisoni* code moderated the conduct and behaviour of the Gusii people starting at the homestead level to entire clans and community at large. The adherence to *chisoni* code ensured and maintained the societal order and stability.

At this point, it is important to point out that the Gusii social structure defined and formed the basis of the Gusii indigenous justice system where the homestead was regarded as the cornerstone of informal legal institutions (see Chapter 11). Finally, it should be noted that, in the face prevailing community interaction and the advent of modernization, the Gusii social structure has undergone changes. In this regard, the Gusii had to embrace social change which allowed the survival of the community to the present.

CHAPTER FIVE

GUSII INITIATION CEREMONY

Introduction

This chapter provides a systematic exposition of Gusii male initiation ceremony. Perhaps there was no other Gusii indigenous ceremony that dramatized the essence of Gusii adult male and female life, for that matter, as circumcision. To allow for systematic discussion of the Gusii male circumcision ceremony, the chapter is divided into various subsections including, initial planning, the actual day of circumcision, the making of the sacred fire, the planting of the ritualistic grass, the mysteries of the *esubo* ritual, privileged freedom and emergence from seclusion. However, it should be understood that until recently (1980s), similar to male circumcision, female circumcision was widely practiced among the Gusii as a major rite of passage.

Rites of Passage and Rituals: Brief Overview

Among the Gusii, adolescent education was the most important stage for skills training and inculcation of knowledge that an individual had to undergo before entering adulthood. Although there was tacit recognition that education was a continuous life-long process, there was clear recognition that education during the transitional period of adolescence was extremely important in shaping the ultimate character and personality of an adult. It was due to this recognition that adolescent life was marked with elaborate and memorable initiation ceremonies, rites of passage, and rituals, such as circumcision, seclusion and other forms of magical-religious rituals. These initiation rites were aimed at transforming an individual from childhood to adulthood status. It was only after undergoing all rites of passage that an individual was eventually regarded as having acquired sufficient educational experience to enable him lead a satisfactory and fulfilling adult life. More importantly, during the period of initiation, an individual received concerted education and training on various aspects pertaining to human sexuality.

Consequently, until an individual underwent all the rites of passage and rituals that marked adolescent life, s/he was perceived as still being a child without a clear understanding of the complexities and mysteries of adult life. However, immediately an individual went through all the requisite rites of passage, s/he was henceforth declared as being an adult ready to undertake all duties and responsibilities as pertains to adulthood.

It is also important to note that after one attained the status of adulthood, any form of weakness and/or unsatisfactory performance of duties and functions, as pertains adulthood, was inexcusable. This would lead to serious sanctions and/or punishment including ostracism. It should be noted that due to recent controversies concerning female circumcision and existing general agreement that female circumcision (sometimes referred to female genital mutilation) is out-modeled.

The Male Circumcision Ceremony

Due to the social and cultural significance that was attached to circumcision among the Gusii, the commencement of this ceremony entailed detailed planning. The circumcision ceremony was usually conducted at the end of the harvesting season, usually the last quarter of the year. This was mainly due to the fact that during this period of the year food was plentiful as these ceremonies involved a lot of celebration, eating and making merry. In addition, at this time of the year most people in the community did not have much work to do. As a consequence, they had more free time on their hands to indulge in leisure activities. During this time of the year, the social situation was ideal for merry-making, celebration, feasting and the performance of various ritualistic activities that accompanied circumcision and other initiation ceremonies.

As the case was with most other communal ceremonies and other important events, circumcision was a community affair transcending individual families, households and sub-clans. The whole neighbourhood was involved, in one way or the other, in the preparation and performance of various aspects of this ceremony. A British anthropologist who conducted research on various aspects of Gusii rites of passage during the mid-twentieth century states (Mayer, 1953):

> In the sense that it takes place all over Gusii at a given season, initiation (circumcision ceremony) may be called a national affair. However, it is not centrally organized.... The main initiation is an affair for the *risaga* (a group of co-operative neighbours). *Risaga* is a small community embracing a number of adjacent homesteads whose members are accustomed to helping one another with co-operative labour and also to share major festivities.

Thus, all members of the neighbourhood (i.e., clan) were involved in performing various duties and assignments designated according to age and gender. For instance, older children were involved in fetching water from nearby streams and collecting firewood from adjacent woodlands. They were also sent on errands to relay important information and messages to and from various adult members in different homesteads in the neighbourhood, and carrying food to guests during the actual ceremony. A solemn responsibility of the boys that had undergone the ceremony was to escort the initiates to and from the place where the surgical operation (i.e., the cutting of the foreskin in the case of boys) took place.

The unmarried young men were also involved in providing guidance and skills training to initiates during the seclusion period that commenced immediately after circumcision. The adult members of the community shouldered the most tedious responsibilities, particularly making detailed arrangements and planning for the intricate activities associated with the circumcision ceremony. The males undertook the construction of huts for the initiates to stay during seclusion period. Apart from making members of a neighbourhood join hands in a co-operative effort to perform intricate tasks, the coming together of members of the clan to perform collective responsibilities provided a special opportunity for all to partake in what can be termed as, "purposive collective celebration". Accordingly, the memorable initiation ceremonies played a crucial role in engendering a strong sense of community, nationhood and affirmed the common cultural identity among the Gusii.

Initial Planning Process

It was required that the boys themselves should show explicit desire and willingness to undergo the arduous initiation ceremony. The boys were supposed to voluntarily tell their parents or guardians that they wanted and were ready to undergo circumcision. This was probably due to the fact that the stakes were quite high, for it was this particular ceremony that determined an individual's long-term social status within the community. Furthermore, circumcision was an extremely strenuous experience that required endurance and courage. However, the final decision as to whether a boy should undergo circumcision rested entirely on the parents.

As mentioned above, the enormity of the work involved in preparation for the circumcision ceremony caused the parents of the boys to come together to plan and assist each other in performing various assignments. For instance, the parents planned and pooled resources and labour to construct seclusion huts and assemble various foods and drinks. In addition, each parent or guardian had to identify an *omosegi* (pl. *abasegi*) - sponsor or mentor - for their son. These were older boys who had already undergone the process and whose role was to assist the initiate go through the ceremony and provide guidance to the initiate on various issues during the initiation period.

Due to the important role that was played by sponsors during various stages of initiation, those selected to act as sponsors had to meet specific stipulated requirements including having already undergone all the initiation rites. In addition, a sponsor should be unmarried and a person of exemplary character. Since sponsors shared intimate relationships with the initiates that lasted for a lifetime, they were supposed to be people who exercised restrained behaviour when interacting with the initiates, see the previous chapter for the Gusii concept governing social behaviour - *chinsoni*.

The duties of the sponsor commenced on the eve of the circumcision day when the boys were required to spend the last night of their "boyhood" at the home of the sponsor. During that night, the boys were confronted with various tasks that were aimed at testing their stamina, courage and determination to go through the rites. For instance, the boys would be sent during the wee hours of the night to look for firewood. The initiates would also be made to strip naked and lie prostrate on cold dew, and they would also be sent to take a bath in a river. All these ordeals were meant to test the initiates' ability and readiness to endure and/or withstand the painful agony of circumcision. After completion of the arduous tests, the sponsor and the other older boys present gave oral narrations of important events that have shaped the Gusii destiny. These included various legendary stories about Gusii heroes or heroines of the past, among other stories.

The legendary figures included individuals who had shown extraordinary courage, wisdom and extemporary leadership skills such as the war heroes who had led the Gusii during major battles against external aggression such as during the Ngarora war against the Maasai and the battle of Osaosao against the Kipsigis. These were unique Gusii personalities and individuals who had stood against all odds and put their lives on the line to provide protection for the Gusii people. These were individuals who epitomized the urge for self- preservation and survival of the Gusii against the various odds that confronted them. Such legendary personalities were perceived as ideal role models whose character needed to be emulated by all Gusii men. After listening to these stories, the boys were allowed to take a brief nap. At the first crow of the cockerel (i.e., at around three o'clock), they were hurriedly woken up by the escorts to start the journey in the outlying woodlands to the venue where circumcision would take place. Circumcision was usually carried out in areas containing ritualistic trees such as *emetembe* and *emiobo*. After reaching the venue of circumcision, the boys were made to lie down on the cold dew in a single line.

The Day of Circumcision

It should also be noted that it was the solemn responsibility of the circumciser, *omosari* (pl. *abasari*), to choose the exact location to conduct circumcision. He would use the location in subsequent years. It was a forbidden to cut the tree under which circumcision was done.

The journey to the site of circumcision was usually dramatic and arduous. Apart from bathing in cold water in the streams that were situated en-route to the venue, the boys were required to submerge their bodies in the cold morning water before continuing to the next stream where they did the same until they arrived at the place. All this time, the boys were required to run at a very high speed, and any boy found lagging behind received a severe beating from the older boys. It is important to note that all these gruelling undertakings were meant to dramatize the whole circumcision process so as to instil utmost discipline and peace of mind for the initiates to confront the knife of the circumciser courageously and in total submission. It was a taboo for any initiate to cry or make any undue movement during the actual circumcision (i.e., the surgical removal of the foreskin of the phallus).

Before the arrival of the circumciser, the older boys escorting the initiates applied further psychological torment that was meant to make the bodies of the initiates numb and unresponsive to pain. For instance, the young men started teasing the initiates that if anyone of them was afraid of being circumcised, he now had the last chance to stand up and run away to Luo land.

These fierce looking young men, who were usually armed with an assortment of crude weapons including spears, arrows, swords, clubs, and knifes, kept informing the initiates that if anyone of them was not ready to face the knife, he should run away before the circumciser arrived. Worse still, the boys were frankly informed that if any of them attempted to cry, he would be speared to death for bringing shame to his clansmen and putting a curse on the circumciser. As the circumciser arrived, walking majestically, carrying his tools of work and making incantations and war cries, the older boys reached a frenzy. They shouted at the top of their voices issuing threats and daring any boy who thought that he was brave enough to demonstrate his bravery and step forward to be the first one to get circumcised. It can be said that, of all the threats, this particular one was perhaps the most daunting.

The initiate who volunteered to be the first one to be circumcised received immediate status as the one who had demonstrated to the rest of the other boys that it was possible to successfully go through the ordeal of circumcision unblemished, thus setting the right tempo for the exercise. He henceforth became a trendsetter and was highly cherished for his act of bravery and courage. He was identified as an individual with the right traits who would in the near future be given onerous communal responsibilities such as leading his age-mates during war. Furthermore, such an individual could also be accorded special social privileges including that of leading members of his lineage or clan in performing important magical-religious rituals and/or ceremonies. Following the completion of all rituals and ceremonies, the boy was given the honour of leading the procession back home.

However, in instances where there was no boy who volunteered to be the first one to be circumcised, the escorts sent forward the boys in the order of age and/or body size. Once the first boy had been circumcised, the other boys followed, one by one, in the order of first come first served. Mayer (1953) describes the occasion:

> The boy stands his back to the tree, his arms grasping the trunk, his legs bent at the knee and held apart; he tries to gaze straight ahead, having been told that the operation will not hurt so much if he does not see it. The foreskin is removed in about half a minute. The boy is to step forward, is a high pitch little cry uttered by the circumciser. One of the older lads gives the returning boy a bunch of *ekerundu* leaves (a common symbol of fertility) to hold in hand as he holds the penis horizontally, waiting for the blood to clot.

During the surgical operation to remove the foreskin, the older boys continued brandishing their weapons at the motionless stiff body of the initiate whose arms grasped a tree trunk. This was done in such a way that it appeared as if the young men were actually going to murder the initiate. They formed a semi-circle around the initiate, and made high-pitched enchantments, working themselves into a frenzy, cutting at the tree trunk with their swords. At the same time, while still pointing their spears and swords at the boy, they made rhythmic gestures as if they were actually going to cut off the boy's head if he made any attempts to cry or made any movement.

It should, however, be noted that all these dramatic acts and enchantments were meant to play on the psychology of the boys so as to direct their attention away from the otherwise painful surgery. All the commotion and loud noises usually succeeded in subduing the boy, and by the time he started feeling any pain, the actual operation was over. Consequently, it can be stated that the dramatic acts in addition to numbing of the initiate's body as he lay prostrate on the cold dew and the chilling morning breeze, acted as, in effect, anaesthesia. After finishing circumcising all the boys, the circumciser signalled the beginning of the journey back home by starting singing the circumcision song, *esimbore*, as Gusii custom demanded. He then handed over the rest of the chorus to the charged and excited young men who chanted the solemn song as they made their way; escorting the initiates to their respective homes.

It should also be noted that this magical-religious song had been passed down from one generation to the other, since time immemorial. This song was only sung during circumcision, and it had a lot of cultural value and symbolism. It was taboo to sing the song at any other time apart from during circumcision. The following are the main verses of the *esimbore* song:

Ekegusii	English Translation
Oyo-oyo-o-o! x2	Here he is! Here he is!
Omoisia omoke mbororo bwamorire	(The circumcised) little boy is experiencing pain
Omosia omoke ateta, ngina!	The little boy, copulate with his mother!
Oyo-oyo-o-o! x2	Here he is! Here he is!
Omoisia omoke mbororo bwamorire	(The circumcised) little boy has felt pain.
Omoisia omoke ateta ng'ina. x2	The little boy, copulate with his mother.
Samokami oirire 'mboro chiaito x2	Circumciser has taken our penises
Tiga aire mbororo bwamorire x2	Let him take he is angry with us.
Oyotarochi tigache kwerorera x2	He who does not believe, let him come and witness
Kwerorera enyamweri ekorwa engoro ime. x2	To witness the one like moonlight, appearing from the cave/hole.
Mboro chiaito indokore rwekonoire. x2	Our penises are like a green tree with its bark peeled off
Oyo-oyo-o-o-o! Oyoo! x 2	Here he is! Here he is! x2
Otureirwe itimo x2	He has been given a spear. x2
Na nguba mbibo x2	And a big shield x2
Arwane Sigisi x2	Fight the Kipsigis x2
Arwane Maasai x2	Fight the Maasai x2
Arwane Sugusu x2	Fight to the north x2
Arwane Irianyi x2	Fight to south. x2
Arwane bobisa x2	Fight the enemy. x2

During the solemn journey back home, the initiates were made to walk in a single line (following the order in which they had been circumcised) sandwiched by their escorts. Care was taken to ensure that no women saw the newly circumcised boys. As already noted, the boy who had volunteered to be the first one to be circumcised, henceforth, became a trendsetter for his age-mates. This act of bravery was given special recognition, and it brought a lot pride to the parents. He was henceforth identified as a person of exceptional courage and could later be called upon to lead his age-mates during crucial occasions, such as when the community was at war with an external aggressor.

Back at the homes of the initiates, the period preceding the initiates' arrival was usually tense with anticipation, especially on the part of the parents. Women kept their ears on the ground as they waited to catch the sound of the circumcision song. It was an act of great shame for a boy to cry while undergoing circumcision. Consequently, hearing the sound of the approaching party singing the circumcision song heralded a big sigh of relief for all people at the homestead who were gathered for the occasion. In the unlikely event of a boy crying and/or making any movement during the operation, he would henceforth be referred to as *enkuri* (pl. *chinkuri*) - one who cried during circumcision. In that unfortunate situation, the circumciser detained the initiate until his parents brought forth a he goat to be sacrificed to cleanse the circumciser.

Thus, immediately the women heard the sound of the *esimbore* song, they started singing and ululating to express great joy, as they ran forth to welcome the returning party of the young men escorting the initiates to the homesteads. However, as the excitable women came closer, the young men formed an impenetrable wall around the initiates to prevent the women from catching a glimpse of the initiates. Gusii custom demanded that married women should not come too close so as to catch a glimpse of the initiates.

The women increased the tempo of their singing and dancing as they approached the main entrance to the homestead. At the same time, the young men escorting the initiates also accelerated the singing tempo of the circumcision song that was now spiced with words of obscenity. It is important to note that, during circumcision ceremony, the *chinsoni* concept of behavioural restraint among people belonging to different generations and genders (see previous chapter) was usually relaxed to allow a freer atmosphere appropriate for merry-making and celebration. The arrival in the homestead heralded the climax of the singing and dancing.

On such occasions, the women went wild with excitement and danced into a frenzy while making high pitched ululations, taunting the young men not to touch them. However, keeping a watchful eye aimed at the excitable women, the young men led the initiate into a specific shed at the edge of the homestead and the *esimbore* song was temporarily halted. The initiates stayed in the sheds until evening and were served with their first meal since undergoing the circumcision. This meal was specially prepared consisting of staple porridge that was served when it was cold, and eaten with a variety of indigenous vegetables, particularly *chinsaga* and *rinagu*. These vegetables have a high nutritional value and they also assisted in minimizing bleeding and energizing the initiates. (Interestingly, this was the same diet which was recommended for newly-wed couples and mothers who had given birth, to assist them to regain their agility and good health.) After taking the meal, the initiates, still in the shed, would be visited by older boys from the neighbourhood who congratulated them and gave them words of encouragement.

Late in the evening, the initiates were asked to remove their fore fingers that had been grasping the hinder skin of the phallus to prevent it from stretching and covering the fore head of the penis. However, there were occasional instances when bleeding persisted. When that happened, it was usually attributed to amorous behaviour of the initiate's mother. In such situations, elderly women ordinarily urged the woman to show honour and spare her son the agony by admitting that she had been unfaithful to her husband. If the woman confessed her sinfulness, a special magical-religious ritual was conducted to cleanse the couple and appease the ancestral spirits.

Associating the incident of bleeding by an initiate to his mother's amorous behaviour does not seem to make much sense. It should, however, be observed that the strong belief that such unfortunate incidents would occur served as a strong deterrent to probable sexual misconduct by married women. This was therefore an effective form of social sanction that was calculated at scaring married women from the unlikely desire of engaging in extra marital amorous behaviour. Interestingly, if the mother managed to prove her innocence, beyond any reasonable doubt, then the bleeding incident would be attributed to certain unfulfilled family magical-religious rituals. In such a situation, the services of a diviner would be sought and remedial action taken to appease the offended ancestral spirits, *chisokoro* (sing. *esokoro*).

Also, this might be accompanied by the administration of first aid to the initiate that involved the use of certain herbal medicines. In addition to all these curative measures, an elderly woman (preferably the grandmother or a classificatory kin) who had already reached menopause removed her waist beads and tied them around the initiate's neck.

Seclusion Stage

When the initiate was being escorted to the seclusion hut, as the Gusii tradition demanded, elders from his father's lineage would, ritualistically, sit in assigned positions between the cattle kraal and the main door leading to the mother's house, *gesieri kia bweri*. Here they were to be entertained and served with food and Gusii traditional brew, *amarwa*. Also during this time (i.e., as the elders were seated in the ritualistic position) the father of the initiate was required to carry a traditional calabash, *egesanda* (pl. *ebisanda*), or a small pot, *egetono* (pl. *ebitono*), containing sour milk to signify the blessing of the initiate to beget many children and abundant cattle. (Note that cattle signified wealth and were a form of currency of the time.) After the initiate entered the seclusion hut, there was a lot of singing, dancing and merry-making that went on until midnight. During such a time, the women once again ran wild with excitement, singing and making high-pitched ululations.

Men, as Gusii tradition demanded, maintained their cool, especially in public. Now they loosened up, after sipping mouthfuls of the traditional brew. They also started singing traditional male songs, *emeino* (sing. *omoino*), and dancing with abandon while the women made ululations in admiration of the singing and dancing prowess of their men. On the way to the seclusion hut, the older boys, while still shielding the initiate from preying eyes of the people, briefly paused near the place where the now excitable elders were seated (i.e., the area between the cattle kraal and the main entrance door to the mother's house). They sang the circumcision song with vigour to signify the entry of the initiate into the seclusion period. The initiate was supposed to enter the seclusion hut through the main door facing the cattle pen. This door was also referred to as *gesieri kia gesaku* (the door of the lineage). Once inside the seclusion hut, the initiate was required to use a breached door, *egesieri kia 'gesaku*, when going out and/or entering the hut. Thus, throughout the seclusion period, the initiate was supposed to use the main door only twice (at the start and end of the seclusion period).

When in seclusion, the initiates were referred to as e*bisimba* (sing. *egesimba*), "wild cats." They were not to be seen by members of the community, especially their parents, married women, girls and uncircumcised boys. In this regard, the only link that the initiates had to the outside world, especially their parents, was through the sponsor, *omosegi*.

The remaining part of this Chapter provides a detailed description of the various stages of seclusion that the initiates (boys) went through. Thus, due to the inherent and in order to avoid unnecessary repetitions, we are going to use the case of male initiates to explain the various stages of the seclusion and the various activities and rituals that were performed during this period.

The Making of the Sacred Fire

On the same day the initiates entered seclusion, the sponsor, *omosegi*, with the help of his assistant, *omosichi* (pl. *abasichi*) – the tamer - lit a ritualistic fire that was supposed to be kept alight throughout the seclusion period. This fire was made by rubbing a dried stick (derived from a hardwood) against a grooved stick (derived from softwood) that lay, horizontally, across the floor. Using both palms, the hardwood stick was vigorously rubbed against the grooved stick until sparks of fire were produced. The sparks were then hurriedly put together to make the ritualistic fire inside the seclusion hut. Interestingly, the hardwood stick that was used for rubbing was referred to as *ekerende egetwani* (the male stick) while the soft stick that was rubbed until it produced the sparks was referred to as *ekerende egekungu* (the female stick). These metaphoric phrases were probably supposed to convey subliminal messages to the novice on the act of having sexual intercourse. That is to say the *ekerende egetwani*, the "male stick," can be figuratively translated to mean the male reproductive organ or phallus. *Ekerende egekungu*, the "female stick," referring to the soft wooden groove that was drilled using the "male stick" can figuratively translated to mean the female reproductive organ.

When starting the sacred fire, both the "male stick" and the "female stick" were vigorously rubbed against each other until they produced sparks which were used to light the sacred, ritualistic fire. The act of rubbing the two sticks against each other was a figurative demonstration of the sexual or procreation act between the male and female which results in conception of an embryo (symbolically the sparks). This later developed into an infant. Eventually, an infant had to be carefully looked after and nourished so that it could develop into an adult. That is to say the sparks that were used to make the sacred fire were supposed to be carefully looked after and nourished to produce the glowing fire that was supposed to be kept alight throughout the seclusion period. The caring and nourishing the sacred fire, figuratively, demonstrated the onus of parental responsibility of looking after a child from infancy until it reached maturity.

The seclusion period was perceived by the Gusii as a form of rebirth. An individual was, ritualistically, reproduced to start a new life of adulthood. Indeed, it was taboo for the sacred fire to go out (during the whole of the seclusion period). This was prescribed by serious sanctions, i.e. it was believed that any initiate whose fire, inadvertently or otherwise, went out could experience serious problems in their marital life in years to come. They might either fail to have a satisfactory sex life or might be barren or impotent. Thus, there were a lot of cultural values attached to the ritualistic fire, and it was the duty and solemn responsibility of the initiate to look after the fire and make sure it was kept lit throughout the seclusion period.

The Planting of Ritualistic Grass

During the third day of seclusion, the *omosegi* with the help of his assistant *omosichi* prepared a ritualistic bed for the initiates. This bed was usually called *riburu* (pl. *amaburu*) and consisted of a main frame that was constructed using small trunks or branches of a particular hardwood; then the frames were covered with a thick layer of a leafy twig from the ritualistic plant, *amabuko*. In addition, the sponsor prepared a bow and arrows (i.e., sharpened sticks) for the initiate to use when going out in the forest to hunt wild game and birds. It was also during the third day that the boys planted *esuguta* near the entrance of the main door, *egesierikia bweri* (as already mentioned, the initiate was prohibited from using this particular door until the end of the seclusion period). During this particular day, the sponsor, accompanied by a few older boys from the neighbourhood, went to a valley bottom where this type of grass grew in waterlogged clay soil. After identifying a suitable stump of the ritualistic grass, the sponsor dug it up using a traditional hoe while the tamer assisted in carefully pulling the grass out. During this whole period, the accompanying boys sang a ritualistic song, e*sabarianyi*. It was only sung on such an occasion. Like the circumcision song, e*sabarianyi* was loaded with a lot of cultural symbolism that was handed down from generation to generation. This song had the following main verses:

Ekegusii	English Translation
Esabarianyi y'esuguta y'abare esabarianyi	Of initiates' esuguta.
Aye, makomoke oremire inchera igoro	Oh, stepmother has cultivated on the main path.
Ee, tiga areme mboremo bwamoborire	Yes, let her cultivate, she has no other garden.
Aye, okwanigwe na moeti na mogendi.	Oh, she gets greetings by passers-by.
Aye okwanigwe nonde ataiitongo	Oh, she gets greetings by passers-by.
Aye, okwanigwe na omoeti na mogendi.	Oh, she gets greetings by passers-by.

After uprooting the ritualistic grass, esuguta, the song was sung continuously until the boys arrived back in the homestead. The singing went on until the esuguta was planted inside the seclusion house, in the specified location. After planting the esuguta, the sponsor demonstrated to the initiate how to take care of the ritualistic grass so that it did not dry. This involved sprinkling the grass with water on a regular basis. After the training, the initiate was given an opportunity to sprinkle water on the grass while singing the esabarianyi song.

The Mysteries of the Esubo Ritual

The esubo ritual, which was performed on the fourth day after circumcision, was perhaps the most dramatic training during the seclusion period. There was a lot of cultural significance attached to this particular ritual which was also loaded with subliminal messages on sexuality and gender specific roles that were at the core of Gusii adult life. The ritual was carried out at the time when the initiate had survived the circumcision ordeal and was now settled down to lead a life of seclusion for the duration of about two months. In preparation for this particular ceremony, the sponsor, accompanied by a few boys from the neighbourhood, went to the forest to look for bitter herbs and wild roots that were supposed to be eaten by initiates during the esubo ritual. After returning from the forest with an assortment of the bitter herbs and wild roots, the sponsor would ask the initiate to assist him in preparing strings that could be used in making ropes. When the ropes were ready, the novice was informed that they were going to be used in tying up a mysterious beast, enyabububu, which was to arrive during the esubo night from its abode in Lake Victoria.

However, the ropes in actual fact were used in the construction of a musical instrument capable of producing an unfamiliar deep groaning sound imitating that which was supposed to be produced by the mysterious beast, *enyabububu*. The instrument was made by tightly tying a wet/soft animal skin (preferably goat skin) around the mouth of a medium-sized pot using the ropes. At around midnight, the sponsor, assisted by his deputy, started administering various activities that marked the start of the *esubo* ritual. The ritual was kicked off by the sponsor, asking the initiate to start eating the "special food" (i.e. the bitter wild roots and herbs). The initiate was required to systematically chew, and digest the food to his fill. In case the initiate showed reluctance in eating the unpalatable concoction, he received a severe spanking from the sponsor.

While dishing out specified quantities of herbs and roots, the sponsor usually used particular Ekegusii terminologies when referring to various parts of animal meat. Thus, for instance, the sponsor started the process by asking the initiate to have the "first course of the meal" by saying, "okay now young man take this *riuga* (pl. *amauga*) - bone i.e., the hardy wild roots - and chew it to satisfaction". Then the sponsor handed over the second mouthful of the food (a concoction of the bitter herbs), saying "now boy take this *ritana* (the juicy meat derived from between the forelimbs and forelegs of a heifer) and eat it".

This process would continue until the older boys were satisfied that the initiate had eaten enough mouthfuls of the unpalatable concoctions.

As would be expected, the initiate found it extremely difficult to chew and swallow the revolting concoctions. Obviously, after chewing the concoction, it was even more difficult to swallow through the throat to the stomach. The bitter concoction could burn the initiate's mouth and throat. The initiate, however, had no option but to continue chewing and swallowing the bitter concoction; otherwise he could receive a severe scolding and/or spanking from the sponsor. If the initiate managed to courageously endure this ordeal without undergoing undue coercion, he received a lot of praise from the sponsor and the other older boys present during this occasion.

By the time the boy finished taking the concoction, however, he would have developed painful blisters in his mouth, lips and throat. As a result, he experienced difficulty in swallowing food for a few subsequent days. Thus, to prevent the initiate from starving following the ritual, he was served with a sumptuous meal before undergoing this ordeal.

No sooner had the initiate finished consuming the unpalatable concoction than he was subjected to another ordeal that involved the rubbing of hot pepper on the healing penis. The sponsor ordered the initiate to stand still as the tamer, *omosichi*, applied the dry pepper mixed with water on the wound on the boy's penis. This process of rubbing the initiate's penis with pepper was referred to as, "letting the snake bite the initiate's phallus," *okoromia omware eng'iti*. As the tamer stretched his hands forward to apply the caustic paste, the sponsor would shout at the initiate to close his eyes so that he did not see the snake that was going to bite his penis. It is noteworthy that, in most instances, the boy actually believed that a snake was going to bite his penis. This belief was usually strengthened by the fact that, prior to the start of the *esubo* night, the older boys menacingly informed the initiate that a big snake was going to bite his yet to heal penis during the *esubo* ritual.

As would be expected, the initiate experienced excruciating pain; however; he was not supposed to touch his penis. Doing so would result in severe spanking. As time went on and the tormenting reached a crescendo, the pain would become unbearable and the initiate eventually broke down and started crying loudly, to the amusement of the older boys. They would laugh while rebuking and ordering him to stop crying as a baby. When it reached this seemingly unbearable level, however, the sponsor stopped the torment. By this time, the initiate would be experiencing excruciating pain and would implore the sponsor to spare him further agony. Looking agitated, the sponsor would harshly retort, asking the initiate to explain why he had been involved in abominable acts such as sleeping on his mother's bed and having sex with "dirty" uncircumcised girls. The initiate would then be ordered to publicly repent his sins and be forgiven. The initiate would then be ordered to take an oath binding him not to be involved in any abominable sexual acts until the end of his life on earth. Otherwise, the ancestral spirit would impose a severe curse on him that might result in him being completely ostracized from the Gusii community.

The taking of the oath brought to an end the administration of this particular ritual. Subsequently, the initiate was ordered to go to sleep.

Immediately before dawn (at around five in the morning), the sponsor ordered the initiate to wake up and confront the mysterious beast, *enyabububu*, that had arrived from the lake. At this time, the other boys, who were already outside in the darkness, started entering the house led by the *omosichi*, the tamer of the mysterious beast. As they entered the hut, they vigorously hit the walls with sticks to create an impression in the mind of the novice that indeed the mysterious beast had arrived, trampling into the house. This impression was further accentuated by the musical instrument which produced a deep strange sound.

As the older boys entered the dimly lit house still hitting the wall, the tamer, *omosichi*, quickly dug a hole in the floor of the house where he buried the musical instrument - the pot with a soft animal skin covering its top. Immediately the instrument was secured in the ground, the tamer began "milking" the "mystery beast" from the lake (playing the musical instrument), *ogokama eng'iti enene yarure roche/nyancha*!

In reality, the milking of the mystery beast involved a systematic tapping on the soft wet skin, producing a deep groaning sound to imitate the voice of the mysterious beast. Then the other boys informed the novice that the tamer was milking the mysterious beast, *enyabububu*, before it swallowed him alive and carried him inside its belly as it returned to its abode in the depths of Lake Victoria. Indeed, the strange deep roaring sound and the intense commotion that followed made the novice believe that the mysterious beast had arrived to take him to the lake.

Overwhelmed by extreme fear of the unknown phenomenon, the novice started crying aloud as the agitating boys continued threatening him that the mysterious beast was about to shallow him and return with him to the lake. Afterwards, the sponsor ordered the initiate to come out of the bed and confront the mysterious beast. When the boy refused to come out due to fear, the older boys forcefully dragged him from his hiding place under the ritualistic bed. Meanwhile, the other boys asked the beast whether it wanted to swallow the boy and take him to the Lake. In return, the *enyabububu* would roar in the affirmative (i.e., this was done by the *omosichi*, manoeuvring the sticks he was rubbing on the musical instrument to produce intonations imitating the affirmative sound of the supposed mysterious beast). Screaming aloud, the novice implored the now excited boys not to let the *enyabububu* swallow him as he continued resisting being dragged out of his hiding place.

This made the sponsor highly agitated, and he started giving the novice a severe spanking for embarrassing his parents and the community at large by his cowardly and/or unmanly crying. Then they forcefully dragged the initiate closer to the *enyabububu*. This was the time it dawned on the initiate that he had been subjected to a major deception because instead of seeing a scary big beast, he realized that the deep sound was being produced by the musical instrument that was partially submerged. The novice once again took another magical-religious oath, swearing that henceforth he will never in his lifetime show any form of cowardice when confronted with difficult and dangerous situations such as the time of war against an external enemy. After taking the oath, the sponsor disclosed all the secrets of the *esubo* night by lighting the fire in the house for the initiate to see with his naked eyes that, actually, what had been making him scream with fear was in reality non-existent. The sponsor then informed the novice that the strange sound was produced by the submerged pot. There was, after all, no mysterious beast that was going swallow him and take him to the lake. The initiate then received training on how to construct and play the musical instrument.

Finally the initiate was asked to step back and relax; everybody broke into prolonged delirious laughter at the height of the deception that shrouded the *esubo* ritual. The initiate also joined in the laughter, wondering aloud why throughout his childhood life, he had been made to have a morbid fear of the time when he was going to confront the mysterious beast during the *esubo* ritual. After the sponsor was satisfied that the enormity of the symbolic meaning of the *esubo* ritual had sunk in, he permitted the initiate to go to sleep. Meanwhile, people in the neighbourhood were awakened by the deep roaring sound of the *enyabububu* that was quite familiar to the initiated adults.

However, when the frightened children inquired from adults what was producing the scary noise, the adults simply informed them it that was the groaning sound of the mysterious beast that had arrived in the neighbourhood to swallow and take the initiates to his abode in the depths of Lake Victoria. However, if the children asked further why the beast should take all the initiates, the elders then clarified that the mysterious beast only swallowed those initiates who had been disobedient to their parents and other community adults. This was supposed to serve the role of influencing all children in the neighbourhood to be obedient to all adults in the community. In other words, they should always accord respect to all people in the community or else when their turn for initiation came, they would be swallowed by the mystery beast and taken to the lake never to return again.

Privileged Freedom

It is important to note at this point that throughout the seclusion period, the initiates were referred to as *ebisimba*, as started previously, indigenous wildcats that are quite common in wooded areas of Gusii land. These wildcats are known for their reclusive behaviour and the stealthy manner in which they stalked their prey. The wildcats roamed at will in their forest habitat and sometimes strayed in Gusii homesteads to stealthily prey on people's chicken, especially during the wee hours of the night when everybody was asleep. Probably, the initiates were referred to as "wildcats" to connote the reclusive lifestyle they were required to adopt during the seclusion period (i.e. they were not supposed to be seen by members of the community). Also, throughout the seclusion period, the initiates were permitted a rare privilege to freely stalk people's chickens in the neighbourhood so as to capture them and roast them for food in their seclusion huts.

Tradition demanded that owners of the chicken should not launch any complaint since the chicken were supposed to have been eaten by the wildcats (the initiates). Thus, whenever an initiate killed chicken in the neighbourhood, it was simply stated that *ebisimba biairire engoko*, the wildcats have taken the chicken; this was not taken as an act of theft. The owner was therefore neither supposed to be compensated nor were the initiates supposed to be punished. Furthermore, the initiates were allowed the privilege of stealthily entering people's fields of maize, arrow roots, cassava and sweet potatoes and stealthily harvest the crops which they took to their hut to cook and feed on with abandon. However, this conduct should not imply that the initiates were not well fed during seclusion; on the contrary, they were pampered with all sorts of delicious meals made up of beef, mutton, eggs, plenty of milk and indigenous vegetables during this period. And these are meals they could call up at will.

During the seclusion period, the initiates were also exempted from all forms of normal daily chores or duties. Throughout the seclusion period, the initiates were supposed, most of the time, to lead a reclusive leisurely life including spending a lot of the daytime hunting smaller game in surrounding woodlands. However, as already stated, when going out of the seclusion hut, initiates were supposed to be extremely careful not to meet anyone or be seen by people in the neighbourhood. Particularly, it was taboo for the initiate to meet or be seen by his parents, uncles and or their classificatory kin. They were also not supposed to be seen and/or interact with uncircumcised boys and girls. Thus, the seclusion huts were a no-go area for most members of the community. The only exceptions to the rule were the already circumcised boys, grandparents and, to a certain extent, young girls who were not yet married.

If the initiates met with uncircumcised boys and girls collecting firewood in the forest, they beat them up and chased them away; nobody questioned them about this unbecoming behaviour. Consequently, during times of seclusion, the uncircumcised boy and girls always avoided venturing into adjacent woodlands because of the fear of encountering the unfriendly "wildcats". It is, however, interesting to note that usually young good looking unmarried ladies from the neighbourhood paid occasional visits to the initiates in their seclusion huts. During such visits, the ladies wore their best attire and were well groomed. While in the initiates' huts, they uttered obscenities that were aimed at provoking the initiate's libido. These particular sexual innuendos were referred to as *ogosonia abare* (arousing the initiates' sexual urge). Since the initiates were still nursing fresh surgical wounds, however, the arousing of an erection usually resulted in pain and agony as some of the unhealed penises' nerves might rupture. Noticing this, the youthful ladies, who seemed to enjoy the whole process knowing that the boys were still quite harmless, let out loud laughter as they ran out of the seclusion huts. As Philip Mayer (1953) put it:

> During the first few days after *esubo*, at which time the wounds of circumcision had not thoroughly healed, parties of girls came to the seclusion huts 'to trouble the novice' (as the Gusii say) by what is called 'arousing desire' (*ogosonia*). Removing all their clothes, they danced around the novice in a provocative manner and challenged them: 'You said you would become a young man (*omomura*) and have intercourse with a girl; now are you ready? Here it is - what you wanted. Come and copulate ('*nchuo ontete*), a direct utterance, employing a verb never voiced in decent speech.

However, it should also be stated that the episode of *ogosonia* (sexual arousal) was meant to serve a special purpose. It was meant to test whether the initiate had the potential of experiencing normal sexual arousal (i.e., having a stiff erection of the penis) and to find out if he was capable of sustaining effective sexual intercourse/penetration as was appropriate for procreation.

Emergence from Seclusion

As already stated, the seclusion period lasted between one and half to two months. Thus, by the time the initiates left seclusion, the wounds on the penis were completely healed. Nearing the end of seclusion (i.e., the last week) special preparations was made for the performance of the final rites or rituals that marked the end of seclusion and final admission of the initiates into the life of adulthood. As part of the preparation for the final initiation ceremony, parents of the initiates would, for instance, busy themselves preparing various food stuffs and traditional beer, *amarua*, to be consumed by guests who would be in attendance to witness the performance of the final initiation rites. Thus, these final rituals marked the end of seclusion and eventual acceptance of the initiates to rejoin the rest of the community as full adult members of the society.

On the last day of seclusion (nearing dawn or at around five o'clock), a swarm of young unmarried circumcised men and women from the neighbourhood descended on the home of the initiate to partake in special feasting which involved singing and dancing, eating and drinking. Eventually, after the party of these young men and women had been appropriately entertained, the initiate's sponsor, *omosegi*, and his assistant or tamer, *omosichi*, would lead the rest of the young men present in performing the following rites that marked the official ending of the seclusion period.

First, the traditional ritualistic bed, *riburu*, used by the initiate during the seclusion period, was destroyed by dismantling it and setting the pieces on fire, outside the seclusion hut. This was an indication that the seclusion period had officially come to an end. Also, as the ritualistic bed was being destroyed, the mysterious beast, *enyabububu*, would arrive in the homestead to make a final roar that signified the end of the seclusion. The roaring of the *enyabububu* was meant to particularly remind all the people in the neighbourhood that the initiates were now getting out of the sumptuous period of seclusion. During this second visit, unlike the *esubo* night, it was the initiates themselves who "made the *enyabububu* roar" (i.e., playing the musical instrument that produced the unique noise imitating a mysterious beast).

As the initiates busied themselves with playing the *enyabububu* outside the seclusion hut, the sponsor, with a group of unmarried young men, prepared a series of verbal questions to be used as the final matriculation. These were to test the initiate's competency and understanding of various forms of Gusii indigenous knowledge and the skills that had been imparted to him during the seclusion period. These pertained to various duties, functions and responsibilities of an adult Gusii man. For instance, the initiates would be asked to identify the leaves of various medicinal plants that were used in the treatment of various ailments, i.e. malaria, pneumonia and dysentery, etc.

The initiates were also asked to enunciate various aspects of the Gusii code of conduct that governed social behaviour and intergenerational social interaction, *chinsoni*. In addition, the initiates would be asked to recall the names of all members of their lineage or genealogy and the various classificatory groups they belonged to, i.e. names of brothers and sisters, parents, and grandparents, great-grandparents, etc. Other forms of competency that the initiates were supposed to have mastered included having a clear understanding of the various magical-religious rituals that were performed during various stages of the Gusii life cycle (i.e., during birth, circumcision, marriage and death). They were required to have a clear understanding of the cultural significance and social meaning of the magical-religious rituals.

The initiates were also expected to have a clear understanding of important historical events, acts of heroism and/or exemplarity behaviour shown by famous legendary Gusii figures. These included important Gusii personalities who, over the years, had played a critical role in shaping the destiny of the Gusii as a people. The initiates were also asked to enunciate the main duties and responsibilities of a Gusii adult male's life (marriage, sex, raising a family and the main skills in agriculture and animal husbandry). Furthermore, specific practical tests were administered to the initiates. These types of tests were particularly meant to assess the initiate's level of courage, stamina and endurance in dealing with difficult life situations. A good example of such a practical test was when the initiate (with his hands tied backwards) was asked to perform what seemed to be an impossible task. This was being commanded to use his teeth to pull out a peg that had been stuck in the ground close to the sacred fire in the seclusion hut. Performing this arduous task required the initiate to have the ability to balance his whole body and bend on his knees. While bending, the initiate made a swift move to pluck the peg while avoiding getting burnt.

After performing this final matriculation, the initiates were finally asked to take a special oath binding them not the leak any of the secrets as concerns the initiation ceremonies (i.e., the various mysteries that shrouded circumcision and other forms of initiation rites) to the uncircumcised lads. After taking this oath of secrecy, the initiates were led to the main house to receive special parental blessings (this was mainly done late in the evening). The initiate's parents (who were already aware that their son was about to visit them in their house for the first time since getting circumcised) were required to lie on their sleeping bed, in a ritualistic position, ready to give the final special blessings to their son.

While approaching the parents' house through the main door, *egesieri kia bweri* (the door facing the cattle kraal), the initiate announced his presence to his parents and then uttered a standard statement, solemnly requesting his parents to give him the special blessings as follows: *tata nababa borania ango* (which literally translates to 'please father and mothertalk to each other and give me blessings'). The father, who all this time was in bed with the mother supposedly having and/or pretending to be having sex, retorted: *ee mwana one borania chiombe n'abanto* (yes, my child, have the blessings of having a lot of cattle and children). After the father finished giving his blessing to the son, it would then be the turn of the mother to follow suit and utter the same words of blessing after being requested by the son to do so.

As already noted, the initiate was supposed to receive parental blessing while, ritualistically, standing on the entrance of the main house that faced the direction of the cattle pen. This implied that the blessings should, appropriately point to ownership of a large herd of cattle which was the ultimate wealth of a Gusii person. Similarly, the blessing by the parents' and the ritualistic act of pretending to have sex, implied the ability to beget many children. Thus the son should look forward to marrying in the near future and eventually having a successful sex life and begetting several children, just as his parents were doing. It should be noted that this visit to the parents' house by the initiate marked the first time his parents saw him since the time of undergoing circumcision. This act of blessing was the first conservation between the son and his parents since entering seclusion. After receiving parental blessings, the initiate would be escorted by his sponsor and tamer to a nearby stream to bathe (this would also be the first bath since circumcision). During the whole period of seclusion, the initiates were not supposed to bathe. The initiate was usually supposed to walk to the stream using any nearby detour route to avoid the prying eyes of people from the neighbourhood.

While going to the river to bathe, the initiates were supposed to carry with them a portion of twigs from the ritualistic bed. The initiate was required to use the twigs to vigorously scratch and wash his body clean. While taking a bath, the initiate uttered standard words as follows, *ekeraboko nekio* (all the uncleanness should be washed away by the river).After finishing bathing, the initiate was given specially prepared new attire. Reaching home after taking a bath, a specially prepared traditional cream was applied on the face of the initiate to anoint him and give him special permission to henceforth join Gusii adult life. It is important to note that all these rituals that were performed at the end of the seclusion period marked a symbolic rebirth of the individual (the initiate). This anointment of oil on the face of the initiate was supposed to be performed by the initiate's grandfather or his classificatory kin (if the grandfather had already died).

This act was supposed to be carried out inside a cattle pen to signify the blessing to have a large herd of cattle. Then, after receiving the anointment, the father of the initiate uttered final words of blessing to his son as follows: *mwana one onywe mache maya na ase ogotachaobonyasi boseboke* (my child drink good water and, may the grass on the ground you step on sprout). The anointment was the final ritual that was performed during this occasion. After receiving the anointment, the initiate joined unmarried young men to take the family cattle for grazing in adjacent rangelands. Later in the day, they took the cattle to the river to drink. While the young men were away tending to the family cattle, clan elders arrived in the homestead to join the parents of the initiate in special celebration and feasting to mark the end of the initiation ceremony. After being served with various traditional dishes and drinks, the clan elders, whom Gusii tradition required should always maintain their cool and carry themselves with decorum, especially when in public, now loosened up. The excitable elders then stood up, at marked intervals, to join hands in singing the Gusii male songs, *emeino*, that were supposed to be specifically sung during such a special occasion. While singing the male songs, the elders started dancing occasional jigs as befitted them. This involved rhythmic shaking of shoulders and systematic stamping of their feet on the floor. As the night approached, the initiate, who had now returned from looking after the family cattle, was finally paraded before the excitable lineage of elders to receive congratulatory remarks for having successfully gone through all the requisite rites of passage, thus bringing the family pride. The elders also reminded the initiate that he was now an adult ready to discharge all the duties and responsibilities of Gusii adult life, including being called upon to go to war to defend his people against any form of external aggression.

Conclusion

This chapter has presented an in-depth description and analysis of the Gusii initiation ceremonies, particularly, the male circumcision. It has been elucidated that this ritual was a public affair where both boys and girls were expected to undergo the ordeal without showing a trace of fear. In addition, the whole process tested the initiate's level of courage, stamina and endurance which prepared him/her for future life challenges with regard to discharging all the duties and responsibilities of a Gusii adult. It is important to point out that despite the wholesome changes in Gusii society nowadays, most of the essential elements of the circumcision ritual have remained in place. The practice of circumcision is, however, nowadays performed in hospitals by medical doctors. Formerly, the *abasari* (sing. *omosari*) *were* the ones who carried out the act of circumcision. Nowadays, their function has been eclipsed by the modern medical practitioners. Furthermore, due to the urban lifestyle brought about by modernization, the initiate stays with his/ her parents in the same house. As a result, the moral lessons learnt during the seclusion period are not observed and therefore they are disappearing. In addition, due to medical reasons, female circumcision has been prohibited by the Government and therefore it is also gradually disappearing. Finally, the Chapter has elucidated that on the most basic level, the social consequence of a boy's and girl's circumcision meant transition into Gusii adult responsibilities and duties.

Editor's Notes:

- *This Chapter was originally developed by the author in conjunction with Prof. Solomon Monyenye.*

- *Female circumcision followed the same process as male circumcision enunciated in this chapter, albeit conducted by women. Male circumcision in Gusii entailed removal of the foreskin; women circumcision related to the excision of the clitoris or part thereof. For an extended treatise of female circumcision in Gusii, see Daniel Momanyi Mokaya's* **Female Circumcision Among the Abagusii of Kenya** *(2nd Edition), Nsemia Inc., 2012.*

- *It is not clear, either from oral tales or the written word, how the Gusii came to adopt circumcision as a rite of passage.*

CHAPTER SIX

GUSII CUSTOMARY MARRIAGE

Introduction

The Gusii, like many communities across the world, had an elaborate customary marriage process. This chapter examines the various stages of the Gusii customary marriage. It also provides an exposition of the intricate stages of the Gusii customary marriage. These stages included the initial identification of a suitable bride, engagement, payment of bride price (dowry), and conducting of the final magical-religious wedding ceremony. Note that once the wedding had been consecrated it was supposed to be binding throughout one's life history.

Brief Overview

According to Gusii customary law, a nuclear family (consisting of wife, husband and the immediate children) was legitimized and received communal recognition only after the payment of bride wealth by members of the husband's family. Gusii customary marriage was an intricate and systematic process that commenced after a young man (the bridegroom) had received consent from his father and paternal uncles that he had met all the obligatory requirements to establish his own family. Young men were only allowed to marry after reaching their early twenties and above. In addition, they should also have undergone all the initiation rites that confer to them the status of adulthood. After the bridegroom had received parental consent, the marriage arrangement had to go through various distinct stages.

First Stage: Identification of a Suitable Girl (*Okorigia Omoiseke*)

Soon after receiving parental consent, a go-between, *esigani* (pl. *chisigani*), was identified by the young man's family. Typically *esigani* was an aunt or a trusted female relative of the family. She was given the responsibility of scouting for a suitable bride. The *esigani* was usually given specific instructions by the bridegroom's family concerning the type of woman they were looking for to be betrothed to their son. The instructions given formed the criteria used when scouting for a bride. A young man was not supposed to be directly involved in looking for a woman to marry. Among the Gusii, marriage was perceived as an important undertaking that had long-term implications on the overall socioeconomic and cultural well-being of the community, it could therefore not be left to the young man alone to determine whom to marry.

More specifically, Gusii customary law on marriage stipulated that a bride had to come from a different clan (a clan was made of individuals of the same lineage; these were considered 'relatives') from that of the bridegroom. In addition, the bride was not supposed to be a blood relative of the bridegroom's mother. Further, she could not be related to the bridegroom's paternal or maternal grandmother. It was considered a taboo for a person to enter into marriage with a blood relative. If such an unlikely abominable act happened, then the man and wife were declared cursed people, and ostracized from the community.

The person chosen as *esigani* was supposed to have a clear understanding of the history and socio-economic status of both the bride and bridegroom's families. She acted as a special link between the two families. In this regard, further arrangements for the marriage were not supposed to proceed until both families of the bride and the bridegroom had received clear information on the history and socio-economic attributes that were acceptable to both parties. Special attention was taken to make sure that there were no negative attributes relating to either of the families. These included, but not limited to, a history of practicing witchcraft, suicidal tendencies or an existing curse on either family.

After identifying a suitable girl, the *esigani* made arrangements to visit the girl's family and broach the subject of marriage. Approaching the girl's family was a delicate affair, and the *esigani* had to carefully gauge the evolving mood to make sure that her mission did not go wrong. If the bride's family was receptive to the news, they usually made a detailed enquiry about the bridegroom's family. If this introductory visit was received favourably, the girl's father consequently asked the *esigani* to go and inform the suitor to pay a visit to his home. This was to give the prospective couple an early opportunity to form a personal impression of one another. Consequently, regardless of the nature of reception from the bride's family, the *esigani* went back to the suitor's family and provided a detailed report regarding her visit and outcomes thereof.

With positive results reported by *esigani*, it was important that the suitor give approval of the proposed girl and accept the invitation to visit her family. After a period of about a week, the suitor, accompanied by a few of his age-mates (mainly close relatives and trusted friends), paid a visit to the girl's home. This visit was specifically referred to as "a visit to see the girl," *okorora omoiseke (ekerorano)*.

This initial visit was extremely important. it was during this occasion when the prospective couple made a personal decision as to whether they were suitable or not for one another. If the girl was not impressed during this initial interaction, she was entitled to reject the marriage proposal by simply informing the suitor, "*karwe isiko riaito*" (leave our compound/ front yard). However, if she was favourably impressed, she expressed her acceptance of the marriage proposal by presenting a token gift (usually gruel/porridge) to the suitor inside her parent's compound. If the suitor, on his part, was dissatisfied, he was not supposed to speak out openly, but to wait until he and his companions got home to inform his people to stop further negotiations. Young people were given a leeway by their parents to either accept or reject an offing marriage at this initial stage. Usually, it was socially unacceptable, among the Gusii, for parents to insist that a marriage goes ahead without receiving consent from both the bride and bridegroom.

Second Stage: The Selection of Cattle

If all went well during the first stage of the marriage process, the suitor then informed his father and paternal uncles that he was willing to marry the proposed girl. This particular consent from the suitor set the stage for the commencement of giving bride wealth to the girl's family. At this stage, the father of the bridegroom sent an emissary to the girl's father to come over to his home on a specified date to "look for the cattle," *okomana chiombe*. This request signaled the start of the process of transfer of bride wealth to the girl's family. On the specified date, the father of the girl, accompanied by a few elders from his clan, paid a visit to the suitor's family.

After initial greetings and introductory remarks, the suitor's father led his visitors to the cattle enclosure where the animals to be given as bride wealth were already gathered. Depending on the prevailing socio-economic circumstances, the suitor's father, in consultation with some of his clan elders, usually made a decision on the number of animals to give as bride wealth prior to the visit by the bride's father. Once at the cattle enclosure, the animals were driven outside one by one, and the elders from the girl's clan closely examined each animal inquiring about such characteristics as age and the number of times the animal has calved (if the animal is female). In the process, they isolated the animals they thought acceptable and those they would reject.

The accepted animals were taken to one side. The suitor's father was asked to provide replacements for those that were rejected. The examination and selection of animals continued until the number set aside for the bride wealth was satisfactory to both parties. It was, however, acceptable for the bride's father to continue demanding for more cattle even if he already knew that the other party had provided the stipulated number of animals. Customarily, the bridegroom's father was not supposed to directly refuse, but was supposed to politely turn down the demand by saying, "we really have no more cattle."

The following are the main principles that were supposed to be followed when giving bride wealth: (a) an animal that has been offered and accepted by the girl's father thereafter passed at once into his ownership and the new owner's rights started to operate there and then; (b) by accepting the animals offered during the selection, the bride's father declared his final satisfaction, and he cannot afterwards, under any circumstance, ask for more; and (c) the finality in bride wealth agreement was symbolized by a special celebration that took place immediately after the selection process was completed.

Composition of Bride Wealth

In most instances, the animals that were given as bride wealth consisted of a number of cows and heifers, one bull and a number of goats. As stated above, the total number of animals that were given as bride wealth mainly depended on the stipulated current rate or standard that prevailed at that particular period, with minimal variation based on mutual agreement by both parties. Thus, the opening statement during bride wealth negotiation usually went like this: "you know that most fathers are asking so much for their daughters, so we are demanding the same." Gusii elders ascertain that in the recent past, the number of cattle that were given as bride wealth usually ranged from eight to fourteen. The number of goats usually did not exceed six. Within the number of cattle that were given as bride wealth, there had to be one standard bull referred to as *eeri y'egesicho,* the apron bull. This was the bull to be slaughtered during the first day of the wedding ceremony (see more below). A cow's offspring that was still suckling was referred to as *omebiara* (pl. *emebiara*) and was never counted as part of the bride wealth. Similarly, goats were usually not counted as part of the bride wealth, but were supposed to be used for sacrifices in various rituals that were performed at various stages of the marriage process, particularly during the wedding.

Apart from the bride wealth, however, there were other customary gifts that were supposed to be given during the various stages of the marriage process. Although these gifts were not supposed to be mandatory, they were usually perceived as a sign of goodwill, and they served to cement and maintain friendly kinship ties between both parties. The marriage gifts included the following:

- *eeri y'omoyega* (the bull for celebration) - to be slaughtered by the bridegroom during the honeymoon period (*egechabero*);

- *embori y'amaseko* (the goat of laughter) - to be slaughtered for the bride's girlfriends, mainly from her father's clan, who paid her a visit in her new home during the honeymoon period;

- *eereri y'egekobo* (bull of returning the bride) - to be slaughtered by the bride's father at the end of the first visit of the bride signaling the end of the honeymoon period;

- *embori y'enyangi* (goat for the wedding) - a she goat given to the bride's father to be slaughtered as a sacrifice during the wedding;

- *eeri y'enyangi* (bull of the wedding) - a bull that was provided by the bridegroom's family and was supposed to be slaughtered before the wedding. The animal's hide was used to make a special head dress (*ekiore*) and a jacket (*esumati*). These were to be worn by the bridegroom on the second day of the wedding, at the time when the marriage was formalized by a traditional priest;

- *embori y'omosubati* (goat of the sister) – given by the bridegroom to the eldest sister of the bride for recognition of her seniority and the special advice/care she had availed to the bride; and

- *embori ya magokoro* (goat of the grandmother) – given by the bridegroom to the grandmother of the bride.

Transfer of Ownership of Bride Wealth

The bride's father was not supposed to take away the animals on the day of selection, although legally the selected animals were now his. Before the animals were driven over to the girl's home, the bride was required to invite the bridegroom to her home for a special ceremony called *ekeria 'boko* (eating at the place of the in-laws). On the stipulated day of *ekeria 'boko*, the bridegroom accompanied by his friends visited the girl's home. During this particular occasion, there was a lot of feasting by the bride and the bridegroom and the invited friends and relatives.

A few days after *ekeria 'boko*, the bride wealth was taken to the bride's family. This process of taking the animals to the girl's home was called *okoira chiombe oboko* (sending the animals to the place of the in-laws). This was usually done by a selected group of young men from the bridegroom's clan and, ordinarily, the suitor was not supposed to accompany them. It was seen as demeaning and a lack of decorum for the suitor to be directly involved in taking the animals to the bride's home. The person who was serving as the go-between (*esigani*) was required to join the young men in taking the animals to the girl's home in her capacity as the main witness in the transfer of ownership of the animals to the bride's family.

Gusii customary law required that on the same day the animals arrived in the bride's home, the young men who had brought the animals should be allowed to take the girl with them after being appropriately entertained. The girl was, however, supposed to offer token resistance and even attempt to hide herself when the young men started the journey back. But she was expected to eventually yield and accompany the young men to her prospective husband's home.

The arrival of the bride in her husband's home signalled the start of the honeymoon period which was referred to as *egechabero* (decorating the bride). During this period, the bride was really pampered, particularly by her the bridegroom's mother (her future mother-in-law) who gave her special ornaments and other gifts. She was also supposed to put on her best clothes and was constantly entertained by her husband's relatives and friends. The *egechabero* was supposed to last for one month. During that whole period, the bride was under no obligation to work, although she could volunteer to assist her mother-in-law in performing housework.

Egechabero largely served the purpose of assessment for "fit". The bridegroom had to deflower the bride and in the process consummate the marriage. His age mates kept close watch of progress to make sure that this happened. Where there were challenges with consummation, the bridegroom's age mates kept a close watch to make sure the bride did not run away.

The bride's side also kept its curiosity to establish how the process was going. As Nyang'era, N. K. (2014) says:

"... It was a tradition that within three days of the bride's [stay] at her husband, [the] mother of the bride was to send another girl or sister of aunt of the bride carrying a delicious meal to the home of the bridegroom to find out about the welfare of the couple.

"This visit by a relative of the bride really was meant to find out about the consummation of the marriage under the pretext of conveying a delicious meal." (pp 46)

There was happiness with news of consummation. Relatives happily consumed the meal from the bride's home and soon the bride's parents would receive the same news to further comfort them that all was going well with their daughter and the marriage.

At the end of *egechabero*, the lady was required to pay a visit to her parents and was supposed to stay at her parents' home for a period not exceeding one month. This visit to her home was quite significant for she was supposed to inform her mother concerning her initial marriage experience. If she had strong objection to (or reservations about) the marriage, she would report it to her father. It was also one of the times when a marriage could be terminated without serious repercussions to any of the parties. In cases where such termination happened, the bride wealth was returned to the groom's home.

Third Stage: Wedding Ceremony (*Enyangi*)

A Gusii customary wedding was one of the most significant and sacred ceremonies in Gusii culture. The ceremony was conducted only after all the outstanding animals, agreed to during the bride wealth negotiations, had been sent to the bride's father. There also could be no objection to the marriage by either party. The wedding ceremony was very elaborate and was usually held for three consecutive days of continued celebration and feasting. It consisted of a series of ceremonies and rituals that were conducted with a lot of decorum and detailed observation of all the required wedding activities. Particularly, attention was paid to the proper conduct of all aspects of the various wedding rituals, with the maintenance of minute details pertaining to all aspects of the wedding ceremony. This entailed a lot of initial planning and preparation of the various activities. The start of the wedding ceremony entailed that the wife, whose bride wealth had been paid and was already cohabiting with her husband, return to her home where the initial rituals of the ceremony were supposed to take place.

The first day of the wedding ceremony was called *egetaorio*, and it involved a lot of feasting, especially the provision of entertainment to the bridegroom and his party, consisting of several of his age-mates from his clan. The climax of the *egetaorio* ceremony was a well-organized wrestling match in the evening (when the sun was about to set). It was usually carried out in a clear open field near the homestead of the bride's father. This important ritual was supposed to test the level of stamina, endurance, determination and tenacity of young men from parties, *abako* (sing. *omoko*) (in-laws), and it usually took place under the watchful eyes of selected elders who played the role of impartial adjudicators. The wrestling match usually pitted young men from both the bride's and the bridegroom's clan. The young men on the bridegroom's side did their level best to win the wrestling match since it would be extremely embarrassing to be defeated by their in-laws and in the face of the bride and her family.

In a situation where the bridegroom's group lost the wrestling match, usually nasty jokes and chides were directed at them, particularly by the bride's girlfriends (i.e. being chided by the girls as to whether they were real men with the required vigour and masculinity). The winning party was also supposed to take charge of slaughtering the bull designated for *egetaorio* ceremony. In addition, the winners were at liberty to choose the juiciest parts of the meat and only give leftovers to the losing party as a sign of humiliation and embarrassment to the in-laws (*abako*). Nevertheless, all this was done with a light touch. As the Gusii saying goes, "in-laws, or people from whose clan you marry, are usually people you fight with". At the end of the wrestling match, there was a lot of singing, dancing and feasting, particularly by the young men and women from both parties.

The second day of the wedding ceremony was called *echorwa*, and it also involved a lot of celebration and feasting. *Echorwa* was a very elaborate ceremony and some writers like Nyang'era, N. K. (2014) term it the "climax" of the marriage process.

More importantly, this was the time when the marriage was solemnized in a magical-religious ritual that was conducted by a recognized wedding priest or priestess, *omokundekane* (pl. *abakundekane*). This ceremony had a lot of religious significance and was supposed to be conducted behind closed doors. Only a dozen guests from both parties were allowed to participate in this ceremony. The ceremony involved the sacrificing of a white goat as a symbol of bestowing the blessings of the ancestors on the couple.

On the third day of the ceremony, the couple returned to the bridegroom's home where final magical-religious rituals were conducted which also involved the sacrificing of a white he-goat. The act of sacrificing of the he-goat symbolized the finality and sealing of the marriage. In addition, during this ceremony, a marriage name was given to the wife, termed *erieta ri'ebitinge*. This is the name she would go by her new home. As well, the traditional priest placed specially designed ankle rings called *ebitinge* on the bride. The ankle rings signified that now the bridegroom and the bride had attained full status of marriage, and the wife was now both legally and spiritually bound to her husband. This marked the end of the wedding ceremony. After the wedding ceremony, it was in rare for the marriage to fail or lead into a divorce.

The Religious and Cultural Significance of the Wedding

It should be stated that the *enyangi* completed the customary Gusii marriage process. As Mayer (1950) states, the *enyangi* was really significant in a Gusii customary marriage:

> Bride wealth emphasized the status of the father (by assigning paternal rights such as the ownership of the children to the man's side). It [was] *enyangi* that emphasized the status of husband. Before *enyangi,* the jural act of returning the bride wealth [was] enough to annul a marriage and restore the *status quo*. It was a far more serious affair to 'cut the marriage

rings' i.e. to break up the marriage after *enyangi*. The wife's father cannot lawfully order her back into his homestead in case of a dispute; the wife herself [was] faced with powerful new mystical sanctions if she should leave her husband and remarry, or even if she committed adultery.

As a consequence of *enyangi* having been solemnized by a traditional priest, a lot of religious and mystical elements that symbolized the finality of the marriage process were now in place. It created a new personal bond between the wife and husband that went beyond the payment of bride wealth and showed that in all purposes the married couple were now legal husband and wife linked together by various magical-religious elements which were taken as extremely important in the Gusii community.

These magical-religious ties placed a special link and maintained almost all aspects of established marriage equilibrium between the respective clans of husband and wife. As Mayer (1950: 115) further states:

Besides emphasizing the substitution of husband for father's authority, *enyangi* marked the entry into a new stage of life.... A woman of any age who has not made *enyangi* was technically a 'girl'. She is distinguishable in everyday life by not having the marriage ankle-rings.... Such a woman cannot pass to any religious or quasi- religious status... as for instance be initiated as a female circumciser or a diviner, or a marriage priestess *omokundekane*. Similar rules applied to men who have not made *enyangi*.

The Privileged Obstruction

At various stages of the *enyangi*, some privileged obstructions of the wedding process were allowed, particularly before the start of the various magical-religious rituals that accompanied the wedding ceremony. These obstructions mainly came from the various actors of the wedding ceremony including the bride herself, her eldest sister and the mother-in-law. Thus, it appears that these privileged obstructions during the initiation of various wedding rites were mainly allowed to the female relatives and other female actors of wedding ceremony and not the men. However, the carrying out of the various obstructions during the *enyangi* were clearly prescribed in the Gusii customary marriage customary rules and regulations. The main purpose of causing obstructions during the wedding process was mainly to extort legitimate gifts that were supposed to have been given to the person causing the obstruction. On the part of the bride, this was done to demonstrate the significance of giving personal consent, which formed the basis of the Gusii customary marriage. It also put to test the level of love that the husband or the other male relatives (i.e. her father) had toward her.

In most instances, wedding obstructions involved overt threats to undermine the smooth running and/or delay of the wedding process by interfering with some of the prescribed wedding rituals. The most dramatic forms of obstruction were those that happened at the time when the initial magical-religious rituals were supposed to be conducted during the first day of the wedding. This was *echorwa* when the bride was expected to symbolically give consent to her marriage and to show the level of love she had towards her husband.

A good example of a wedding obstruction that symbolically demonstrated that the bride may not have absolute love towards her husband was if she decided to show reluctance or refuse, for some time, to be shaved or put on her wedding regalia, thus delaying the beginning of the *echorwa* ceremony. Such forms of obstruction would really be embarrassing to the bridegroom and his party.

However, there wasn't much the bridegroom's entourage could do at such a time except to present a particular gift to the bride, such as a specially made bracelet or bangle to appease her and make her stop the obstruction. But even after accepting to be shaved and putting on the wedding regalia, the bride could further decide to refuse to walk through a group of assembled elders in her entry into the inner room of her mother's house where the initial magical-religious ritual was supposed to be conducted. She could also refuse to kiss the especially prepared calabash containing some traditional porridge that she was supposed to hand over to her husband. During the second day of the wedding, moreover, the bride could refuse to kiss the love-cup *egesingero* that was supposed to be handed over to the wedding priest.

During the third day of the *enyangi*, conversely, when the woman was escorted to her husband's homestead, where the final rituals of the wedding ceremony took place, the bride might find herself in a similar situation. She might be faced with various forms of obstructions that were usually directed to her by the female relatives of the husband, particularly his mother and her daughters. They could publicly accuse her of all sorts of things such as being a lazy woman who has been disrespectful to her mother-in-law. While hurling all forms of accusations towards the bride, they delayed or refused to allow the bride and her party entry into the homestead. It was taboo for the bride to enter the husband's family homestead without receiving permission from her mother-in-law since returning to the husband's home symbolized her second rebirth. Even after entering the homestead, the mother-in-law could decide to refuse to take part in the final wedding rites until she was placated by being given a gift such as a goat or specially prepared bracelets.

The privilege of obstruction was supposed to be reciprocal in nature (i.e. it was supposed to be directed at both parties of the wedding ceremony, usually done by the female relatives on both sides). Various forms of gifts were usually extorted by the use obstructions. For example, during the *echorwa* ceremony (aside from the obstructions mentioned previously) ceremony at the bride's home, her elder sister or grandmother might demand to be given her rightful gift (i.e. a goat and/or specially made bracelets) through obstruction. If this had not yet been done as required by the rules and regulation that governed the conduct of Gusii customary marriage, usually it took a lot of persuasion by elders and other family relatives to placate the person who was doing the obstruction. She was promised that she was going to receive her rightful gift as recognized in Gusii customary marriage or wedding law.

The giving out of gifts to the various relatives of both parties was also supposed to be reciprocal since the individual who made the obstruction was required to provide some forms of gifts, *ebitoro* (sing. *egetoro*). Although these were not necessarily equal in value, they were supposed to be involved in performing various forms of tasks during the wedding ceremony. In this regard, the duality or parallelism of various forms of obstructions (i.e. that were directed to both the bride and the bridegroom) were recognized and accepted. Furthermore, various other actors in the wedding rituals could also cause obstruction in order to extort some form of payment for the roles that they played in the wedding ceremony. For instance, a number of young girls (who were not yet circumcised) were involved in assisting the wedding priest in performing certain rites during the various stages of the wedding ceremony.

These girls included a special girl from the bride's clan *omoimari* (pl. *abaimaari*) who was supposed to assist the wedding priest when conducting the *echorwa* ceremony. The other girl was the one from the bridegroom's place *omotang'ani* who was supposed to lead the wedding procession when the bride was being escorted back to husband's home. This girl was also required to sleep on the same bed with the couple (by sleeping between the husband and wife) for three days after the wedding ceremony. There was also a young uncircumcised boy *omong'wansi* (best man) who was always supposed to be with the bridegroom all the time the various magical-religious rituals were being conducted. Finally, there was a young man who was the blacksmith or "the boy of the *ebintere*" who assisted in the making of the iron tube used in the marriage ankle rings. He was also supposed to be in charge of overseeing the various journeys to and from both the bride's father's homestead and the home of the bridegroom.

It can also be stated that, in the usually long drawn-out wedding ceremony, the various forms of obstructions provided some dramatic highlights and added more excitement to the wedding process. They also reflected the tenseness and sometimes the existing ambivalence from both the bride's and the bridegroom's people. These clearly demonstrate that there was always some form of struggle between affection and animosity and/or between gratitude and dislike that went on during the wedding ceremony. Consequently, the various forms of paroles provided an ideal opportunity to vent all forms of hostile feeling. They teased and provoked the other party (i.e. the bride refusing to show love to her husband by refusing to hand over the love cup, *egesingore*, which was supposed to be handed over by the husband to the wedding priest). As a consequence, the various obstructions provided a means of releasing emotions during these extensive and exhausting processes of the wedding ceremony. The giving of gifts based on reciprocity was also directed towards smoothing the long-term relationships between the two different clans that were linked by the marriage (before the marriage the different clans may not always have been in good terms with one another).

Conclusion

This chapter has shown that the customary marriage was a very intricate affair involving systematic processes that commenced after a young man (bridegroom) received special consent from his father and paternal uncles that he met the conditions to get married. The conditions included reaching the requisite age, and meeting all the obligatory requirements including having undergone the various initiation and/or training initiatives that a Gusii young man was supposed to undertake as he was being prepared to take over the honourees and increasing demanding responsibilities of adult life including giving birth and taking care of children. After conducting the magical-religious wedding ceremony, the marriage was deemed to be irreversible except under vary rare circumstances such as one being unable to give birth. It is further enunciated that each of those marriage stages were meant to serve specific purposes in the intricate processes of Gusii customary marriage.

Editor's Note: *some writers (notably N. K. King'oina 1999) have broken the marriage process down into finer-grained stages. However, the entire essence of the process, which is well-captured in this chapter, has no contradiction with that of other writers. As well, note that as the Gusii population increased, and dispersed to different parts of the Gusii territory, variations happened. However, the core of the process remained, only to be interrupted by colonial administration and various religious groups.*

CHAPTER SEVEN

GUSII INDIGENOUS EDUCATION SYSTEM

Introduction

This chapter deals with Gusii indigenous education system. It is articulated that the indigenous education system was meant to transmit critical social, cultural, economic and religious values and apprenticeship skills to the youth using various modes of formal and informal learning and training systems. In addition, it presents the different learning methods and training strategies that were used to impart various forms of knowledge, skills and competencies.

Role of indigenous Education: Brief Overview

The main role of indigenous education among the Gusii people, as was the case with most other African communities, was to transmit the requisite social, political, economic and religious aspects of the community through systems involving the adult members of society and the youth. This was done through various forms of formal and informal learning and training processes. An important aspect of Gusii indigenous education was that it was based on a gradual progression of the human life cycle. As an individual went through various stages of the life cycle from childhood to adulthood, the individual was confronted with different informal learning experiences and skills training. The learning process was also mainly based on practical experiences and apprenticeship at various stages of life that was aimed at transmitting to the learner the actual life experiences and the various social, economic and political aspects of the community life. These practical forms of training and learning processes were anchored in real life experiences that moulded a person's character to fit into the psychological orientation, social behaviour and cultural obligations that were acceptable to the community.

Consequently, as a child went through various stages of physical and mental growth, different forms of educational experiences and various learning models were introduced at each stage of growth in the human life cycle from birth, childhood, and adolescence to adulthood. In this regard, it can be argued that Gusii indigenous education was a lifelong learning process that started at one's birth and continued up to one's death. By the time an individual reached adulthood, the person would have evolved into a well-balanced and appropriately socialized member of the community inculcated with various appropriate emotional and moral forms of behaviour.

Furthermore, there were various forms of formal and informal education that were based on apprenticeship and practical learning experiences. These included the acquisition of various skills involving, for instance, agricultural practices, the art of tool making, how the tools were used, and house-building skills. On top of that, all the young men received various forms of military training that were supposed to be used in their later stages of life to fend off any form of perceived internal and external aggression against the community. These were practical skills and appropriate forms of knowledge that were important for the survival of the family, clan and indeed the whole community. Furthermore, an individual required these forms of learning to enable the individual to successfully confront various lifelong challenges.

It should be stated that, in most instances, Gusii indigenous education was conservative and conformist in nature. Consequently, as an individual progressively developed various forms of social norms, physical skills and moral values, the individual was expected to conform to existing long-term tested forms of cultural, social, moral and religious values relating to social behaviour and personal conduct. As an individual progressively developed through various stages and eventually became a young adult, the individual was supposed to conform to all aspects of the Gusii lifestyle. The individual was required to adhere to all explicit and implicit forms of regulations, moral and religious values and rules of religion, inheritance, and family relationships based on the Gusii concept of *chinsoni*. This code entailed certain behavioural avoidance and restraints when dealing with people of different generations, age-sets and genders.

When imparting various knowledge and skills, the conduct of community elders as role models to be emulated by the youth, was very important (i.e. based on the principle of what you preach is also what you practise in your daily life). More importantly, the role of adults as role models of the youth was very crucial due to the fact that they were important depositories of knowledge and skills that they had already acquired in their various stages of growth. Consequently, elders were highly respected because they were perceived as people with a lot of life experiences and knowledge about Gusii culture and socio-economic practices.

In all the various Gusii clans, members of different generations (i.e., children, parents and grandparents) were supposed to be well grounded on the proper forms of intergenerational interactions and individual behaviour. The youth were particularly always expected to show respect to elders, visitors and other members of the community. Showing obedience and respect to people belonging to higher social hierarchies based on age and inter-generational differences was an important requisite in the provision of Gusii indigenous education. Children were supposed to show obedience and respect to older people. Any form of disobedience and/or disrespect to older people was forbidden, and showing such unbecoming tendencies would lead to severe punishment.

The Gusii therefore taught their children consciously and subconsciously, through the conduct and behaviour of adult role models, various aspects of Gusii life as pertains to emotional, social and spiritual conduct. On the other hand, the children were expected to emulate and practise these forms or models of social behaviour as demonstrated by the adults and to eventually base their individual lives and social behaviour on the accepted communal values and cultural practices. Consequently, most learning processes and training for various aspects of life, such as culture, history, natural environment, the philosophy of life, various norms and traditional customs were usually systematically and progressively imparted to the youth.

The young people were always challenged to make responsible and wise judgment when confronted with various forms of life experiences and challenges in the social and physical environment. The appropriate language skills of *Ekegusii* were, for instance, imparted to the youth through the daily narratives of the people around them and also through the presentation of interesting stories such as legends, myths and folklore concerning their family, clan and indeed the whole Gusii community. Similarly, the learning of abstract and imaginative thinking was encouraged through the acquisition of various interpretational skills as presented in Gusii riddles and proverbs.

Stages of Gusii Indigenous Education

The Infancy Stage

As already stated elsewhere in this book, childbirth and the raising of children were the hallmarks of a successful Gusii customary marriage. Children were highly valued as they represented the future progression of a family and lineage; they were also an important source of labour. In addition, as children (especially the male children) grew older, they were expected to be defenders of their family, clan and indeed the whole community from any form of internal and external aggression. At the initial stage of life, infants, usually between the ages of one to six years, were educated both formally and informally within their respective homesteads. During this stage, the child's mother was expected to be the principal trainer; the mother taught the child various psychomotor skills such as walking, talking and toilet usage skills. In addition, the mother was usually the most important figure in the child's life. This was because she was supposed to breastfeed the child and train him/her the various skills.

The mother also provided warmth, physical and emotional protection to the child and provided the child with motherly love acts such as fondling and kissing of the child. Furthermore, the mother was expected to sleep with the child on the same bed, and during daytime, the child was not supposed to be far away from the mother; the latter also taught him or her basic language skills and behavioural norms. Consequently, a child acquired appropriate language skills through practical experience of hearing the various sounds of *Ekegusii* intonations and proper pronunciation of different words of the language. As the child grew older, the mother would use concrete life examples to train him/her in mastery of the language, feeding, walking and toilet usage skills. The mother always motivated the child to learn various abstract and practical skills through positive reinforcement such as praising the child whenever he or she managed to perform certain basic functions and activities.

Children were weaned by their mothers when they reached the age of three years. From that period, learning usually happened through interaction with other children and peers. More so, grandparents and other adult family members taught the children various ways and experiences pertaining to Gusii life through riddles, folklore, myths and legends. In most instances, these forms of training took place in the evening when children were seated near the fireplace in their mothers' or grandparents' houses. Furthermore, the grandparents taught the children various community songs and dance performances, and narrated to the children interesting stories that were centred on important community history, events, rituals and the forms of important social activities and cultural practices.

They also taught the children stories and legends of family and community heroes and heroines. Most of the stories and songs were usually based on themes such as the importance of hard work, generosity and shunning selfishness. These were taught to the children in an interesting and entertaining manner. These forms of social and cultural values were cherished in the Gusii community. The stories taught the children the various forms of punishments that befall the people who go against the expected social, moral and religious norms. Furthermore, a child's intelligence and level of imagination was tested through the presentation of riddles, myths and legends.

Parents were particularly conscious of the fact that these forms of knowledge which children acquired during the early stages of life usually left an indelible mark on their youthful minds. They would eventually serve as reference points during the later stages of life, and, as a consequence, they played an important role in shaping children's characters and social behaviour. The youth were also inculcated with practical skills such as the use of various tools, the art of fire making and how to use and manage various items that were usually found in the homestead. Avoidance of different forms of bad behaviour, such as dishonesty, stealing, laziness, disobedience and being disrespectful to others, were also inculcated to the children during the earlier stages of life. The Gusii concept of *chinsoni* that emphasized behavioural avoidance, modesty and restraint, and taboos was also taught to the children from a very early stage.

The Childhood Stage

The childhood stage fell between the ages of six to twelve years. This was the period when the children were supposed to start to receive broader exposure beyond that of their families and homesteads. It was at this stage that the children started to interact with children and other people from adjacent homesteads. It should also be emphasized that at this stage, peer interaction and role-play were the most important modes of the children's learning experience. Particularly, from the age of six, the children were also allowed to perform simple tasks. They were also expected to perform various family chores such as looking after their younger siblings and being able to feed them (especially during the absence of the mother), collecting firewood and fetching water from nearby streams and rivers. Eventually, with the passage of time, through role-play and practical encounters with various life experiences, the children started to gain mastery of how to perform various chores in the homesteads.

It was during this stage that parents started to introduce children to various gender specific roles and functions. For instance, fathers started to encourage their young sons to undertake various male-specific assignments such as herding, hunting and clearing of fallow land to make it ready for cultivation. Mothers started to introduce their daughters to various female specific chores such as cleaning the homestead and housekeeping, fetching water and collecting firewood, and how to use a hoe for crop cultivation and weeding. With the passage of time, the children progressively learned how to perform many of these gender specific roles and they were always encouraged to gain confidence and have mastery on how to perform various activities. This was done through different forms of positive reinforcement from parents, older siblings and other members of the community in general.

Consequently, at around the age of ten, most children would have managed to master and had sufficient expertise to effectively perform various gender specific basic occupations. Most children were particularly encouraged and continuously reinforced to competently perform various life sustenance skills such as the clearing of fallow land for cultivation, herding, and crop cultivation and weeding. Furthermore, the boys started to imitate other forms of male specific functions such as acquisitions of basic military techniques and hunting skills, by closely following and/or watching their fathers when they were undertaking various gender specific activities. The girls also started to learn from their mothers, mainly through apprenticeship, to gain mastery in performing various female specific functions such as fetching water and collecting firewood, grinding of finger millet and sorghum, crop cultivation and weeding. Thus the children started to progressively acquire mastery of various life sustenance knowledge and skills through practical training and apprenticeship.

More importantly, the male child was expected to master various herding skills, starting with looking after goats and sheep near the homesteads. The boys made sure that the animals were always taken to proper grazing ranges and also that the animals did not go astray and destroy neighbours' crops. The male child was also encouraged to acquire important personality traits such as being courageous and brave when confronting difficult situations. In order for them to develop other forms of masculinity traits, the boys were usually encouraged to perform mock fights with other boys from the neighbourhood. In addition, in these forms of mock fights, the boys learned and/or acquired fighting and defensive skills. These skills eventually became handy in their later stages of life when all the young men were required to put their life on the line to defend their families, clans and indeed the whole community against any form of aggression. However, it was of utmost importance that the boys did not injure one another when conducting mock fights. In addition, the boys were expected to acquire other attributes such as the importance of group co-operation and teamwork when confronted with an external aggression. As one Gusii saying puts it, "one shield has never taken cows to the river," (*nguba emo tiyana koira ng'ombe roche*). This Gusii saying emphasizes the importance of teamwork, particularly at the time when people are confronted with extremely difficult situations that require group effort.

All these forms of military skills and defensive techniques that the boys acquired through role playing initiatives and masculinity traits, such as courage, bravery, endurance and stamina, were absolutely necessary during their later stages of life. These would come into play when their community might be attacked by their war-like neighbours, especially the Maasai and Kipsigis cattle raiders.

It should also be stated that these forms of military training were supposed to be undertaken in a more professional manner at the later stage when the young men were supposed to join various military encampments, *ebisarate*. Furthermore, especially when the boys had reached the age of eight years and above, they were supposed to join older boys in taking cattle for grazing in ranches that were usually in outlying frontier land that were usually located far away from the homesteads. Here, the boys learned more detailed knowledge on animal husbandry, such as knowing the exact names of all the family cattle, their distinct and other special features.

In addition, while grazing cattle, the boys had an opportunity to know the names and characteristics of various wild animals, birds and plants. The older boys narrated to them various interesting myths concerning various wild animals. Furthermore, the young boys came to know the names and characteristics of various animals and were informed through various legends as relates to various forms of humans and wildlife interacting, and the unique animals taken as totems by various Gusii clans. More so, the boys got to know which animals were dangerous to people and the ones that were edible.

In addition, the boys learned about the names of various plants and herbs, which ones were edible or had medicinal value and the various forms of ailments they were supposed to treat. Furthermore, the boys got to know what types of trees were used in the construction of houses, the making of various tools and implements.

While grazing the cattle, the boys were supposed to make sure that the animals did not go astray, especially enter other people's cultivated fields to destroy crops and other forms of property. When being taught various life sustenance skills, the boys who showed negative behavioural tendencies such as laziness, sluggishness and being unable to graze the livestock in the proper manner (including being able to take the livestock to adjacent rivers to drink water) were usually given a stern warning. Repetition of such unbecoming behaviour, particularly after receiving several initial warnings, would lead to severe punishment including spanking. The main purpose of these various forms of learning processes was to inculcate a proper work ethic and to demonstrate that, in many instances, life was not easy. As a consequence, for one to be able to earn a decent living and to be successful in life, he or she had to work extremely hard to overcome various challenges and probable dangers. The rearing of cattle was highly cherished among the Gusii people, particularly since they were the main source of wealth and were used in paying bride wealth. They were also seen as symbols of wealth and prestige.

Consequently, all the sons in every homestead were supposed to develop high affinity and attachment toward their household cattle to the extent of being able to put their lives on the line to protect and defend the herds from cattle rustlers, especially Kipsigis and Maasai raiders. They were also supposed to protect the cattle against attacks from wild animals such as lions and leopards. Moreover, every young male was supposed to be able to easily identify their cattle whenever they got mixed up with cattle from neighbouring homesteads, especially in the grazing field, and when they had been driven to the river to drink water. They were also supposed to know all their family cattle by their specific names, main features and characteristics, such as colour and age.

The Stage of Initiation into Adulthood

It should be stated that no Gusii person was seen as being a fully socialized and grown up individual until he or she had gone through the various initiation rites, particularly circumcision and other accompanying traditional rituals that conveyed to an individual the important status of adulthood. Consequently, in order for any Gusii person to be accepted as a full adult, he or she had to undergo various initiation ceremonies. These conveyed the rite of passage that was seen as a second rebirth that, symbolically, transformed an individual from childhood and/or adolescence to full-fledged adulthood status. These initiation rites of passage were usually undertaken when an individual had reached the age of between fifteen years and their early twenties. These rites conferred to an individual the important status of manhood and/or womanhood with all forms of duties, rights, responsibilities, power and prestige that accompanied such status.

The Role of Circumcision in Gusii Education

It has already been stated that in Gusii customary law, male circumcision and female clitorectomy were taken as extremely important cultural and sacred rites. Through circumcision and the seclusion period that followed immediately, the boy, *omoisia* (pl. *abaisia*), was transformed through a symbolic rebirth from being a boy to being a young man, *omomura* (pl. *abamura*). Similarly, through the same process the girl, *egesagane* (pl. *ebisagane*), became a young woman, *omoiseke* (pl. *abaiseke*). The seclusion period used to last for a period between one to two months. During this important period of seclusion, the initiates were required to go through various rituals, *chinyangi* (sing. *enyangi*), where they were diligently taught the various rights, obligations and duties of grown up men and women.

After undergoing all the required rituals, the initiates graduated into full-fledged men and women, ready to be involved in the undertaking of all responsibilities as pertains to adulthood. Women would be expected to undertake such responsibilities as child bearing and appropriate childcare practices. Men, on the other hand, would be expected to undertake male roles as raising a family and protecting the community.

They were also accorded the rare privilege of attending and participating in all forms of Gusii rituals as related to community governance, and social and religious values around which Gusii life revolved. Each initiation rite consisted of an elaborate formal and informal educational initiative that enabled the initiate to shed his or her past behavioural experiences as a child and to go through a symbolic rebirth and enter into a new life of adulthood.

It should also be stated that the initiation period throughout Gusii land was usually undertaken towards the end of the year (between August and December). This was after the end of harvesting season when there was plenty of food and other resources to be used for feasting and to be used in diligently feeding the initiates during the seclusion period. It can also be argued that the circumcision and *clitorectomy* rites formed the climax of Gusii formal and informal education system. As discussed in the chapter on circumcision, during this period, the initiates went through various forms of education that were based on dramatization of various important Gusii social values and cultural practices. During the seclusion period, the initiates were taught that they should always show respect to their parents and other community elders. It is during seclusion that the initiates were prepared to take their expected roles and responsibilities in society. It can therefore be stated that the seclusion period provided an opportunity for an uninterrupted and continuous formal training process where the initiates went through systematic education and acquired various forms of instructions that eventually conferred to them full status of young men and women in the society.

Boys were usually circumcised by traditional circumcisers, *abasari* (sing. *omosari*), who were well-trained in the art of conducting circumcision. The actual circumcision of boys was usually done under specifically recognized trees that had ritualistic value, such as *omuobo* (pl. *emiobo*), whereas girls underwent clitorectomy while seated on a specially designed stone called *orotuba*. Traits of courage, bravery and endurance were highly encouraged at the time of circumcision. More particularly, boys were forewarned by the young circumcised men who escorted them to the circumciser that, should they dare make any form of sound or movement when they were being circumcised, they will be speared to death, in this regard, boys were not supposed to show any sign indicating that they were in pain, when the traditional circumciser was carrying out the actual operation (i.e., cutting of foreskin of the phallus).

Various techniques were used to test the initiates' level of endurance and courage including applying acceptable methods of inflicting elements of pain to the initiates, especially boys. These included being stripped naked and covering their bodies with stinging leaves of certain herbal plants such as *enyanduri* (pl. *chinyanduri*) (stinging nettle) and being submerged into extremely cold water in the adjacent rivers during the wee hours of the night. Subjecting the initiates to these forms of pain and severe conditions of endurance was supposed to train and make the initiates develop high levels of courage and stamina. These were seen as important modes of training that were aimed at moulding the young men to be able to withstand difficult situations and hostile environments such as confronting the enemy during times of war and/or being able to withstand various life threatening situations whenever they occur.

During the whole period of the seclusion, a ritualistic fire that was made by rubbing or drilling of two dry sticks until they produced sparks of fire burned continuously. The fire was usually started and maintained by the initiates under the supervision of the young circumcised men who guided them in the making of the sacred fire that was not supposed to go out until the end of the seclusion period. It was taboo for the fire to go out during the seclusion period. This was supposed to teach the initiates to develop a high sense of duty and responsibility. More important were the various forms of education and training that were provided to the initiates during the seclusion period and afterwards. Through these formal educational processes, the young men and women were taught and achieved a mastery of various aspects of Gusii social values and cultural practices. The young men were also instructed to have a clear understanding as to who the traditional enemies of the Gusii people were, particularly the warlike neighbouring communities of the Maasai and the Kipsigis. The young men were taught that they should always be ready to confront their traditional enemies at any time and at any place whenever need arose, especially during cattle raids and various land disputes.

Immediately after circumcision, the young men who escorted the initiates to their respective homesteads sang a special Gusii circumcision song, *esimbore*. This song particularly dramatized the level of enmity that existed between the Gusii and their external adversaries. The initiates were supposed to internalize special messages that were song. Some of the phrases that were contained in the circumcision song informed the initiates that they were now men who should be ready to carry weapons of war such as shields, spears and arrows. These could be used to confront their enemies and defend their people from any forms of external aggression.

In most cases, the songs that were sung when the circumcised girls were being escorted to their homesteads were quite different in content and message compared to the boys' circumcision songs. The girls' songs usually revolved around themes that emphasized the fact that they had now become women and they should always guard their virginity until they got married. Moreover, specific women were appointed to teach and provide training, during the seclusion period, to the female initiates on specific gender duties such as being a good housewife and other functions of motherhood including pregnancy, childbearing and childcare. In addition, various forms of sexual education were imparted to the initiates during the seclusion period. They were informed that they had now acquired the full status of men and women. The women initiates were also taught that they should now have sexual relations with only circumcised men; men initiates were similarly advised: to have sex with only circumcised women. It was a taboo for a circumcised person to have sexual intercourse with uncircumcised ones of the opposite gender. These forms of sexual training were supposed to reinforce the fact that the Gusii community only permitted marriage and sexual relationships to circumcised and initiated young men and women.

At the end of the seclusion period, the young men were eventually supposed to start living in a military encampment, *gesarate*. A typical *gesarate* was made of a number of huts, *ebisarate*, in which the men and boys lived. Here, they received further training that was provided by experts on various war skills and fighting techniques. They were once more emphatically informed that they were now mature men who should always be ready to put their lives on the line in defending the Gusii community against any form of internal and external aggression. Through strict supervision by experts, they received further instruction and drills on how to handle and use various weapons such as shields, spears, bows and arrows. Such important fighting skills were imparted on the young men by allowing them to take part in pseudo-fights with other young men from the neighbouring *ebisarate*. However, the trainer made sure that each trainee was always alert, and they did not cause injury to one another. Furthermore, the young men were trained on various skills such as how to make shields, spears, bows and arrows and how to maintain those weapons of war. Once the trainees had acquired all the necessarymilitary skills and knowledge, they were allowed to join other warriors during times of war with the neighbouring communities.

At *gesarate*, the young warriors also looked after cattle and were supposed to be always alert to detect the arrival of nocturnal cattle raiders especially the Kipsigis and Maasai. On the whole, the young warriors were taught that they had to work hard in order for them to be able to own their own cattle; they should always be ready to protect their animals against cattle raiders and rustlers. In general, the young warriors stayed in the *gesarate* for a period of between three and five years. It was only after they had served in various military regiments and graduated from the *ebiesarate* that the young men were allowed to return to their respective homesteads and were now free to marry. Consequently, it was only after the young men had gone through all the initiation rites and had served in various military initiatives against perceived and real enemies that they were now seen as having received a full education. They were now ready to undertake family responsibilities and establish their own homesteads. They were also seen as having matured into adult men with the requisite knowledge and wisdom. As a consequence, people in the community accorded them respect and loyalty. By this time, the young adults would have reached the age of 25 years and above.

Conclusion

In this chapter, it has been enunciated that an important element of Gusii indigenous education system was that it was based on gradual progression throughout the human life cycle. Thus, as a person went through the various stages of life starting from childhood, adolescence to adulthood, he/she was confronted with different formal and informal learning experiences and practical skills that were relevant and/or useful to one's life.

CHAPTER EIGHT

GUSII INDIGENOUS MEDICINE

Introduction

This chapter provides an illumination into various types of Gusii indigenous medical practices and highlights Gusii perceptions and philosophies as relates to different diseases and medical conditions. It also provides a classification of different categories of Gusii healers who performed various preventive and curative medical practices. It is particularly articulated that, as is the case with many Bantu and other African communities, disease and/or illness was intricately interwoven with the peoples' socio-cultural fabric and religious/spiritual values and beliefs.

In this regard, what may originally have been perceived as a physical ailment could eventually became a communal issue affecting a multiplicity of social groups starting from the family or village to the clan, and sometimes, the whole Gusii community.

Indigenous Medicine in the Face of Modernization: An Overview

An aspect of Gusii culture that has withstood the onslaught of Western influence and modernization is the practice of indigenous traditional medicine that is widely practised in many parts of rural Gusii land and many other parts of Kenya. It is possible that this widespread practice and usage of indigenous traditional medicine is due to the extremely high costs (for the common man) of Western medicine. In many parts of rural Kenya, moreover, health facilities and infrastructure are limited and may, to a large extent, be non-existent. As Sindiga (1995) puts it:

Kenya's modern health facilities are spatially inequitable and favour urban areas where only 15 per cent of the country's 25 million [now over 43.5 million] population lives. Some 57 per cent of the households in Kenya must travel more than 4 kilometers to the nearest health facility.

...Countrywide, the ratio of health centers to population is quite low, varying from 1:200,000 to 1:5,000. . ..Even where health facilities exist, medical services are not always available. Many facilities suffer from inadequate personnel, shortage of drugs, transport problems, lack of water, delays in repairs and even lack of stationery.

Due to the limited nature of modern medical facilities, services and infrastructure, it has been estimated that over 90 per cent of Gusii households seek some form of non-licensed and non-institutionalized traditional medicine. Due to existing stereotypes and the stigmatization attached to traditional medicine that is the result of the predominate Western influence and widespread Christianity, most of the people who seek this form of medicine, including making payments and visitations to "witchdoctors", are unwilling to admit openly that they consult traditional healers and medicine men.

What is Traditional Medicine?

Gusii traditional medicine may be defined within the broader context of indigenous African traditional medicine as:

> "the totality of all knowledge and practices whether explicit or not, used in diagnosing, preventing or eliminating a physical, mental or social disequilibrium and which rely exclusively on past experience and observation handed down from generation to generation, verbally or in writing" (Ampoto and Johnson-Romauld, 1978).

For the Gusii, as the case is with most African societies, disease or illness is intricately interwoven in the social fabric of the people. This attitude derives from the fact that within the African social milieu of the extended family, when an individual contracts an illness and/or is attacked by disease, he/she cannot perform his or her duties or functions within the social context (Sindiga, 1995). As a consequence, the group, comprising of family members, neighbours and/or friends, is affected by the individual's illness and will be driven to seek treatment and other forms of remedies for the patient.

Thus, what was initially an individual problem or physical manifestation transforms into broad social and cultural issues affecting a multiplicity of social groupings extending to broader spatial and temporal locations. As Wisner (1996:82) ascertains, "understanding the social significance of disease and illness is the key to comprehensive understanding of the various aspects of African traditional medicine." Thus in the broader African context:

> Disease is not merely something resulting from malfunctioning in this or that organ or a lesion therein..., but essentially of a rupture of life's harmony, to be imputed either to a material cause instinct with some 'intangible force' or directly to that intangible force in itself. It is... necessary in traditional medical practice to confront the symptomatology and aetiology of diseases not only in the material but also the immaterial world (Ampofo and Johnson-Romauld 1978).

The Gusii have an elaborate traditional medical system with a variety of practitioners, specializations, pharmacopoeia and medical paraphernalia.

This system exists side by side with modern medicine, a demonstration of its resilience over time. It is used almost exclusively when measles (*omokururo* or *ekanyamoguku*) appears in children. In fact, the Gusii do not take measles victims to the hospital before the rash appears. Other conditions for which the Gusii do not seek modern medicine are evil eye (*ebibiriria*); and *orosao rwa abana* (infant diarrhoea) (Nyamwaya, 1986) which, they believe, is caused by abnormal development of milk teeth (*ebisara*). The foregoing indicates that the Gusii make a distinction between diseases or conditions which have to be drawn to modern medical attention and those that are preserved for traditional medicine. How is the distinction made? Who makes the distinction? To understand this phenomenon, one must delve into the disease etiologies of the culture concerned.

Disease Causation and Therapy

The Gusii do not distinguish between disease, illness or misfortune, although diseases (*amarwaire*; sing. *oborwaire*) are believed to be caused in a number of ways. When a person falls sick or even dies, the Gusii tend to tag a human-induced cause, especially witchcraft, to the case. Equally important are the supernatural causes of disease. In this regard, the Gusii, as the case is with many African communities, attribute the occurrence of diseases both to natural and supernatural causes. Consequently, people may resort to seek the services of traditional healers and/or "witchdoctors" who are present in almost all Gusii villages and/or townships. As Mbiti (1969) succinctly puts it, traditional healers (or witchdoctors for that matter) are the friends, pastors, psychiatrists and doctors of traditional African villages and communities. A traditional healer is:

> "A person who is recognized by the community in which he or she lives as competent to provide health care by using vegetable, animal and mineral subsistence and certain other methods based on the knowledge, attitude, and beliefs that are prevalent in the community regarding physical, mental and social well-being and the causation of disease and disability (Ampofo and John-Romauld, 1978).

The Gusii traditional healer performs multiple functions including acting as herbalists, diviners, seers, spiritualists, traditional surgeons and birth attendants, among others. More importantly, the Gusii use a holistic approach to the understanding and treatment of diseases and/or any form of misfortune whereby both organic, nutritional, and psychological attributes of disease or illness are considered together. In the realm of the supernatural, ancestral spirits (*chisokoro* sing. *esokoro*) may cause diseases. It is the duty of the living Omogusii to lubricate relationships between them and the departed ancestors. This takes the form of livestock sacrifices, usually cattle, sheep, goats and chicken. In normal circumstances, once a father has offered a sacrifice to the ancestral spirits (*chisokoro*), the son or sons need not do the same. But the grandsons are obliged to do so. Failure to 'remember' the ancestors may lead to the punishment of family members. They may remain poor or they could be afflicted with ill health and sometimes death.

The anger of *chisokoro* may be expressed through evil spirits (*ebirecha*; sing. *ekerecha*). If, for example, a father is not buried properly on his death, his spirits could become angry and affect a family member. Such would show themselves in madness (*ebarimo*) or make a woman barren/ infertile (*omogomba*; pl. *abagomba*) or make a child to contract epilepsy (*endurume*). A father's proper burial consists of first slaughtering a cockerel (*etwoni*), followed by a he goat (*egoree*) after three days. After two to three months, another *egoree* or *emingichi* (ram) is slaughtered to cleanse the home. At this stage, another man, for the purpose of continuing procreation in the dead man's name, may inherit a surviving fertile widow.

According to the Gusii, there are a number of other causes of *ebirecha*. These include spotting a python, killing a person, or killing *omogere* (a Luo). The affected family is expected to go to a diviner (*omoragori*, pl. *abaragori*) to find out the underlying cause. Family members then take the required action, usually herbal medicine and sacrifice. In the case of killing a person, a black sheep is usually slaughtered. This is believed to chase away the evil spirits (*ebirecha*). The Gusii also believe that witchcraft is responsible for certain medico-social problems. These include mental disturbance (*ebarimo*), female infertility (*obogomba*), and developing a chronic wound (*rikwege*; pl. *amakwege*). Other problems believed to result from bewitching (*ogokonwa*) are epilepsy (*endurume*) and evil eye (*ebibiriria*).

Both witches (*abarogi*; sing. *omorogi*) and sorcerers (*abanyamosira*; sing. *omonyamosira*) are well known within Gusii society. Witches are particularly feared and their actions appear to be motivated by jealousy (LeVine and LeVine, 1966). Sometimes, *abanyamosira* also act as healers to deal with the effects of witchcraft in society. Moreover, certain diseases are believed to be inherited (*ororeria*). Such diseases may be passed down the lineage to the offspring. A good example is *enyaini* or *endonge* (liver cirrhosis). The liver enlarges and hardens, ultimately developing a wound. Chronic *enyaini* causes oedema of the feet. At this stage, a person will die. *Enyaini* is treated by Gusii traditional medicine.

Another cause of disease and ill health among the Gusii is breaching taboos, taking perjured oaths, and sexual offences, especially adultery. These sets of offences draw the anger of ancestral spirits, which administer punishment. Adultery is punished by *amasangia*. The latter is the supernatural punishment against the infidelity of a married woman. The actions of an adulterous woman affect her husband and children and may lead to death of any of these. Men's extramarital relations with married women are also held in check by *amasangia* (LeVine and LeVine, 1966).

Finally, the Gusii believe that the environment may cause disease demonstrated by swelling all over the body (*enyamo*). It is believed that changes in seasons may bring 'bad air' from distant lands. The Luo have a similar condition called *yamo*. In general, naturalistic diseases are picked in the environment. They are amenable to herbal remedies. Such include asthma (*ekeera* or *egekuba egeku*), splenomegaly (*endwari y'anda*), malaria (*esosera*) and diarrhoea (*orosao*). Although this is an attempt to delineate clear disease etiologies held by the Gusii, such classification is only useful for analysis and greater comprehension of the culture's conception of disease and illness.

In reality, the Gusii: "maintain contradictory explanations of disease. On one hand, there is the view that disease is punishment for sexual, aggressive, property and ritual offences. On the other hand, there is the view more frequently used, that blames disease on the unwarranted malevolence of others" (LeVine and LeVine, 1966). This is what makes the Gusii pragmatic about treatment, and they will try anything that promises help and that has the faith of someone they respect. When one remedy fails, they try another, running through injections, tablets, sacrifice and sorcery with no feeling of inconsistency (LeVine and LeVine, 1966). Nyamwaya (1986), notes that many Abagusii first seek meaning in the physical causation, or what he calls the "how" explanation of illness. Only in cases of mental ailments or chronic disease is a "why" explanation sought. According to Nyamwaya (1986), there are two categories of causes which are attributed to the "why" explanation, namely interpersonal (witchcraft, curse or breaching of a taboo or custom) and spiritual (ancestors). The interpersonal factors are "the stresses, guilt and emotional disturbances which are consequences of sins or crimes committed by the patient or his fellow men". He concludes that: "the 'why' type of causation deals with social responsibility for an illness. An individual who deviates from the social norms cherished by the community will bring punishment on himself or his family."

Thus, the Gusii look to the various possibilities of causes when an illness strikes. They may utilize modern medicine together with herbal remedies. The latter are to protect them against evil people. Simultaneously, they may sacrifice an animal just in case the problem comes from the supernatural. In other words, the Gusii make an open-ended search for treatment within the medical systems which are accessible and available until the disease/illness is cured. Rather than providing a key to simple and swift selection of a medical system, the diverse disease etiologies tend to provide the basis for the uncertainty as to the actual cause of a given illness. The result is a rather diffuse pattern of therapy-seeking behaviour.

Practitioners of Traditional Medicine

The Gusii traditional medical system comprises several specialists. These are listed in Table 16.1. The basic traditional healer is *omonyamete* (pl. *abanyamete*), literally a herbal dispenser. He or she is found everywhere and usually dispenses herbal remedies for conditions that are believed to be natural. The healer who deals with love charms is called *omoebia* (pl. *abaebia*) and dispenses *amaebi* (love portions). Another category of healers is the diviner (*omoragori;* pl. *abaragori*). *Abaragori* usually unravel the cause of a given condition, especially one emanating from either supernatural or human-induced causes. After diagnosing the cause, an *omoragori* also advises on a course of action to avert the problem.

There is also a category of people who foretell the future through prophecy called *ababani* (sing. *omobani*), who are like seers. There is also another category of healers comprising traditional birth attendants (*abarabi;* sing. *omorabi*). These provide a variety of services including antenatal, prenatal and postnatal care and counsel expectant mothers on the appropriate foods to eat. *Abarabi* are significant in the Gusii society because of the high demand for children. Gusii men and women share a "strong desire for offspring" (LeVine and LeVine, 1966). Among the Gusii, childlessness is believed to be a consequence for perjured oaths, punishment for breaking a taboo or custom, and displeasure of the ancestors for failing to appease them.

Perhaps the most remarkable feature of Gusii traditional medicine is surgery. The surgeons (*ababari*; sing. *omobari*) are particularly known for the surgical procedure called craniotomy or head trephining which really is the opening of the brain case to relieve pressure which causes headaches in brain tumours (Thairu, 1975). *Omobari* has deep knowledge of the human body, suturing and antisepsis, essential for his surgical work. Such specialization is also well known among the Meru, Kuria and Marakwet people of Kenya (Nyamwaya, 1992).

Table 16.1: Gusii Medical Specialists

Category		Function
Singular	Plural	
Omonyamete	Abanyamete	Herbalist
Omoragori	Abaragori	Diviner
Omoriori	Abariori	One who unearths magic/witchcraft materials and medicine a "witch smeller"
Omorabi	Abarabi	Traditional birth attendant
Omorabi	Abarabi	Surgeon
Omosari	Abasari	Circumciser
Omoromeki	Abaromeki	One who performs localized bloodletting to relieve pain
Omoebia	Abaebia	Dealer in love medicine
Omwati	Abati	Performs autopsies
Omonyibi	Abanyibi embura	Rain maker
Omokireki	Abakireki	One who uses medicine to prevent diseases and misfortunes
Omobani	Ababani	One who foretells the future
Omonyamosira	Abanyamosira	Sorcerer

Source: LeVine and LeVine (1966)

Other specialists in related areas are *abasari/abakebi* (circumcisers), *abati* who drain abscesses and undertake autopsies and *abamoreki* who puncture a part of the body to release pressure thereby relieving pain. Male circumcisers operate on boys whereas the female circumcisers conduct clitorectomy. Female circumcision is still very much a revered tradition among the Gusii. As explained above, witchcraft is quite feared among the Gusii. The Gusii believe that witches use certain magical materials to inflict suffering on their targets. However, such harm can be undone by *abanyamosira* or *abanyanabi* (sorcerers). Sometimes the sorcerers can play the role of healers. In this capacity, they utilize their medicines to retaliate against witchcraft or to protect a family from it by performing a protective ritual called *okoosia* (LeVine and LeVine, 1966). Witches usually consult *abanyamosira* to obtain protective medicine to sniff out and unearth the magic or witchcraft materials and medicines causing illness. Medicines neutralize their potency and render them useless. The *omoriori* (pl. *abariori*) is sometimes dubbed a "witch-smeller" (LeVine and LeVine, 1966), although he works only to remove the paraphernalia of witchcraft rather than smelling the witches themselves.

Profile of a Practicing Traditional Healer

Some 10 kilometers to the Southwest of Kisii town along the Kisii-Kilgoris road at Boburia village, Boronyi Sub-location, Nyaribari Chache, lived Pastor (retired) Abel Nyakundi Onchoke. Born in 1901, Nyakundi earned a Diploma in Evangelism at the Seventh Day Adventist (SDA) Training School, Kamagambo, in 1942 after two years' study. He was ordained as a pastor in 1948 and retired in 1975 after working for 27 years. I interviewed Nyakundi in the month of September, 1989 at his home.

Nyakundi was a herbalist but he mixed this with Christian prayer. His father was a traditional healer working as *omoriori* and his mother was a diviner. This background enabled Nyakundi to work as an apprentice to his parents as he grew up. He said that he inherited the knowledge of the treatment of various medical conditions from his mother. He intimated, however, that the knowledge of certain herbal medicines was revealed to him by God. Nyakundi believed that faith and herbal remedies work together to control a disease or illness. After retiring from his religious duties, Nyakundi took to full-time work as a herbalist. He had practised as a traditional healer for 20 years, suggesting that he combined his pastoral work with herbal treatment for some time. When I interviewed him in 1989, he had four assistants - his wife, son and two grandsons. The assistants were going through a training programme and had mastered various herbs used in treating different conditions.

Nyakundi listed about 40 diseases that he was able to treat; among these was women infertility (*abakungu bateneine*). He also said that he could provide medicine to women who gave birth to female children consecutively so that they could get a male child and vice versa. Other diseases he treated were diabetes, hypertension, nose bleeding, chronic headache, asthma (*egekuba egeku gekoera*), gonorrhea (*enyamosono* or *enyamorero*), boils (*esamusamu*), miscarriage and premature births, poisoning (*esumo*), and abdominal pains in women who miss their menses. Nyakundi kept a strict record of his patients. On average, he made consultations with 10 patients every week. His patient records showed the name of the client, place of origin, problem, diagnosis, treatment/ herbs administered or provided, the amount of fees paid and the balance to be paid in future. Concerning the issue of consultation fees, Nyakundi said he charged inexpensively because of his belief that his knowledge of herbal medicines was a gift from God. He could not exploit it for profit. The healer noted that many of his patients came to him after seeking treatment in modern facilities. This suggested that either the problem could not be handled successfully in biomedicine, or the patients did not wait through the course of initial therapy before looking for an alternative.

During the week preceding our interview, Nyakundi had been consulted by patients suffering from infertility (women), asthma, malaria and amoeba. He treated women's infertility with the roots of *mote o'itimo* herbs, asthma with the leaves of *mote o'kebaki*, and amoeba with the leaves of *omonyantira* or *ekemwa*. Malaria was, however, treated with 22 different herbs. Nyakundi collected herbal medications from the bush himself. Nevertheless, owing to his advancing age, his assistants had increasingly taken over the chore. He also noted that bush land was receding, forcing him to walk long distances in search of the herbs. He had planted a few herbs, which were very difficult to obtain.

Pastor Nyakundi represents the contemporary workers in Gusii traditional medicine. Most of them are herbalists; other cadres are scattered widely apart. Both men and women practice Gusii medicine, many of whom are older people, usually over 50 years of age. Gusii healers are experienced and each has practised for a median of 20 years. Again, most practitioners inherit the vocation from their family members and/or work as apprentices to practising healers. Unlike Nyakundi, most of the Gusii traditional healers practice medicine as a part-time activity while cultivating their land holdings for food and/ or cash crops. A survey of traditional healers in Bonchari in 1993 showed that they attended to a median of four patients per week (c.f. ten for Nyakundi). They treated a large range of medical conditions with herbal remedies collected by the healers themselves. Most of the herbs were collected from the bush although many healers also planted some herbs.

Conclusion

This chapter has outlined Gusii traditional medicine and highlighted the community's concept of disease causation, illness and misfortune, and the practitioners in this medical system. Although distinctive disease aetiologies are articulated, therapy seeking behaviour tends to be pragmatic. The average individual moves from one medical system to another without a sense of contradiction. Gusii traditional healers have many specializations; however, herbalists form the dominant group. In addition, it has been elucidated that the gap between the accessibility and availability of modern health services and the demand for these services is filled by traditional medicine. Finally, the chapter has concluded with a profile of a Gusii traditional healer to add breath to the

The Gusii of Kenya

Author's Note: *Isaac Sindiga obtained his Ph.D. degree from Syracuse University. Before his sudden and untimely death in May 1999, he had originated the idea of compiling this manuscript detailing Gusii culture. It is in recognition of his initiative and scholarly commitment that his chapter on Gusii indigenous medicine has been included in this book. Most of the material in the chapter was drawn from the book he edited,* Traditional Medicine in Africa *published earlier by East African Educational Publishers.*

Editor's Note: *- Practitioners of Gusii medicine often took their role as a (spiritual) calling and hence a duty to the community. As such, they made their rates very basic and hence affordable to the majority in the community. This was, in part, because of the belief that they could lose the "power" to treat as this came from the ancestors. Greed, they believed, would anger the ancestors and bring a possible curse on them and/or their families. In addition, these practitioners had a duty to pass the knowledge and expertise down generations. A practitioner usually had a younger person on apprenticeship.*

102

CHAPTER NINE

GUSII AGRICULTURAL SYSTEMS

Introduction

Main aspects of Gusii indigenous agricultural systems are presented in this chapter. It is also enunciated that, over the years, the Gusii had evolved various farming strategies that involved organized division of labour and diverse farming techniques and land tillage. Particularly, the Gusii had developed a division of labour system, termed *risaga* (pl. *amasaga*), which involved establishment of well-organized indigenous co-operative working parties consisting of people drawn from similar lineages. Last but not least, the chapter looks into the influences of contemporary farming methods (most of which came with the onset of colonialism) on Gusii indigenous farming systems.

Traditional Productive System

The highland environment, in which the Gusii found themselves, exercised the most significant influence on the system of production that had emerged there by the end of the nineteenth century. The highlands were quite heavily forested at the time the initial groups of Gusii settled there. The environment required considerable adaptation for those who made their homes in that region. Dense forests had to be cleared to open the way for agricultural occupation. The clearing of trees was normally a communal activity mainly involving people with kinship ties. As noted in earlier chapters, the main bases to claims of land before the colonial era were either first clearing or initial hunting rights.

As a result, kinship units occupied a ridge or succession of ridges. These came to be regarded as clan land, and individual households gained rights to land through kinship. Moreover, the rights of a household over land extended to the area that could be effectively cultivated, including fallow land, over a number of years. This kinship-based land tenure provided a head of household with rights to cultivate a variety of crops, using household labour. On the other hand, rights to grazing lands, forests, and salt licks were communal. Households shared use of these with other kin.

This distinction between individual use of a household's arable land and the communal use of grazing land was important. Arable lands were under the direct control of the household head, while grazing land and the protection of cattle were shared. This meant that allocation of household labour took different forms when directed towards agriculture and cattle rearing. It also meant that differing cultural values came to be applied to cultivation and livestock herding. Cattle rearing, in particular, had substantial economic and social significance. It not only overshadowed cultivation in social significance, but large numbers of cattle provided greater status to the owner than sheep and goats. Wealth and economic strength was thought of primarily in terms of the number of cattle a household possessed. Cattle were raised for milk and for meat with hides also being utilized within the domestic economy. Cattle were also the currency of dowry, a significant element in the Gusii marriage tradition.

Cattle could be obtained by breeding, raiding neighbouring ethnic groups, through receipt of animals as dowry when a daughter got married, or by trade, especially with the Luo living to the North and West of the Gusii highlands. Such trade was usually a barter exchange where surplus grain or vegetables was traded for the livestock, which was part of the complex commercial links the Kisii had with the Luo that involved a variety of other items. Another indication of the importance of cattle was the special measures taken to protect this resource. In many parts of the Gusii highlands prior to the first decade of the twentieth century, cattle were kept in *ebisarate*, which fortified cattle against loss through raids. The cattle villages were walled enclosures where cattle could be kept at night or when not grazing or in potential danger from neighbours, such as the Kipsigis. Several adjacent households kept their cattle in such *ebisarate*. Unmarried men belonging to those households lived at the cattle village so as to care for and defend their livestock. The young men could also use the cattle village as a base for launching raids by which they sought to increase the size of the herds held at the *ebisarate*.

While cultivation enjoyed less economic and social significance than cattle rearing, the importance of cattle keeping in the Gusii economy was declining by the start of the colonial era. This was because the cool, wet highlands, made up of many rolling hills and ridges, generally lacked extensive open pasture land. Thus, the region the Gusii came to inhabit during the nineteenth century was not well-suited for raising large herds of cattle. Settlement in the highlands made cattle herding less feasible while the rich soils and reliable rainfall that characterized the highlands made cultivation relatively more attractive to most Gusii households (Ochieng' 1974; Were and Nyamwaya 1986).

Cultivation required households to mobilize available land and labour for the growth of crops that could be consumed by the household together with a surplus. The surplus was utilized for exchange and for protection against risks in case of crop failure. Prior to the twentieth century, land for cultivation lay close to, and included, the household's homestead. Cultivated land often consisted of a long strip running from the top of a ridge down toward the valley bottom, possibly touching a river or stream to ensure each household had access to water. This pattern was facilitated by the soils in the highlands which maintained a high level of fertility under traditional cropping patterns. This was one important factor that was responsible for a general lack of fragmented holdings in the Gusii highlands at the start of the last century (Uchendu and Anthony 1975). The crops for which land was used and labour mobilized were varied. The two most important staple crops at the end of the nineteenth century were finger millet (*obori*) and sorghum (*amaemba*). Both were sown through broadcasting. When harvested, these formed an important element in household diets as they were consumed after being ground into flour and boiled in water. *Obori* was also extensively used in beer-making. By the early twentieth century, this grain had considerable value in exchange relations. It was a trade item often in strong demand from the Luo neighbours.

While finger millet and sorghum were the major grain crops cultivated, some planted and consumed maize. This "traditional" maize was small in stature and produced multi-coloured kernels. If cultivated, it was planted on the edges of millet and sorghum fields. Root crops, such as sweet potatoes, yams, and cassava, were cultivated by households as well; in most cases, these crops were viewed as providing protection against environmental risks, for example, the depredations of locusts. Pulses, such as peas and beans, were also grown by most households. These provided important supplements for the grain crops in balanced household diets. On the other hand, bananas were not very extensively planted prior to the twentieth century. The relatively small number of households which cultivated bananas did so for "snacks" or fruit rather than as a staple food (Uchendu and Anthony 1975; Were and Nyamwaya 1986).

Traditional cropping patterns fit these varied crops into the two rainy seasons experienced by the Gusii highlands. The long rains begin in February or March; this was the time of the year for bush clearing and land breaking. The sowing of *obori* and *amaemba* normally took place just prior to or after the outset of the long rainy season. The actual planting time was determined by the amount and pattern of rainfall. Beans and peas were also planted at this time, often intercropped in the same fields as the grain crops. At the start of the colonial period, the general pattern of polycropping was to plant *obori* first with a thin admixture of *amaemba*. The finger millet ripened first and was reaped; after this, beans were planted between the sorghum stalks (Northcote, 1909). This intercropping had several advantages: it allowed for the concentration of labour in the cultivation process and it helped to provide soil renewal through the action of the leguminous crops. Following weeding, the long rains crops were harvested in August and September.

At the same time this work was going on, those households that planted crops for the short rains that began in October or November started breaking ground for planting. Although most households did not plant the short rains crops in the same fields as the long rains crops, the practice once again allowed for a concentration of labour in the cultivation process. *Obori* and *amaemba* were the most widely planted grains. However, it is clear that far from all households in the Gusii highlands planted these grains during the short rains period. Many households had abundant land and labour resources to produce sufficient food crops during the long rains to last throughout the entire year (Maxon, 2003). In this productive process, Gusii households had developed techniques for maximizing yields. In addition to the inter-planting of legumes noted above, households sought to maintain soil fertility through the practice of fallowing. Fields that were used for crops were left fallow for several rainy seasons before being returned to production. This pattern, which characterized the practice of the majority of Gusii households, has been termed shifting cultivation or a "rotational bush-fallowing system" (Maxon 2003).

Planting patterns also took account of other risk factors besides the danger of the depletion of soil fertility. Factors governing when and what to plant were determined by household risk aversion as well as subsistence needs. In terms of risk, the unpredictable variation in some ecological variable was the most important. Household practices for dealing with risk were the result of historical experience as to the crops and techniques that were most appropriate for household needs, though patterns of reciprocity and other "culturally defined" exchanges also played a part. Risks that households were concerned with included the late start or failure of one of the rainy seasons, loss of crops due to drought after the rains had started and planting had taken place, loss of crops to hailstorms, or destruction of crops due to predators such as locusts.

Households responded to such risks by adjusting times of planting, harvesting later or earlier than normal, or shifting concentration to a particular crop with known advantages in the face of ecological threats (e.g. planting sweet potatoes when famine threatened). In times of severe environmental damage to cultivation, households were forced to fall back to livestock. Although these were also subject to risks such as disease, cattle could be exchanged for grain in times of severe ecological stress.

In this productive process, there was a clear division of household labour along gender lines. Men cleared the fields for planting; women and girls undertook most of the other tasks associated with the cultivation process, such as weeding and harvesting. They often received assistance in these chores from members of other households related to them by ties of kinship. Young, unmarried men herded cattle, often using *ebisarate* as the focus for this activity. Uninitiated boys herded their household's sheep and goats.

Co-operative Work Groups (*Risaga*)

The traditional organization of labour also included other significant forms of assistance and work sharing. Among the most notable was the institution of *risaga* (pl. *amasaga*). *Risaga* represented cooperative working parties drawn from neighbouring households, not necessarily related by ties of kin. These households pooled their labour resources for certain specific purposes (Mayer, 1951). As noted in an earlier chapter, important examples of pooling of labour through *risaga* included the uniting of diverse Gusii sub-clans for defense against external raids. It is important to emphasize that the *risaga* was bound by neighborhood and economic dependence, not just by kinship (Mayer, 1951). The institution represented a means by which labour could be deployed as efficiently as possible in periods of peak demand (Tosh, 1980).

As a result of the research he carried out in the late 1940s, anthropologist Philip Mayer concluded that a network of *risaga* units covered the whole of the area inhabited by Gusii. The boundaries of each unit were "clearly defined and semi-permanent;" established territorially; the *risaga* included all households within the area (Mayer, 1951). Members of the group were termed *abanyaisaga* (sing. *omonyaisaga*), people of the *risaga*. The *risaga* unit was a permanent structural group, even though working parties were not activated very often at that time. The work carried out by the members of the working party included all the major agricultural tasks, though it was more usual for the *risaga* to undertake projects that were especially heavy or significant (Mayer, 1951).

An important characteristic of the *risaga* was that of the activation of these cooperative working parties involved a measure of reciprocity. Every head of the household belonging to the group had the right to call on others in the group to help with the task he wished to be completed, but the *omonyaisaga* was expected to provide participants in the working party with what Mayer termed "the usual reward - a sociable beer drink held at his home as soon as the work has been done" (Mayer, 1951). The reciprocity enshrined in the beer drink represented the wider concept of mutual obligations within the area covered by the *risaga*. Each main *risaga* area was recognized as the "large *risaga*" and it was sub-divided into units known as "small *amasaga*." Working parties could be called from either the large or small units. The boundaries of each were clearly recognized by the households concerned. Names of groups were usually geographically determined (Mayer, 1951; LeVine & LeVine 1966).

For the *amasaga*, there was no formal authority structure. A group sprang to life when a working party was required. This occurred often throughout the year, particularly during the growing seasons. Any household could call upon others in the unit to participate at any time. The usual practice was for household heads to invite others for the work projects, but as the initiative came from the person responsible for a particular plot of land, a woman could also initiate a call for assistance directed to the plot for which she was responsible. Thus if the working party was to be made up of women and girls, the woman could invite them herself, but if men were to participate in the work, then the household head was to make the invitation (Mayer, 1951).

Most tasks undertaken by the *risaga* were agricultural in nature, though house building could be tackled as well. While the former were expected to be completed in a day, the latter would not usually be accomplished in such a short time. Working parties drawn from the large *risaga* usually consisted of both male and female participants, though working parties for small *risaga* were often only females (Mayer, 1951). Members of the group were expected to turn up for the work as few excuses could be viewed as valid reasons for not taking part. Only by sending its full labour force could a household fulfill its obligations to the group (Mayer, 1951). One could be excused from participating in the group's work because of illness or mourning.

Among the common reasons for the calling for help from *risaga* was the need to take advantage of favourable weather, ill health among members of the homestead initiating the call, the failure to take note of environmental changes or inefficiency. The tasks, mostly "heavy and monotonous," carried out by the group included the clearing of fields and tilling for planting, the sowing of crops, weeding, especially if young plants were threatened, or harvesting. The *risaga* was particularly important in the latter process when harvesting in a short period of time was deemed necessary to avoid the risk of crop damage, for instance, by excessive rain or subjected to attacks by insects.

Few other obligations took precedence over the call to work as part of a given *risaga*. Nevertheless, a key element in the process of calling the *risaga* unit for common tasks was the availability of beer. Invitations to work could not be sent out until there was sufficient beer ready for consumption by members of the work party on completion of a day's work. *Risaga* workers were supposed to arrive at the site of the task soon after breakfast, each bringing the implements that they felt would be needed for the specific job at hand. Work was carried on through midday. The entire afternoon was then left for the beer drink (Mayer, 1951).

Working together was also expected to promote a sense of accomplishment and hard work. According to Mayer, reciprocity was important in promoting hard work and team effort in undertaking the tasks set for the *risaga*. He wrote: "The person who is conspicuous for slacking when [he/she] works for his *abanyaisaga* can scarcely expect them to put forth their best efforts when [his/her] turn comes for helping him" (Mayer, 1951). Participation in the beer drinking can be seen as in a sense a reward for participation in the joint project. In "normal" circumstances, four pots of beer were provided for *risaga* workers. However, gender and status governed who could participate in the drinking. If the working party was composed exclusively of women, for example, "traditional etiquette" forbade women to drink too much beer. Where women and men both worked, the men and women drank separately with men having much more beer provided to them (Mayer, 1951).

This system of neighbourhood work groups was functioning all over the Gusii highlands at the time Mayer carried out his field research. The anthropologist recognized, however, that some fifty years' experience of influences brought by colonial rule had produced some changes. He viewed the "occasional" payment of money for work, instead of the beer drink, as a reflection of European influences (Mayer 1951). Wage labour had emerged within Gusii society, but the practice of hiring others to carry out agricultural work, such as plowing and fencing, was used only "to a small extent." Even wealthy household heads preferred to use *risaga* for weeding and harvesting as this did not require the use of cash.

Colonial Attempt to Use *Risaga*

Nevertheless, Mayer believed that the institution of *risaga* had survived the four decades of colonial rule intact. Thus *risaga*, touching every corner of the Gusii highlands, presented the colonial administration with a vehicle that could be very useful in carrying out various forms of agricultural improvement schemes deemed desirable. As Mayer puts it:

> "the system of *risaga* groupings provides a series of ready-made units through which the Agricultural Department could maintain contact with a known number of neighbouring cultivators" (Mayer, 1951).

As their main function had been co-operation in agricultural work, the *risaga* could be used for "agricultural improvement measures." The cooperative nature of the work groups could be used, he went on, for anti-soil erosion measures, manuring schemes, coffee growing, and tree planting. The *amasaga* "should also provide a good starting point for group farming and other new forms of agricultural co-operation" (Mayer, 1951). Mayer enthusiastically placed these ideas before the colonial state in 1948 and 1949.

They met a warm reception since the late 1940s was a period characterized by the agriculture department's strong interest in promoting agricultural improvement through group farms. The idea was to combine several household holdings into a single unit as a means to promote "improved" farming practices in the form of crop innovation and soil conservation measures. On the group farm, for example, land could be terraced over a wide area with a single crop planted in large fields and a system of scientific crop rotation worked out. It was further held that new cash crops could be effectively introduced through the vehicle of group farms (Maxon, 2003). This approach attracted the support of some colonial agricultural and administrative officers as an efficient means of promoting agrarian change while avoiding reliance on market incentives to bring about desired alterations.

They feared that the uncontrolled play of market forces would promote individualism and bring in its wake all manner of economic and social problems, such as soil degradation and increased differentiation between rich and poor households. Such officials believed that Gusii households constituted a rural population of egalitarian peasants who lacked responsiveness to market forces. As such relying on customary practice, as suggested by Mayer, would allow the introduction of innovations through traditional institutions. Significant innovations could be made without economic, social and political disruption. When the colonial officials attempted to introduce the idea of group farms in the Gusii highlands in 1948, little success was achieved. At the urging of the District Commissioner and District Agricultural Officer, Mayer took a direct part in trying to convert *amasaga* to group farms in 1949. This effort as well as those of the colonial state to use the institution in new ways quickly proved a huge failure. None of the group farms established in the Gusii highlands succeeded. Some never got off the ground. In no instance did the households targeted have any interest in becoming a part of a group farm.

The attempt of the colonial state to harness *amasaga* so as to promote group farms that would lead to the adoption of improved technology and greater productivity did not amount to anything. The colonial officials, and perhaps Mayer himself, had mistaken the purpose of *amasaga*. Such groups entailed labour sharing, not the sharing or common ownership of land. The group farm ideal did not allow the individualism that had taken root among Gusii households to flourish. Most such households desired to make some profit from agriculture and to utilize it within the household.

It was a reflection of the considerable impact capitalism had made in the Gusii highlands (Fearn, 1961). Mayer's research actually reinforced this point as he reported that even wealthy household heads preferred using the *risaga* work groups rather than having to pay workers to carry out the tasks (Mayer, 1951).

Colonial Rule and Agricultural Change

The onset of colonial rule unleashed new forces that encouraged a process of peasantization. Households continued to use family labour to produce for their own subsistence and commodities for the new markets established under colonial rule. Down to 1930, this process had produced a relatively modest impact. It was characterized by an "abundant supply of land relative to labour and the introduction of simple farm implements" as well as limited engagement with markets (Uchendu and Anthony, 1975). The main technology adopted during these initial decades of the colonial impact was the utilization of hoes produced in Europe in place of the traditional implements used for turning the soil. The period witnessed no extensive change in production patterns. This was the result of several factors: the late conquest of the highlands and the lasting legacy of hostility to British rule; the provision of little in the way of specialist extension services in the Gusii highlands (only in 1929 was a trained Agricultural Officer stationed there); the relative isolation of the highlands from the main communications link in early colonial Kenya (i.e. the Uganda Railway); lack of direct links to the principal areas of European settlement, and the main urban areas of the colony.

Nevertheless, new crops were introduced during this period, partly by state action and partly as a result of market forces. Two examples of such crop innovation were maize and wheat. These were made available to Gusii households, particularly colonial chiefs and headmen, through the issue of seeds. Despite distribution by colonial officials both before and after World War I, wheat never became a significant crop in the Gusii highlands. This was primarily due to the crop's failure to find a place in household consumption patterns. The maize seed provided was quite different from that traditionally cultivated by Gusii households. Hickory King was distributed at the start of the colonial administration, and thanks to its more rapid growth and better yields, it quickly replaced older varieties.

Later, Flat White maize came to supplant Hickory King. By the close of the 1920s, households planting maize no longer did so along the edges of fields; it was inter-planted with other grains and beans. By that time, households in the Gusii highlands had discovered that maize could be sold as a means of gaining the cash required for taxes and other needs and to supplement the household diet. Nevertheless, it is important to recognize that maize had yet to become a major item in the diet of most households. *Obori* and *amaemba* continued to have greater importance (Great Britain, 1934). Nor was there a consistent demand for maize at prices that encouraged households to grow and market surpluses of the crop. The primary reason for this situation was distance from the market and poor communication in terms of roads that set transportation costs high and producer prices low so as to discourage exports of maize within the colonial marketing structure (Great Britain, 1934).

The 1930s, marked by the Great Depression and consequent low prices for produce, did not bring a dramatic alteration in this pattern. Nevertheless, more maize was produced and sold to the neighbouring district of Kericho (for supplying the tea estates now coming into production) while the introduction of market regulations brought about what colonial officials viewed as improved quality of maize grown in the Gusii highlands. Still, generally low prices for maize meant that the region was not a major exporter of maize through the colonial marketing system during the decade. However, the 1930s were quite significant in the agricultural history of the Gusii. This was because the decade witnessed the introduction of a high value cash crop that could bear the costs of transport and still bring a profit to the grower, coffee.

In 1939, for example, a ton of coffee returned slightly over 622 shillings to the grower while a ton of maize returned 50 shillings (Maxon, 2003). First planted in 1934, coffee growing was marked by strict state control and gradual adoption by a limited number of households. By 1941, just less than 200 households had planted coffee totaling 102 acres (Maxon, 2003). The first sales of coffee at the end of 1937, however, spurred interest in further planting. By the end of the decade, coffee had been established as a cash crop that could be grown in the Gusii highlands, thus opening the way for increased cultivation.

The onset of World War II, however, held back the expansion of coffee planting as the colonial state gave priority to the production of food crops in aid of the war effort. This had a significant impact on the highlands for, although the war ended in 1945, the decade marked the start of a huge agrarian transformation. Higher prices, increased marketing facilities, and better roads in the region combined to greatly spur production of maize. The result was that during the 1940s maize became a profitable crop for many Gusii households as increasing amounts were exported from the highlands. The crop was now planted during the short rainy season as well as the long rains season. Maize came to play a much more central role in household diets, further spurring production. By contrast, the end of the decade found less than 250 acres of coffee planted by 530 households (Maxon, 2003). This proved a springboard for greatly expanded coffee planting in the 1950s and 1960s. Although production and sale of maize in the Gusii highlands continued to increase, coffee surpassed maize in value returned to households through sales by the mid-1960s. Planting and production expanded further in the 1970s; many Gusii households reaped substantial benefits with the boom in prices in the latter portion of that decade.

Coffee was not the only high value cash crop cultivated in the Gusii highlands at that time. Pyrethrum was introduced to Gusii households in the 1950s, and over the next two decades, the region became the leading producer of small farm pyrethrum in Kenya. In the 1960s and 1970s, extensive planting of tea was undertaken. By the end of the century, tea was the most important high value cash crop grown in the highlands in terms of consistent returns to the grower. No wonder the area inhabited by the Gusii became a part of what has been termed Kenya's "agrarian revolution zone" (Orvis, 1997). The three cash crops were cast within a co-operative framework by the state. That is; co-operative societies served as the vehicle for marketing the crops grown by thousands of households on small plots and as a means of putting inputs into the hands of growers.

The latter was one significant change in productive patterns that marked the 1940s and subsequent decades. Another was the change in land holding arrangements, especially beginning in the 1960s, that witnessed the introduction of individual land tenure. Thus the predominant pattern of production by the end of the twentieth century was characterized by a consolidated household land holding devoted to the production of maize and other grains and vegetables as well as one, and in some cases more, of the cash crops noted above. During the second half of the century, bananas assumed an important role in those planting patterns. This reflected increased consumption by Gusii households, but bananas from the Gusii highlands were increasingly exported to Kenya's urban areas during that period. Despite these changes, the impact of the traditional productive system continued to be significant in terms of crops, planting choices, and household allocations of land and labour. Although some households began to utilize ploughs after World War II and hybrid varieties of maize were widely adopted by the end of the century, cultivation in most households was still carried out via the hoe. As in earlier periods, family labour continued to be widely used in the productive process.

Conclusion

This chapter has demonstrated that the Gusii indigenous agricultural systems existed in natural environment, and was also influenced by Gusii historical and cultural experiences including existing social networks and economic linkages with neighbouring communities in Western Kenya. Gusii historical traditions, as recounted earlier in this book, relate to a series of migrations by which families and clans came to settle in the highlands. In the course of these population movements, Gusii experienced contacts with such people as those who came to constitute the Southern Luhyia, particularly the Logoli, as well as the Luo, Kipsigis and Maasai. These contacts influenced settlement patterns and productive systems. As the Gusii moved to their current homeland, they developed techniques of production which stood the test of time in providing for household subsistence needs. It is important to note that traditional productive norms were not completely eliminated by the colonial experience; rather, these were altered. Changes in crop preferences and technology were the result of market forces and pressure from the colonial state. These began with the inauguration of the colonial rule in 1907-08 and continued to be the case through the remainder of the twentieth century as new crops, such as hybrid maize, coffee, pyrethrum and tea, were adopted by many households together with new productive techniques.

Author's Note: This chapter was written with Robert Maxon. He is distinguished Professor of African History at West Virginia University and has over the years written widely on Kenyan history and culture.

Editor's Note: Over time there were variations of the risaga concept. A good example of the egesangio (pl. ebisangio) where members of the group helped with chores on a "merry go round routine". Here, all members would go from a member homestead to another until the circle was closed. Like risaga, ebisangio were convened as and when the need arose, especially around the start of the season when there was need for labour tilling the fields.

CHAPTER TEN

RECENT EXPONENTIAL GROWTH OF GUSII POPULATION
Introduction

This chapter focuses on the various factors that have contributed to the recent exponential growth of Gusii population. In order to provide systematic elucidation of Gusii demographic trends, the Chapter is divided into specific historical eras (i.e., pre-colonial, colonial and post-colonial era).

Demographic Growth Rates: Brief Overview

In the recent past, particularly from the 1950s, the population of the Gusii people has been growing at a rate of over 4% per annum, one of the highest demographic growth rates recorded anywhere in the world. Currently, most of the Gusii population of over 3.5 million people, falls within the youthful age bracket of less than 15 years. It can therefore be postulated that due to the youthful nature of the overall population, it is expected that the Gusii population will continue growing at high rates into the foreseeable future. This growth rate is quite phenomenal bearing in mind that as recently as 1948, the Gusii numbered less than 300,000. This means that within a short duration of about 50 years, the population has increased more than tenfold (Ankar and Knowles, 1982; Frank and McNicoll, 1987; LeVine, et.al; 1996). This phenomenal growth of the Gusii population underscores the fact that the region has, in the recent past, experienced extremely high fertility rates. What are the underlying factors that have caused this phenomenal growth and high fertility rates? Human fertility is basically a biological function that is usually constrained by physiological and social processes that function within the context of socio-economic structures and cultural values (Frank and McNicoll, 1987).

Consequently, human fertility and population growth, unlike other fecundity, is basically constrained by both physiological and socio-cultural factors. In that matter, allowing full fecundity potential, a normal female is capable of giving birth to 15 infants, assuming that there is an average of 30 years reproductive period between the age of 15 to the time of menopause, approximately the age of 45. Even among the Gusii with such high rates of population growth, the number of births per female rarely exceeds ten (10). The major socio-economic factors that influence human fertility among the Gusii, and other communities, will be briefly presented in the following section.

Social-Demographic Factors Causing Rapid Population Growth

1. The age of marriage which determines the length of the time that women are exposed to the probability of child bearing within the reproductive period. As will be discussed later, there was a drastic reduction of the age of marriage, particularly with the start of colonial rule in the region at the turn of the twentieth century. In this regard, the younger the age of marriage, the longer the period a woman's reproduction capacity, and the greater the number of children that she is likely to have.

2. Yet another factor is the number of women ever married within a given period. It can be said that until recently, all ladies who had reached the required age of marriage were usually married since there was widespread practice of polygamy. Further, the Gusii place a high emphasis on marriage and fertility. Therefore, as the number of women who got married at a particular time increased, conversely the fertility rate also increased as more of the existing reproductive capacity was utilized.

3. The voluntary factors affecting the exposure to conception or to maturation of a pregnancy to a live birth is yet another cause. Some of the most effective voluntary factors include modern methods of family planning such as the use of contraceptives and other preventive techniques such as condoms, diaphragms, oral pills and injection, Inter Uterine Devices (IUD) or the coil. Probably up to the present time, these voluntary methods are rarely used in Gusii communities, as is the case with other parts of Kenya, particularly in the rural environment where most of the Kenyans live.

4. According to Gusii customary laws of marriage, women are supposed to deliberately pursue continuous reproduction accomplishments in their marital behaviour to increase chances of having more children to justify the well-being of marriage. Rather than considering reproduction as more of a by-product of routine sexual encounters among married couples, inversely, it is usually seen as a time to conceive another child. In this regard, a woman, who is customarily married with the required bride wealth paid, is culture-bound to become pregnant on a regular basis that maintains a birth interval of not more than 3 years.

5. Gusii customary marriage law requires almost all women who have reached the required age of marriage actually get married. This cultural practice guarantees almost universal entry of most women into a reproductive marital union, at the ideal age for conception and then childbirth. It also guarantees, almost universally, that entry into marriage assures a reproductive continuity until the period of menopause is reached.

Demographic Trends in the Past 300 Years

There are no existing conclusive studies that have been conducted in recent years to determine the causes of accelerating high fertility rates, and mounting population pressure leading to the deterioration of existing sustenance resources such as land. Such pressure may lead to stagnating standards of living and increasing levels of poverty. This study does not claim to provide answers to such a complex and emotive topic concerning the causes of high fertility rates among the Gusii people and related socio-economic and cultural factors that perpetuate the rapid increase of population. This study, however, provides a systematic analysis of historical and longitudinal demographic trends among the Gusii people in the last 300 years. As already stated, it is generally accepted among most demographic researchers, development experts, and government officials that the rate of population growth among the Gusii and most other rural Kenyan communities appears to be unprecedented in the world demographic history (Anker and Knowles, 1982).

Particularly, from the 1950s to the 1980s, there were very high birth rates of 53 live births per thousand people, and the crude natural increase of the population among the Gusii during that period exceeded 4% per annum. According to the theory of demographic transition, derived from historical trends of population growth rates in the Western world, population growth in most Western countries has gone through three main stages of demographic transition namely: pre-industrial, transitional and urban-industrial (Caldwell, 1976).

The pre-industrial stage was characterized by both high fertility and mortality rates; the transitional stage was characterized by high fertility and declining mortality rates; whereas the urban- industrial stage was characterized by both low fertility and mortality rates. Comparing the Gusii and the Kenyan demographic trends in general, they appear not to fit this Western model of population growth. This is particularly demonstrated by the fact that even before entering the industrial stage, Kenya has been experiencing phenomenal population growth over the last 50 years. Current population growth rate trends in most parts of Kenya are still quite high, although in the recent past, there are emerging indications, particularly among families living in urban centers, showing that the number of children per family has gradually been going down. This is, however, different from what is happening in most rural areas of Kenya in general and Gusii land in particular. It should be stated that this phenomenal population growth rate among the Gusii, is a very recent phenomenon and does not conform to the transitional growth trends as contained in the demographic transition theory.

Consequently, the recent abrupt phenomenal population growth rate in Kenya in general, and in the Gusii community in particular, cannot be appropriately explained using the theory of demographic transition. In this regard, the Gusii demographic growth trend can best be conceptualized as having gone through the following historical stages:

Firstly, the pre-colonial stage when the population growth rates were probably similar to those of pre-industrial stage in the Western world. This initial period was characterized by both high fertility and high mortality rates. Secondly, the colonial stage was characterized by high fertility rates and the start of inverse reduction in infant mortality rates. Thirdly, the post-colonial stage, which shares similar characteristics with the former stage. Nevertheless, the average size of most families went up to eight children per family due to a continuous reduction in infant mortality rates. We are going to apply these three stages or periods to analyze the demographic growth trends among the Gusii community in the last 300 years.

The Pre-colonial Period

When the Gusii settled in their current homeland about 200 years ago, their population was relatively small, consisting of approximately 20,000 people. As discussed elsewhere in the book, the Gusii were organized into eight contiguous clans and each of these clans consisted of several sub-clans that occupied distinct ridges that are separated by low-lying valley bottoms and rivers. Most historians contend that the dispersal of the Gusii from the Kano Plains and eventual settlement to their current homeland was involuntary settlement. It was occasioned by constant attacks by Maasai cattle raids in the initial expansive Gusii settlements in the low-lying Kano plains where the Gusii had lived for a period of about 200 years. As is also discussed elsewhere in the book, the most basic Gusii socio-economic and political organization was usually based on distinct or autonomous homesteads, *emechie*, that consisted of a family patriarch, his wife or wives and their immediate children. Several homesteads belonging to the same closely knit kinship groups or sub-clans, *ebisaku*, lived adjacent to one another and it was a conglomeration of these several sub-clans that forms the eight distinct Gusii clans.

It can be posited that a number of socio-economic and environmental factors, particularly in the period before the Gusii started experiencing ferocious nocturnal Maasai cattle raids, caused a relative increase in Gusii population associated with relatively high fertility rates of about 2% per annum. There were also enhanced infant survival rates due to favourable climatic conditions, an abundance of milk and meat supplies from the large herds of Gusii livestock that grazed the wider expanses of the park-like country of the Kano plains.

In addition, there were several other foods, including millet, sorghum, pumpkins and sweet potatoes that augmented the Gusii diet. Furthermore, the Gusii had a basic understanding of herbal medicine that they used to cure and prevent common infant ailments. Most of this herbal medicine is still used by Gusii people, especially in rural areas; and it appears to be effective in the treatment of common ailments that afflict infants. Consequently, the initial Gusii populate that had settled in the Kano plains increased from a mere 1000 people to over 20,000.

It is probably an understatement to say that when the Gusii were forced to disperse from the warmer low lying areas of Kano to the cold, wet and dense forested high altitude areas in the Gusii highlands region, the people must have experienced a major cultural-cum-environmental shock and socioeconomic disorientation. By the time the Gusii moved to the high altitude areas, they had already lost most of their livestock to the marauding Maasai raiders. Worse yet, the Gusii found the high altitude areas too cold and wet. The densely forested areas were also invested with several disease carrying vectors, unlike the open grassland region of the Kano Plains where they had lived for many years.

It also required a lot of intensive labour and tenacity to clear the thickly forested lands in order to make them habitable for human settlements and growth of subsistence crops. As a consequence, the Gusii suffered high infant mortality rates in their initial settlement in these highlands. Furthermore, the overall Gusii population, especially that of the elderly people who could not withstand the cold weather conditions, succumbed to various ailments. Probably, it can be estimated that by around 1800, the Gusii population had been decimated from the original population of about 20,000 to less than 15,000 people due to these unfortunate physiological and socio-economic factors.

As William Ochieng' (1974) succinctly puts it, most Gusii clans decided to move further southeastwards to the Kipkelion plateau (in the present border between Kericho and Bomet districts) due to hostile environmental conditions of the high altitude areas. From their new settlements in the Gusii highlands region, these plateau areas may have appeared as being a lower lying region with probable warmer and hospitable climatic conditions that would be conducive to the long term survival of the Gusii people. As a consequence, most Gusii people decided to move and settle in the Kipkelion area. Unfortunately, when most Gusii families moved to Kepkelion, the region turned out to be even colder with extremely wet conditions.

Furthermore, the Gusii once again started experiencing increased raids and attacks from both the Kipsigis and the Maasai. In this catastrophic situation, the Gusii had no option but to make a do or die decision and they started retracing their way back to the Gusii highland and adjacent areas. It can be estimated that by the time of their second resettlement in the Gusii highland region, their overall population had been reduced to less than 13,000 people. Having a strong urge to survive as a distinct ethnic community against all odds, however, the Gusii eventually evolved various survival techniques that made it possible for them to fend off external aggression (see Chapter Two).

Consequently, by the 1830s, the Gusii had managed to adjust relatively well in their settlement in the cooler high altitude areas of Gusii land. Through group and corporate efforts (*amasaga*) of various kinship groups, the Gusii started extensive clearing of the forest vegetation and establishing new settlements on the various ridges and cascading hills of the current Gusii land. By the twentieth century, the Gusii had managed to transform the previous dense forest lands into habitable human settlement areas, rich grazing ranges and productive croplands. More so, by around 1800, the Gusii people as a community had evolved various defensive mechanisms that appear to have been quite effective in defending themselves against their belligerent and more warlike neighbours, especially the Maasai and the Kipsigis.

As a result, it appears that during this period there was relative tranquility and prosperity in Gusii land, and the population started to increase once again. Eventually by the 1830s, various Gusii sub-clans had succeeded in clearing the forested land in several adjacent ridges and hills. This enabled the people to move and settle in adjacent frontier territories where they cleared the forested land for cultivation and grazing. The transformation of former forest areas into productive pasturelands enabled the Gusii to start rearing increased numbers of cattle and other forms of livestock. Consequently, this ecological transformation provided an improved socio-economic environment quite conducive for increased population growth. As LeVine (1996 et.al. 60) states:

The Gusii entered the colonial period with a history of economic and military success over several challenges to their survival. In their fertile and abundant territory, the Gusii lived like frontiersmen on the defensive in dispersed and mobile homesteads, and with a portable culture. Their lives were organized around three priorities; food production, military defense, and childbearing. Food production was achieved through shift cultivation of indigenous (finger) millet (eleusine and sorghum) and the raising cattle for milk and goats and sheep for meat. Local defense was necessary in the absence of a central authority to protect against cattle raids and other military actions, requiring all able bodied men to be prepared (confront any act of war) and the young warriors to act as militia. Bearing of children was necessary to maintain both food production and defense.

Consequently, it can be posited that due to the small number of inhabitants relative to the available frontier territories, most Gusii families and various kinship groups, that were settled in distinct ridges and cascading hills had very fertile soils and well distributed rainfall suitable for the growth of several subsistence crops and livestock grazing, must have had an extreme urge to replenish and increase the number of their people. Particularly the various Gusii families, kinship groups, and clans had a very strong urge to increase the number of their people for defensive purposes and in order to enable themselves to clear more forested land and establish new homesteads in existing abundant frontier territories that were unoccupied. It can therefore be argued that in initial settlement and eventual successful adaptation to the new high altitude ecological region, high fertility rates and increased childbearing became a cherished goal among the Gusii people.

In this cultural and socio-economic situation, a family patriarch who had many wives and children was generally perceived as a successful person who was accorded a great deal of respect and prestige in the Gusii community. Conversely, a person who had very few children and/or no children was generally perceived as a very unfortunate person in the community and had very low self-esteem.

Moreover, the main purpose of Gusii customary marriage, as was the case with most other African communities, was to give birth to as many children as possible to replenish the population of the immediate family and fellow kinsmen. As already stated elsewhere in the book, according to Gusii customary law, an immediate family consisting of husband, wives and the children was only legitimized and received communal recognition after the payment of bride wealth by members of the husband's family to their in-laws. The giving of bride wealth conferred upon the husband and his kinsmen the right to claim ownership to all the woman's children including those who may have been conceived elsewhere and/or after the death of the husband. In this regard, the giving of bride wealth conferred all the reproductive functions of the wife to the husband and his immediate kinship. Based on the extremely high premium that was placed on having many children, the success or failure of a man and woman was mainly measured by the number of children which they managed to sire, especially the number of sons in the family. Consequently, in each Gusii homestead, the husband and his wives placed an extremely high value to their fertility and the number of their children who managed to survive into maturity to foster and perpetuate the name of the family into the future.

It can therefore be argued that Gusii welfare and socio-economic well-being was to a large extent associated with the level of fertility and the increasing survival of the children to maturity. In cases of infertility, it was seen as a major imbalance in the welfare of the family and the kinship group, and was usually associated with existing displeasure of the ancestral spirits and/or as being brought about by an act of witchcraft. Immediate remedies were always sought to offset this imbalance by conducting religious rituals to appease the offended ancestral spirits. In the case of suspicion of witchcraft, remedies were sought from traditional medicine men who were supposed to provide magical-religious remedies to counter and forestall the evil spell brought about by suspected witches in the neighbourhood. Within the Gusii communal set up, the social ranking of a man and woman and the level of their communal progress within the kinship unit, generational and gender hierarchy, particularly among age-mates, depended to a large extent on the level of their reproductive achievements. Consequently, a man or woman usually achieved communal recognition and social esteem based on the birth of children, the circumcision of those children, the marriage of the sons and the giving birth to grand and great-grandchildren. As a consequence, life lost all meaning if a married woman was unable to give birth. If in such a situation it was eventually proved beyond any doubt that the woman was barren and therefore not capable of bearing children, Gusii customary law required such a woman to "marry another woman" who will bear children on her behalf. According to Gusii customary law, a respected male member of the kinship unit was discretely identified and was allowed to cohabit with the newly married woman. Usually children born out of such a marriage arrangement were culturally figuratively said to belong to "a deceased son" of the childless woman. Thus, these children were referred to as the woman's grandchildren and were accorded all the rights within the homestead and the immediate kinship group.

The Gusii perception of socio-economic well-being and spiritual harmony was therefore based on progressive reproduction within the family and its kinship. Therefore, a successful model of a Gusii homestead was based, to a large extent, on the number of children in that homestead (especially sons), the existing social harmony and tranquility among those children, and the level of respect and obedience they bestowed to the family patriarch. Moreover, most Gusii traditional rituals were mainly centered on the enhancement of family fertility and successful progression of the reproduction process in the homestead. In this regard, most Gusii rituals, such as various religious ceremonies during childbirth, circumcision and even during the death of a member of the family, were directly or indirectly centered on the appeasement of the Gusii Supreme Being (*Engoro*). Any other recognized kinship religious rituals were usually supposed to symbolize the enhancement of fertility and reproduction accomplishment in the homesteads and the kinship group as a whole.

Furthermore, Gusii fertility and reproduction accomplishment was usually maintained through the functions of the kinship system (*ebisaku*) and the existing Gusii cultural values and practices that used to continuously accord each married woman proper social interactions through the practice of avoidance behaviour, *chinsoni*, which restricted a woman's extramarital sexual activities. These socio-cultural practices also guaranteed that a married woman's reproductive continuity was maintained until menopause. Moreover, in instances where a woman became widowed or a husband was incapacitated in child bearing, reproductive continuity was facilitated through acceptable and discrete arrangements with an identified male within the kinship unit. The male cohabited with the woman and she bore children on behalf of the deceased husband and/or impotent man.

Colonial Period

The establishment of colonial rule in Gusii land in the early parts of the twentieth century started social, economic, cultural and political processes that assisted to enhance fertility rates and reduce the level of infant mortality. Although the establishment of colonial rule brought about major socio-economic, cultural and political transformation in most African communities such as the Gusii, it did not succeed in the long run in eliminating most of the traditional practices such as the value attached towards having many children.

The initial introduction of colonial and western cultural values, for instance, did not assist in reducing the traditional urge of Gusii families and their kinship groups to have as many children as possible. As a matter of fact, a man or woman's social status and prestige continued to be measured by, and in most instances is still, the number of children they have who have managed to survive to maturity; this is particularly the case in the rural areas like Gusii land. Consequently, most of the cultural factors and values that favour high fertility rates and having more children as discussed above still persist among most Gusii families and other African communities. Another good example which shows the persistence of traditional practices, particularly relating to child bearing, is the fact that, even at the current time, women who are unable to bear their own children are still allowed by members of their kinship groups to "marry another woman". The latter would bear children on her behalf and perpetuate the name of the family.

In most parts of Gusii land, however, one of the initial significant impacts of the establishment of colonial rule was the compulsory destruction of the traditional military encampments, *ebisarate*, for what was purported by the colonial government to be due to security reasons. Thus within a very short time frame very many Gusii young men found themselves freed from the customary obligation requiring all young circumcised males to stay in the military encampment in order to maintain the requisite defense system against internal and external aggression. Finding themselves staying in their parent's homestead, in many instances without any major obligations imposed upon them, most young men started marrying at a very young age. This was unlike what happened during the pre-colonial period when most Gusii young men were only allowed to marry after spending between 3 to 5 years in the *ebisarate*. As a matter of fact, by the time most of the young men graduated and were allowed to leave the *ebisarate*, they were usually above the age of 25 years.

The demand for more young women for marriage also meant that the age of marriage for the girls was drastically reduced, and many girls started to be married as early as the age of 15 years. This meant that by the time these girls eventually reached menopause at the age of 45 years, they would possibly have given birth to as many as 15 children. Furthermore, the survival of children per woman started going up significantly to an average of between 8 to 15 children surviving to maturity compared to an average of less than 5 children during the pre-colonial period (LeVine, et.al., 1996).

It also appears that from the beginning of the twentieth century, payment of bride wealth was seriously impacted by the changing socio-economic and political circumstances. Since there was a large cohort of young men who were ready to marry, the net effect of this situation was the severe shortage of livestock in most families that could be used in the payment of bride wealth for the sons who wanted to marry. In the evolving situation, new forms of marriage arrangement emerged that were at variance with the strict regulations that governed a Gusii customary marriage. For instance, girls at the tender age of less than 15 years started to elope with relatively young men who were also in their mid-teens. This form of marriage was usually initiated by the young couple without any consent from their parents and/ or without the payment of bride wealth. Consequently, these very young couples started giving birth to children at a very early age. This meant that since all other factors, such as infant mortality and survival to maturity, was also quite favourable during this period, most young couples were destined to have large families, in many instances exceeding ten children surviving to maturity per married woman.

Furthermore, with the changing circumstances, many parents also started circumcising their children at a very early age, usually at the average age of eight years. According to Gusii tradition, a girl who has undergone clitorectomy and the accompanying initiation rituals was ready for marriage. As a result, most young girls started to get married at a very tender age, thus enhancing the probability of having many children before reaching menopause. All these factors created a situation of unprecedented rapid population growth rates among the Gusii, as is the case with most other Kenyan ethnic communities during the colonial period.

Post-Colonial Period

Particularly during the early stage of the post-colonial era, there was unprecedented growth of the Gusii population, probably surpassing most other ethnic communities in Kenya. On average, between 1963 to the 1980, most Gusii women had a fertility rate of more than eight children. It can also be stated that over the years, the independent Kenyan government improved and increased the number of health centers and district hospital facilities in most parts of the country. With improved health care, most Gusii women had the opportunity of between eight and fifteen children surviving to maturity. The excessive birth rates over death rates resulted in phenomenal population growth rates, in the whole of Gusii land, of over 4 % per annum during the initial 30 years of Kenya's attainment of independence.

For instance, Gusii women under the age of 45 years reported having more children in the 1970s compared to the 1960s (LeVine, et.al. 1996). Furthermore, within a very short time frame, there was a drastic reduction of infant and child mortality rates thus propelling rapid growth of the Gusii population. This was mainly due to the overall economic improvement in Gusii land, especially during the 1970s and the 1980s. The good overall performance of the Kenyan economy during this period was also accompanied by improvements in health care and general living conditions. Because of improved health care, for example, the proportion of child deaths for women between the ages of 15-45 went down drastically to an average of 2 deaths per 10 children per family. The infant mortality rate in Gusii land and most other parts of Kenya (i.e. the number of children who died in the first year of life for every thousand live births) went down from 140 in 1963 to 89 in the late 1970s and to less than 60 in the 1980s.

Other socio-economic factors that have led to the rapid increase of the Gusii population in the recent past include the limited period of postpartum abstinence after giving birth, a widely followed cultural practice. This practice of reduced postpartum abstinence led to a reduced interval of giving birth from over three years in the pre-colonial period to about two years. Furthermore, there has been a reduction in the period of breastfeeding from about 2 years in the pre-colonial period to currently less than 12 months, thus increasing the chances of conception. Due to the above stipulated factors, Gusii population has grown exponentially in the recent past. These population growth trends have astounded demographic experts since there are no known examples that can be compared to the Gusii situation anywhere in the world.

In this regard, it should be stated that Gusii population has grown from a pantry less than 400,000 people at the time of attainment of Kenya's independence in 1963, to the current population of over 3.5 million people, an increment of over 3 million people in a duration of about 50 years. Most of this population is crammed in a very small land mass of Gusii land of about 800 square kilometers. Thus, the current Gusii land population density is over 4,000 persons per square kilometre. This translates to per capita land ownership of less than 0.15 hectares or 0.3 acres of land per person. Consequently, in all practical purposes, this makes the whole of Gusii region to qualify not to be called a rural area any longer, but a sprawling metropolis that is almost the size of Kenya's capital city-Nairobi, at least, in terms of human population density. In this regard, it can be postulated that if similar demographic trends are to continue to be experienced unperturbed into the foreseeable future, the Gusii population is going to exceed 40 million people (that is equivalent to the total current population of Kenya) by the year 2040. Obviously, this is going to have far reaching social, economic, cultural, political and environmental consequences affecting not only Gusii land but the whole of Kenya and beyond.

Particularly, unless the Gusii and other Kenyan people are able to transcend the current mode of economic production which is predominantly agriculture based (i.e. currently over 80% of the Gusii people live in rural Gusii land where they eke a living through small scale substance farming), and the country enters the status of a newly industrialized economy, as envisioned in vision 2030, the prospects of this exponential population growth are indeed frightening, to say the least. Thus, the end result of **exponential population growth** is going to be increased levels of poverty, malnutrition, youth unemployment with the attendant consequences of increased insecurity, high crime rates and general breakdown of law and order.

Conclusion

In a period of less than 70 years, the Gusii population has exemplified unique demographic trends that have probably not been witnessed anywhere on the face of the earth. Thus for instance, in a very short time frame, the Gusii population increased from a pantry 200,000 people in 1940s to the current population of over 3.5 million. It is argued in the Chapter that if similar demographic growth trends continue uninterrupted into the foreseeable future, the Gusii population will reach 40 million people in the next 30 years resulting in far reaching social, economic and political consequences. In this regard, due to the current exponential growth of Gusii population, perhaps, the critical question that should be asked is: What will be the socio-economic, cultural and political consequences if Gusii population continues to grow at the current exponential rates in the foreseeable future?

CHAPTER ELEVEN

GUSII INDIGENOUS JUSTICE SYSTEM

Introduction

This Chapter tackles the topic of Gusii indigenous justice system. It posits that the Gusii indigenous judicial system and customary law were closely linked and intertwined with the people's social, economic, political and religious values. Furthermore, the Chapter enunciates various forms of Gusii indigenous judicial structures starting with the *etureti* court which was made up of respected Gusii village elders.

Administration of Justice: Brief Overview

The administration of justice among the Gusii people started at the homestead level. The head of the homestead was responsible for settling family disputes and dealing with any form of violation at the homestead level. The homestead head commanded a lot of power and respect from his wives and children. Any orders involving the social, economic and religious welfare of the homestead coming from the family patriarch were taken as commands to be obeyed. Disobedience of the order emanating from the homestead head led to various forms of socio-economic and religious sanctions directed to the offender. By his position as the immediate link of the homestead to the family ancestors, the family patriarch had powers to curse any offender in his family.

The homestead head would also apply a number of economic sanctions. He could publicly reprimand his wives and sons in case they committed any form of defiance or offence. Furthermore, the family patriarch used his authority and applied sanctions to deter conflicts and quarrels among his wives and children and to reinforce his authority over them. It should, however, be observed that in most instances, the homestead head rarely used specific sanctions because family members usually had a lot of respect towards him and as a consequence they rarely disobeyed his authority. Petty jealousy and infractions among his wives and children usually provoked the issuance of a threat by the homestead head. It was only the committing of serious offences such as physical aggression causing bodily injury or incidents of incest and continuous repetition of minor offences (e.g. constant use of abusive language or show of disrespect among family members) that led the family head to effect economic penalties or to invoke supernatural sanctions through the issuance of a curse.

In most instances, homestead heads applied their powers sparingly with the aim of promoting peace and harmony in the family, and not to enhance or perpetuate such conflicts by being seen as favouring one side over the other. In instances where an offence involved members of more than one homestead, then the case was supposed to be handled by the lineage elders, *abagaka b'egesaku*. However, this body was not a formally constituted institutionalized unit. Rather, it was usually an informal meeting of homestead heads as dictated by the nature of the offence. In case of a land dispute between two homesteads, for instance, closely related lineage elders would convene to hear the dispute. In the case of more serious offences, such as murder or witchcraft involving distant relatives, the composition of the lineage elders would be expanded to include elders of the whole clan.

Whenever lineage elders convened as a court, however, there were no specific organs of cohesion to enforce their ruling. Thus, the powers to invoke the use of a curse and communal authority was bestowed to the lineage elders due to their age recognized wisdom, self-help action from the aggrieved party and the fear of invoking a supernatural oath, *emuma*. Additionally, the lineage elders had power to curse any presumed offender such as a thief, a murderer or a witch. In case of cursing, the elders would slaughter an animal such as a goat and use its blood to sprinkle at the site of the crime while issuing a curse, "let the person who committed this offence die". The ancestor spirits were the ones who carried out the curse. Another method that was used by the elders to settle an offence was to the litigants to sue/ take an oath, which would be enforced by the ancestors.

Judicial System and Law Enforcement

The Gusii judicial system and customary law enforcement were closely linked and intertwined with the people's social, economic, political and religious practices. As was the case with most other Kenyan Bantu communities, the Gusii never had centralized formal institutions dealing with various legal issues, and following clearly structured and formalized regulations concerning law enforcement. Similar to other Gusii social, political and economic activities, indigenous Gusii informal judicial system followed hierarchical informal structures that started from the lowest level, the family homestead, and progressed upwards to the clan level, and eventually the whole Gusii community.

Informal Legal Institutions

The Homestead

Throughout Gusii, most judicial matters were usually handled at the homestead level by the patriarchal, the founder, of that homestead, *omogaka bw'omochie*. It can be reiterated that a Gusii homestead was made up of the head of the family, his wives, married sons, their wives, and the other unmarried children of the homestead. In certain instances, the homestead also included people such as visitors and other individuals who had, over time, been incorporated into the homestead, *abamenyi*. The head of the homestead was highly respected by all members of that homestead and he commanded a lot of prestige and authority over all those people.

All members of the homestead were supposed to abide by the orders and guidance provided by the family patriarch on various aspects of Gusii life including the judicial, economic, social and political issues. More importantly, the head of the homestead had the authority and duty to settle all forms of social, political and economic disputes that confronted his family. The family patriarch was, however, not an autocratic leader, always arbitrarily making decisions on legal issues affecting his family. In most issues, including those dealing with judicial matters, the Gusii people generally applied egalitarian principles of equity, consensus building and the law of natural justice.

Consequently, when dealing with important disputes, such as those involving the use of various family resources (including land and payment of bride wealth), the head of the homestead usually consulted widely with other members of his family. Those consulted included the patriarch's grown up sons before making a decision or judgment on the issue at hand. Most disputes that were handled at the homestead level were usually domestic in nature such as the ownership and use of the family land and issues involving the payment of bride wealth for his sons who were already eligible to marry.

Invariably, the rulings that were made by the head of the homestead on disputes involving his family members were taken as final and were supposed to be strictly obeyed by the concerned parties. In this regard, the complainant or the defendant had no right of appeal. Due to the intricacy of most of the domestic judicial issues, the head of the homestead was expected to deal with disputes impartially. Indeed, even in large polygamous families, where there was a likelihood of many disputes, the patriarch was expected to act in a manner that collectively advances the well-being of the bigger collective: his family. Patriarchs who managed to steer their families towards economic progress and wealth creation were usually perceived as men of great wisdom. They were highly respected and held in very high esteem by the community. Such elders were always consulted on broader judicial issues affecting the whole clan and were always called upon to assist in settling disputes involving two and more homesteads.

Etureti

The second level of the informal hierarchy of the Gusii judicial system consisted of a cohort of informal courts, *etureti,* that were usually made up highly respected elders in a sub-clan. The elders who were appointed to members of these informal courts were usually people who had managed to personify and/or portray themselves as 'ideal' Gusii elders. They were all perceived as role models whose behaviour and conduct was supposed to be emulated by other members of the community, especially the young men aspiring to become future community elders.

The other criteria that were used in selecting elders to be members of the *etureti* was how successful they, themselves, were in settling various disputes in their respective homesteads. Also important was their considered level of wisdom as people who were supposed to make impartial and wise judgment on disputes involving the whole sub-clan. At the sub-clan level, the *etureti* was supposed to handle important judicial issues involving members of two or more homesteads, and other important social and political issues involving the whole sub-clan.

At the *etureti* level, the complainant was supposed to report his/her case to the senior most member of the *etureti* who was seen as the upper leader among equals. Before the elders started hearing evidence from the various concerned parties, the senior elder was usually supposed to have briefed the other elders of the nature of the case before them. After the *etureti* had received the litigant and the defendant's points of view, they also received evidence involving the case from witnesses. After receiving all the information and evidence concerning the case, the elders usually conducted detailed consultations amongst themselves and; they also sometimes allowed members of the public who had important information on the history and nature of the case to join them in the consultation before making a ruling. Most of the cases that were handled by the *etureti* involved issues concerning witchcraft, boundary disputes and assault. In issues involving land disputes between two homesteads, for instance, the elders fixed the right boundaries and/or ordered the immediate destruction of any structure that had been put up on the disputed land.

Additionally, the *etureti* had the authority to impose specific fines commensurate to the nature of the offence. The elders also had the authority to publicly reprimand an offender. This was supposed to serve as a warning to the offender and the general public on the seriousness of the offence; it should, therefore, not be committed in the future. However, it should be stated that the *etureti* never had powers of cohesion to enforce their rulings. In this regard, the elders mainly used magical-religious powers that were supposed to have been bestowed on them by the ancestors due to the nature and importance of the work they were dealing with on behalf of their community. Thus, the elders used their traditional authority to invoke a curse and/or take an oath, *emuma*, to oblige the culprit to pay the required fine. In addition, as Kenani (1976) states: "There was no difference between criminal and civil proceeding, nor was there a particular form of pleading which varied with the nature of the claim of the complaint as is in [the] present legal systems."

The leader of the *etureti* usually convened the court, and when congregating such court meetings, all the concerned parties, including their witnesses, were required to attend the proceedings. The court proceedings were usually held in public under the shade of specific types of trees that had ritualistic value to the Gusii people such as *omotembe*. The court's proceedings were also held at specific sites that were considered as being sacred and/or places that were associated with the presence of the ancestral spirits. During the court proceedings, any form of evidence was usually admissible, and all those people who were supposed to be familiar with the dispute or crime were also allowed to participate in the proceedings. Direct or indirect forms of evidence were also admissible and, in most instances, the conducting of the court proceeding was usually based on principles of reconciliation and not on retribution, unless it was a serious offence such as murder, witchcraft or incest.

Moreover, the court proceedings were not supposed to be conducted ex-parte (Kenani, 1976). The complainant and the defendant were both supposed to be present during the hearing of the case. It should also be stated that due to the high regard, respect and prestige that the elders who were members of *etureti* commanded, any summons that were given by these elders, in most cases, was obeyed. It was usually only in extremely exceptional circumstances (i.e., in the case of illness) that any summons to attend the court proceedings was not honoured.

Moreover, failure to attend the court proceedings without giving an acceptable reason would always tend to prejudice the individual's case or evidence. It was also an important requirement that before a complainant and defendant gave any evidence as relates to the case, he/she was supposed to take a customary oath binding him/her to say the truth on all matters concerning the case. Such an oath was usually taken by holding a particular traditional regalia or touching a specific tree that had ritualistic value, and uttering specific words such as, "If I, as a complainant or defendant tell a lie in this court proceeding, I should be stricken by lightning". These forms of magical-religious oaths were usually taken very seriously. Most of the Gusii people had strong beliefs that if one lied after taking a traditional oath, he/she will be stricken by lightning, or any form of serious misfortune will befall the person or members of his/her immediate family.

After the administration of the magical-religious oath, the complainant was allowed to start giving information concerning his/her case before the *etureti*. Next, the defendant was allowed to give his/her testimony. After that, they were each allowed to call their witnesses. Usually the members of the *etureti* were not supposed to cross-examine the witnesses. After all the evidence had been given, the members of the *etureti* made serious consultation among themselves before they eventually made a ruling based on the adduced evidence and the elders' personal understanding of the nature of the dispute. However, if a defendant maintained his/her innocence after the elders had made their ruling that he/she was guilty of the particular offence, another magical-religious oath was administered. But it should also be noted that, in most instances, the fear of the consequence of telling falsehoods after taking the oath usually made the guilty person confess before the elders.

Handling of Criminal Cases

If an individual killed another person willingly and with premeditated intent, the murderer was automatically termed a cursed person. The person who had committed such a heinous offence was also required to give to the bereaved family a stipulated fine that usually took the form of cattle, goats and sheep. The fine was usually given if the murdered person was an adult. In cases that involved murder, moreover, a special form of sacrifice was supposed to be offered to appease the ancestral spirits, and to chase away the evil spirits so that such a crime should not occur again. The offering of a sacrifice was also supposed to bring about social harmony and tranquility to all the involved parties in particular, and the whole community in general. Furthermore, it was socially acceptable for the deceased's family to take matters into their own hands and kill the person who had murdered a member of their family. In such instance, the case ended there and then.

However, if an individual killed another person by accident and without any premeditated intent, this form of crime was taken as manslaughter, *ogoita kwamosiabano*, and there was usually no specific form of punishment that was imposed on the offender. Nonetheless, the person who had committed manslaughter was usually required to provide an animal (e.g. a goat) that was used by the elders to perform a reconciliation ceremony, *ogosonsorana*.

This was particularly supposed to appease the ancestral spirits and bring peace and harmony between the members of the affected families. According to most Gusii elders, cases involving assault tended to be quite common, particularly during various interactions among age-mates where the concept of the *chinsoni* code of conduct that promoted avoidance and restraint (when dealing with people of different generations), was usually relaxed. For instance, age-mates were allowed to make all sorts of jokes and innuendos against each other. They would also make humorous light-hearted statements to one another that would sometimes appear to be rather offensive. In such situations, sometimes the jokes and innuendos would go a bit too far, particularly during occasions of beer drinking among age-mates. These led to physical confrontation and to real bodily harm or injury. In most assault cases involving age- mates and/or members of the same generation, the elders were supposed to reconcile and make peace among the affected parties.

In instances where there was bodily harm, however, the assailant was usually supposed to give some form of compensation to the injured person, mainly consisting of one or two goats. The concerned persons were also required to reconcile with one another by offering a sacrifice to bring peace and harmony between the parties. For cases involving rape, particularly if the rapist was caught in the act by a relative of the victim, the relative had the right to kill the rapist on the spot. This settled the matter and no further steps were supposed to be taken since raping a woman was a very serious offence among the Gusii people, equal to murder.

Handling of Offences Related to Arson and Theft

Gusii customary law also allowed that if the cattle rustler was caught in the act of stealing livestock, he was supposed to be killed instantly. However, such cases were usually quite complicated when dealing with livestock theft cases involving two or more clans. It appears that the stealing of livestock from other clans was, somewhat, acceptable. For instance, if livestock was stolen from a clan, and the offenders were not caught by members of the affected clan, most often such livestock was allowed to remain in the other clan, even if it was common knowledge to most people that those were stolen animals.

However, if the clan from whom livestock had been stolen got to know and eventually traced their stolen livestock to the other clan, the animals had to be given back voluntarily. If this did not happen, then the two clans would declare war against each other. A clan whose cattle had been stolen and were found in the possession of people of another clan, and the animals were not voluntarily returned, normally felt quite offended and humiliated by this kind of act. In this unfortunate situation, the elders of the offended clan would call for a public meeting where they would immediately declare war or any other form of retaliatory measure against the offending clan. It was considered a taboo for a person to steal livestock belonging to a member of his own clan, and this rarely happened. If such an abominable act happened, however, then the clan elders had the power to invoke a magical-religious curse on the offender, even if the stolen animals were voluntarily returned to the owner.

Similarly, in most forms of theft involving other forms of property, the offender was supposed to be killed on the spot if he was caught in the act of committing the offence. This form of punishment was allowed; even if the person caught stealing was a member of that clan. In most cases involving arson or destruction of property, the offender was supposed to be publicly condemned by the elders and was usually ordered to repay the complainant an equivalent of what had been destroyed. As already stated, there was no difference between the criminal and civil offences. In this regard, the two forms of offences were usually handled in the same manner. Some of the most common forms of cases that were civil in nature included disputes over land ownership, non-payment of debts and the recomposing of bride wealth. If the *etureti* found the defendant guilty of the offence, he was ordered to return the property to the rightful owner and/or pay the required fine.

If the defendant refused to return the stipulated property or pay the fine to the complainant, then the elders invoked a magical-religious curse against the offender. In some instances, the elders might decide to ask for co-operative assistance from other members of the clan to forcibly recover the stolen property and return it to the owner. It should be stated that in most cases of civil nature, the main goal of the elders' court was to try to make sure that their ruling provided for the complainant to be returned to the same condition he/she was in before the event that caused the loss of property that had taken place. Furthermore, civil cases were usually carried out with the eventual aim of establishing reconciliation among the affected parties.

Egesaku

This was sort of an informal court of appeal that was based at the clan level. Elders who sat in this court were chosen using criteria similar to the ones that were applied in selecting the elders who served on the *etureti*. In most instances, however, the people who constituted this court were usually selected from the senior-most elders of the various *etureti* within the clan. Most of the cases were handled by the *egesaku* courts were cases of appeal where litigants' were not usually satisfied by the judgment that was handed down by the *etureti*. *Egesaku* had the powers to reverse any form of ruling that had been made by the *etureti*. The elders were also supposed to handle cases that involved members of different clans. Most of the cases that were handled by the *egesaku* courts included land or border disputes between two or more clans, fratricide, and incest cases. The elders who were members of the *egesaku* courts were also supposed to have the utmost magical-religious power that put them in a position to invoke a curse or oath that may affect the whole sub-clan or clan depending on the level of magnitude of the committed crime or offence.

Abakumi

This was a sort of informal Supreme Court for the Gusii people. Elders who managed to acquire the status of *abakumi* or *abanguru* automatically qualified to become members of these courts. People who managed to acquire this highest status in Gusii society were usually extremely rare individuals who eventually became part of community legends. Their recognition, respect and authority usually went beyond the clan level and extended to the other Gusii clans. This was based on their unique leadership qualities and major achievements, such as having high quality military skills, and they were usually given the rare honour to declare war against external aggressors. They particularly became very famous if they managed to lead people to successfully repulse the external aggression and/or win the war. In addition, such people had immense wealth in terms of children and livestock and were perceived as having a lot of wisdom and foresight in dealing with issues affecting the whole Gusii community. Due to the nature of legitimate authority and honour that was bestowed upon them by the whole Gusii community, such leaders were also supposed to have a lot of magical-religious powers.

As already mentioned above, an elder who became *omokumi* was usually automatically anointed by the other clan elders to become a member of the informal Gusii Supreme Court. As a symbol of recognition to his authority, a person who became *omokumi* was usually supposed to receive various forms of traditional regalia or items that symbolized the level of magical-religious power and prestige that the individual commanded in the whole Gusii community. These forms of regalia included a ritualistic staff or walking stick called *enyimbo y'obogambi*, special stools, and a ritualistic head cup known as *egobia y'obogambi* (no other person was supposed to sit on this stool and/or put on the head cap).

They were particularly required to use these ritualistic items when deliberating on important legal issues that had significant implications to all Gusii people such as declaration of war against external aggressors. They also used the regalia when making rulings or public declarations on important issues such as the amount of livestock that were supposed to be paid as bride wealth in a particular time. They also were involved in making rules concerning important socio-economic, cultural, political and religious issues that would have implications in the whole of the Gusii community. Such forms of rules or public declarations also dealt with important issues relating to Gusii customary marriage and the manner in which the Gusii customary wedding, *enyangi,* was supposed to be conducted. They also had authority to make various public pronouncements on the important issues affecting the whole Gusii community. They also had powers to invoke the injection between the Gusii community and their ancestors, eventually the Supreme Being or God, *Engoro.*

The declarations by the *abakumi* court, for instance involving the number of cattle that should be paid as bride wealth by every Gusii family, were usually taken very seriously in the Gusii community. The *abakumi* always guarded particularly against arbitrary or rapid increases in bride wealth, which might cause social and economic imbalance in the Gusii community and destabilize marriage. The latter was one of the important institutions among the Gusii people. As stated elsewhere, customary marriage was usually not recognized as being legitimate until the payment of the bride wealth. The *abakumi* were supposed to have supernatural powers bestowed upon them by the Gusii ancestors and Supreme Being (*Engoro*), including the invocation of the ultimate curse of death on anyone who went against their public pronouncements and/or rulings regarding important issues affecting the Gusii people.

Abakumi Supreme Court Rulings on Bride Wealth Payment

One of the things that linked all the Gusii clans together were the informal rules and regulations that controlled the amount of cattle that was required to be paid as bride wealth. The Gusii people attached a lot of significance to the payment of bride wealth as a means of giving legitimacy to any form of Gusii customary marriage. According to Gusii elders, from 1800 to 1890, the number of animals that were paid as bride wealth usually consisted of six cows, one standard bull and not more than twelve goats. At the turn of the twentieth century, however, the number of animals that were being paid as bride wealth started to rapidly increase. As a consequence, by the 1940s, most Gusii families were paying as many as sixteen cows, one standard bull and several goats. Over time, there appeared to be general consensus among most of the Gusii people that the rate at which the payment of bride wealth was being inflated was quite unhealthy to the overall socio-economic and cultural well-being of the Gusii community.

The upward trend of bride wealth rates were particularly causing forced bachelorhood among many young men who were eligible to marry but could not afford the requisite bride wealth. This led to greater occurrences of unfortunate incidents of young men abducting young unmarried women. The men then forced the women to cohabit with them without the payment of bride wealth. As well, some young ladies willingly eloped with young men, causing their parents to miss the payment of bride wealth. Such situations were quite embarrassing and socially unacceptable. As a consequence, these negative effects that were brought about by the rapid increase of bride wealth led to a general consensus among the Gusii people that common action should be undertaken before the situation got out of hand. Although there used to be a strong urge for bargaining over the number of animals to be paid as bride wealth, in most instances, the number of animals that were eventually given at any particular period depended largely on the prevailing rates at that particular time.

This condition of bride wealth payment uniformly applied in the whole Gusii community without any form of discrimination based on the level of family wealth or any other socio-economic factor. The main reason for this situation was the fact that the bride wealth that was received for a girl was similarly handed over in its entirety for another marriage usually for one of the sons of the bride's immediate family. Consequently, this form of Gusii customary regulation stipulated that the number of animals that were paid as bride wealth should be relatively the same for all Gusii families. It came about as a practical experience that the cattle that was expended as bride wealth for a married sister was, in most instances, the only source of bride wealth for her brothers who were eligible to marry. However, it was natural that the rate of bride wealth had to rise during periods when the overall economy was doing well and livestock was plentiful. Likewise, the rate inversely went down during periods of scarcity, such as when there was an outbreak of a cattle epidemic or during periods when the people incurred heavy losses of cattle due to Maasai and Kipsigis cattle raids.

However, the Gusii always undertook deliberate measures to create a state of equilibrium or control over the rates of bride wealth from time to time depending on the existing economic situation.

These measures were mainly spearheaded by distinguished and influential Gusii elders who were perceived as people with a lot of wisdom and who also had a lot of wealth (in terms of cattle and children). They were also successful in managing various affairs of their respective homesteads. In most instances, elders who managed to acquire this highest level of social, political and economic status, in any given time, were usually few in number, and their authority and influence usually transcended the clan level. The elders who managed to reach this social status were referred to as *abakumi* or *abanguru* (people of immense wisdom, influence and authority) and, as already stated, such elders automatically became members of the informal Gusii supreme court; the *abakumi* court.

Usually, decisions reached by such influential elders on important issues such as customary marriage regulations, rates of bride wealth payment, land disputes involving more than one clan, and declaration of war against external aggression carried a lot of weight. Most Gusii people accepted these decisions. Such important decisions were usually based on the principles of consensus building and popular community agreement, especially among those respected in the other Gusii clans. Consequently, on various occasions when there was general communal consensus on an important issue, such as the need to reduce or raise the rate of bride wealth at a particular time, the *omokumi* from the senior most Gusii clan had the authority to call for a meeting consisting of all the *abakumi* from the other Gusii clans. In addition, other influential individuals, particularly those people who conducted important magical-religious Gusii rituals such as rainmakers and traditional wedding priests or priestesses, were also invited to such meetings.

It was during such occasions that *abakumi* from different Gusii clans constituted the informal Gusii Supreme Court. At such meetings there was usually a lot of consultation among all elders present on the issue at hand. It was only after these consultations and consensual agreement that the *omokumi* from one of the senior most Gusii clans (i.e., the Abagetutu clan) made a public pronouncement of the agreed decisions or rulings. Such public declarations were always accompanied with specific sanctions against any transgressors to the agreed ruling. These sanctions involved the performance of a magical- religious ritual that was supposed to bind all Gusii people to follow the agreed decision. The following are examples of various *abakumi* rulings that were made in different periods, as regards to the reduction of the rates of bride wealth payments. The rulings were based on general consensus among the Gusii people that the rates had become too high and there was an urgent need to reduce them to acceptable levels (Mayer, 1951).

Bogonko's Ruling

As already stated, towards the end of the nineteenth century, the rate of bride wealth had tremendously increased. It stood at over eighteen cows, one standard bull and several goats. Bogonko, who was the *omokumi* from the Abagetutu clan (one of the senior most Gusii clans), invited all the *abakumi* from the other clans to attend a meeting to deliberate on theissue of the rapidly increasing rates of bride wealth. The meeting was held at a place called Sesi in Kitutu. At that meeting, Bogonko (whom most Gusii elders concur was a belligerent leader) made an announcement that the number of cattle to be paid as bride wealth should be reduced to ten animals. The other *abakumi* who were present demurred; they started making murmurs opposing the unilateral decision made by Bogonko, who himself had already married off most of his daughters at inflated bride wealth rates.

Bogonko went ahead and made a public declaration on the reduction of bride wealth and he also issued a magical-religious sanction by performing a ritual involving the invocation of a curse to the effect that "all the people who went against his pronouncement, their cattle will become skins" (i.e. die). Indeed, most Gusii elders attribute to Bogonko's curse the cause of the cattle plague of the late 1890s where most of the cattle in Gusii land were wiped out. However, it is interesting to say that, ironically, the cattle plague eventually brought down the rate of bride wealth during the late 1890s to as low as one cow.

Ogeto's Ruling

In 1906, Ogeto, who was also *omokumi* from the Abagetutu clan, summoned all the other *abakumi* to attend a meeting that was held at Getuanyasi in Kitutu. All the elders present took part in carrying out a magical-religious ceremony that was aimed at consensus building concerning the reduction of the number of animals paid as bride wealth. After discussion, all the elders reached a consensus on the issue. Ogeto made a public declaration that "due to the prevailing economic situation in the whole of Gusii land, the number of animals to be paid as bride wealth should be reduced to three cows, one standard bull and not more than four goats".

All the other elders present voiced their agreement to the pronouncement by shouting in *unison eee twanchire* (yes, all of us have agreed). A magical-religious sanction was also declared against any transgressor.

In conducting the magical-religious ritual, Ogeto was assisted by his eldest wife who was a famous wedding priestess, *omokundekane*. They both declared "let us all now agree to 3 cows and may any man die who disobeys this order". According to Gusii elders, Ogeto's declaration was faithfully followed by most Gusii clans for more than five years.

Inchwari's Ruling

By the 1920s, once again the rate of bride wealth had increased substantially to over eight cows. Inchwari, who was also *omokumi* from the Abagetutu clan, accompanied by a famous rainmaker called Obwoge and his brother who was a wedding priest (*omokundekane*), summoned the Abakumi from other Gusii clans to a meeting in Kitutu. After reaching a consensus, all the elders present declared that, "bride wealth should once again be brought down to three cows and one standard bull". As was usual when elders reached a consensus in such a meeting, they all shouted in unison *eee twanchire* (yes, all of us have agreed) and a magical-religious ritual was conducted by Inchwari assisted by the rainmaker and his brother. They also made a proclamation to the effect that, "let the people [sprout] and become wealthy, let the Gusii country be healed from Ogeto's curse and let the number of cattle to be paid as bride wealth be reduced to three". It is still recalled by the Gusii.

Consequently, it can be stated that there were two main elements that were essential for the public declaration made by *abakumi* court on the reduction of bride wealth, and on any other important issue to be affectively adhered to by all the Gusii clans: authoritative action from a leading *omokumi* to summon a meeting (an informal Gusii supreme court) involving all the *abakumi* from the other Gusii clans and democratic consent where all the elders present expressed their overall agreement on the issue at hand by acclamation.

Conclusion

In this Chapter, it has been elucidated that the homestead, headed by *omogaka bw'omochie*, was the pinnacle of the indigenous system of justice. Further, it is presented that in overall, the elders who sat in the Gusii informal court systems were people who were perceived as role models; people whose behaviour and personal conduct was beyond reproach. It is also indicated that the Gusii informal court proceedings were usually held in the open; mainly, under the shade of specific African indigenous trees, such as the Nandi Flame, *omotembe*. These were trees that we perceived as having ritualistic values to the Gusii community. Lastly, it is shown in the Chapter that the highest level of Gusii informal court structure (which can be likened to the Supreme

Court) was referred to as the Court of *abakumi* (i.e. the Court of Lords). The elders who sat in the *abakumi* court were highly venerated individuals who had achieved the highest socio-economic status in the Gusii society. The *abakumi* elders eventually became part of the Gusii legends that were to be remembered for many generations to come.

CHAPTER TWELVE
GUSII INDIGENOUS INDUSTRIES: THE CASE OF SOAPSTONE PRODUCTION

Contextual Analysis

The Gusii soapstone industry is one of the oldest indigenous industries in Kenya, and perhaps in the whole of Africa which dates back to more than 4000 years. This is based on historical and anthropological dating of soapstone rock art inscriptions, that have been discovered in the Gusii region, particularly in the Tabaka area, in the present South Mugirango Sub-county; the area where most of the soapstone production is presently being carried out (Eisemon, et al, 1988; Hodder, 1992). Currently, the industry is one of the largest contributors to economic development for the Gusii people of Tabaka in particular, and Kenya in general. As an indigenous industry, it has over the years undergone various transformational processes such as handicraft modeling, product design and usages.

Within the broader context concerning the evolution of indigenous industries, it should be noted that technological advancement is one of the major ways in which humans have utilized the environment for the improvement of their livelihoods and overall social and economic development. For instance, the development of tools in the Stone Age period led to the development of various tools made of materials such as bronze and later iron (Ochieng, 1974; Rodney, 1982). These ancient tools greatly enhanced the living conditions of the early people who inhabited different parts of the world, particularly in the African continent which has been recognised as the cradle land of humankind (Rodney, 1982). Initially, technology developed through a process of trial and error, but as humans travelled from one place to another, they spread their technological knowledge with them. This is how the knowledge of iron smelting came to be known to various indigenous people in Africa and other parts of the world.

Consequently, in most instances, the local environment largely determined the forms of technology that was developed by specific communities in different parts of the world. However, as is the case today, there was no ethnic community which was completely self-sufficient. In this regard, different communities especially those that lived in close proximity with each other engaged in various forms of barter trade in order to meet their diverse needs.

For instance, by 500 B.C. iron melting was highly developed in indigenous communities, including the ancestors of the Gusii, Buhaya, Tatoga, Maasai, and Nyakyusa in Eastern Africa (Hodder, 1992). Iron was also a major item of trade obtained from the Pare smelters in Southern Tanzania. The Fipa community also exchanged their iron products with their neighbours for food stuffs and other items.

Salt was also acquired by burning specific types of indigenous grass, a widely practiced method of salt production in Sub-Sahara Africa. The other industrial activities included the production of traditional mats and various types of household utensils by many indigenous communities in Africa such as the Gusii community.

Consequently, it can be ascertained that pots, cloth, iron, salt and mats were major commodities of trade in most parts of Kenya, Uganda and Tanzania. It should also be noted that since Gusii land lies close to the border with Tanzania, traditionally, the Gusii traded with ethnic communities from both present Kenya and Tanzania.

Ochieng (1974) provides insights into the various indigenous industrial products that the Gusii used to trade with their neighbours especially the Luo, Kipsigis and Maasai. The Gusii produced implements such as soapstone utensils, hoes, axes, spears, arrows, knives and razors. These items were especially manufactured by the Gusii clans of Kitutu and Abagirango. Ornamental iron items such as arm rings, leg rings and earrings were also produced in Gusii land. Iron work was also found in other parts of Gusii land, including Bobasi, Machoge and South Mugirango. Apart from iron work, Ochieng (1974) also mentions the manufacturing of various soapstone products such as smoker pipes, bowls, and models of animals, snakes, birds and human beings as part of the products that were manufactured by the Gusii.

The Gusii sold the products to their neighbouring communities in exchange of cattle, salt, hides and skins, ghee, milk and drums. A critical analysis of Ochieng's (1974) findings suggest that Gusii soapstone was initially used to produce items of functional value, such as pipes and bowls. Later, soapstone was carved to make art objects including statues of people and animals. The discovery of iron and agricultural advancement were mutually beneficial, as secure food suppliers gave cultivators free time to develop other skills, while iron tools enabled them to put more land under cultivation, and increase food production.

However, it should be stated that although African communities such as the Gusii produced various types of high quality manufactured goods, they had not made a break-through with regard to high speed production and nd mass manufacturing of industrial products. As Rodney (1982) says, "It was in the level of scale that African manufacturers had not made a breakthrough" in their industrial technological development. For instance, the indigenous cotton looms, pottery and iron smelters were micro-scale in nature, and soapstone sculpturing was done slowly by hand.

Nevertheless, it should be noted that, using quality as a criterion, African manufactured goods were at par with the rest of the world. It is even possible that mass production would have developed in Africa, given sufficient time. Industrial production initiatives such as specialization and division of labour were already taking root in many parts of Africa at the time of the start of European colonialism in the late 19th Century (Rodney, 1982). Indeed, before the establishment of colonial rule over Gusii land, the production of soapstone items had shown a certain level of the division of labour, which was particularly organized according to various gender roles and age groups.

Within this broader historical context of indigenous industrialization in the African continent, it should be stated that, if indigenous African communities such as the Gusii continued working in their industries, it would have denied pioneer European settlers a source of much needed workforce for their large scale farms. Thus, the colonialists felt compelled to suppress African industries in order to eliminate competition for the industrial products from their home countries and; also, to ensure a steady supply of the requisite labour force for the large scale settler farms, mining centres and other capitalistic activities. In this regard, large quantities of raw materials were taken to Europe where they were transformed to various processed industrial goods that were later exported to Africa and other parts of the Third World where they were sold at exorbitant prices, making the European countries lurk in inordinately urge profits.

African iron manufacturing provides a good example of systematic suppression of indigenous industrial production. Kinyanjui (1997) has shown that the colonialists used suppression of conflict among African communities as an excuse to close down traditional blacksmiths, who were producers of swords, spears and arrows. The blacksmiths were further disadvantaged by the importation of foreign manufactured tools, which limited their work to the making of ritual items like circumcision knives. The Abagusii blacksmiths found themselves in a similar predicament, and so they turned to soapstone sculpturing, which did not threaten any of the European industries because it was considered unique art work that did not compete directly with the manufactured goods.

In the long run, importation of mass-manufactured goods satisfied the existing demand for manufactured goods in many parts of Africa and other parts of the Third World. Consequently, the European goods eventually suffocated indigenous production, cutting off the local producers from the existing domestic and regional markets. This unequal competition for markets between mass-manufactured goods and small scale indigenous products led to eventual stagnation of most indigenous manufacturing industries (Rodney, 1982). In this regard, soapstone sculptors were fortunate because they did not have to compete with similar unique artwork from European countries. However, it should be noted that the functional uses of soapstone (such as the production of pipes, vases and bowls) disappeared as foreign manufactured goods started dominating the existing market.

Resilience of the Soapstone Industry

Ironically, one of the main factors that played a critical role in the survival and overall resilience of the Gusii soapstone industry is the underlying conception of the soapstone products whose value was transformed from goods of utility to items of amusement and admiration by British colonial administrators, missionaries, adventure seekers and other agents of European colonialism (Eisemon, et al, 1988).

In this regard, the Gusii soapstone products that were over the years being produced by the local people for their socio-cultural value and economic functions were gradually turned into items of amusement for the European gentry and adventure seekers who came to catch a glimpse, albeit transiently, and amuse themselves with the uniqueness and presumed exotic nature and artistic value of such locally produced pieces of unique African art.

Drawing of a mysterious creature on a soapstone rock

Bao Game

Traditional utility items: smoking pipe, bowls and pots.

Modern artistic items: from left flamingo carving, statue of Mary, chicken, eggs, flower vase and a carving symbolizing unity.

In this regard, with the passage of time the Gusii soapstone products that the local people had produced for hundreds and perhaps thousands of years due to their utility function, social and economic value were all over sudden turned into exotic items of amusement for European colonial administrators, missionaries and adventures seekers intending to make transitory glimpse and/or purchase the indigenous items due to their perceived exotic and aesthetic value (Eisemon, et al, 1988).

In particular, places in Gusii land where these soapstone items were being manufactured, particularly in Tabaka, became instant hedonistic centres of attraction as more and more European travelers started visiting these areas to admire and purchase these locally crafted soapstone products. Thus, as Europeans travelled and visited these centres of production of Gusii soapstone carvings, they marveled at the exotic, artistic and aesthetic value of these items and purchased them as unique pieces of African art that were transported to far flung locations in Western countries and other parts of the developed world.

Over the years, these pieces of African art that were conspicuously displayed in living rooms and arts museums as symbols of prestige showing that the people who owned the items have had the rare privilege and opportunity to travel to far flung destinations in Africa and other Third World societies to participate in various touristic activities including visiting unique environments such as Tabaka in Gusii land where the unique soapstone items are being produced (King, 1977).

Elite Carvers and Globalization of Soapstone Production

In both the colonial and post-colonial era, there were and/or are several local elites who have distinguished themselves locally and internationally due to high quality and aesthetic value of their soapstone art products. A good example of an individual sculptor's inventiveness is provided by Alexander Mogendi, who produced the so-called "snake box" in the 1940s. This was a soapstone box from which the head of a snake would pop out when the box lid was slid open. This design is still popular and copies of the snake box have over the years been sold all over Kenya and many other parts of the world.

Apparently, older soapstone carvers tend to be more innovative compared to younger sculptors. In this regard, some older carvers hold the view that originality fetches higher prices for their work.

However, various researchers have also noted that innovation is only possible when one has a stable income from commercial production and possesses great insight into the art market, both of which require great experience, and are therefore the preserve of the older sculptors (Eisemon, et al, 1988).

One particularly prolific soapstone sculptor is Elkanah Ong'esa. The sculptor recalls that while he was in school, he would make a few carvings for sale in order to support himself (personal communication). After completing high school, Ong'esa opted to go to Makerere University in Uganda to study Fine Art at degree level rather than go to study accounting at the University of Nairobi where he had received admission after passing the Kenya Advanced Secondary Examination. Ong'esa recalls that his interest in Fine Art had developed while he was a student librarian at the current Kisii High School where he got the opportunity to read several books and magazines on Fine Art. While at Makerere in the mid-1960s, he acquired new knowledge and managed to purchase a few tools for soapstone carving. Later, he joined McGill University in Canada for postgraduate studies in Fine Art and Sculpturing.

Perhaps more importantly to the soapstone industry, Elkana Ong'esa also became aware that a carving could be made around a specific theme, and that this would increase its artistic value. He then endeavoured to impart this critical knowledge and skills to other soapstone carvers in Tabaka. Consequently, it cannot be gainsaid that currently Elkanah Ong'esa is one of the most prolific soapstone artist and, over the years, has managed to generate gainful income from the soapstone industry.

In addition to his scholarly credentials in Fine Art, Ong'esa is primarily known as a sculptor and a painter. In the years 1976-1978, while he wasteaching at Kisii College (then a college for primary school teachers and currently Kisii University) he made a soapstone sculpture called *Bird of Peace*, currently on display at the UNESCO headquarters in Paris. Laterin 1982, Ong'esa made another sculpture known as *Freedom Fight*, which represents important Kenyan history on the struggle for independence. This particular piece of art is on display in the UN headquarters in New York.

Ong'esa's other pieces of art work include a two (2) ton soapstone sculpture called *In Search of Water*. The theme of this sculpture is drawn from a popular Gusii folklore which narrates that during a dry season mega animals such as elephants and buffaloes could dug for water until they gave up, only for the little hare to come along and strike water with his first effort.

Elkanah Ong'esa further narrates that this sculpture (and the story in which it is based) represents the way in which big oil companies search for oil and give up prematurely, only for other companies to benefit from their major efforts. He made the sculpture for the Caltex Oil Company in 1984, and a special plane was chartered to transport the heavy sculpture to its final destination in the USA.

In 1996, Mr. Elkana Ong'esa made a sculpture named *Bottle Dance* for the Olympic Games in Atlanta, Georgia. It is in the shape of a bottle with people dancing around it, and it is displayed at the entrance of a state museum in Georgia. He has also made another sculpture known as the *Dancing Bird* which is on display at the entrance of the American Embassy in Nairobi.

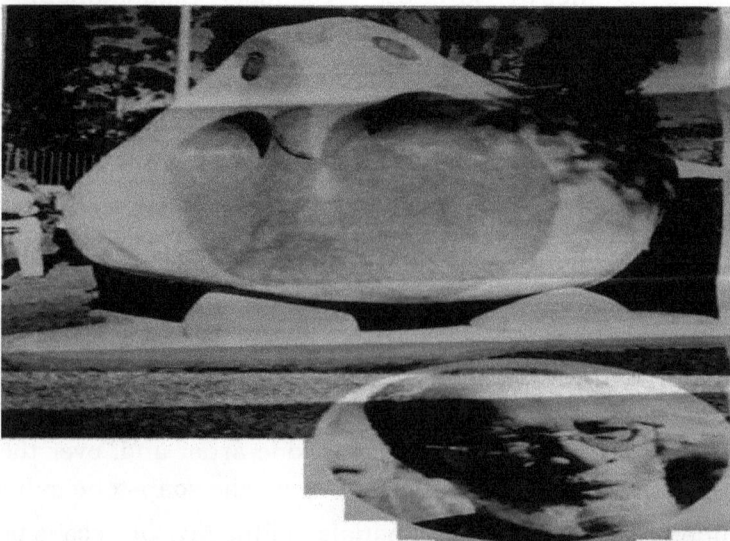

A piece of Elkanah's work at the USA Embassy in Nairobi: The Dancing Bird

The bird sculpture has a flock of other smaller birds engraved in it symbolizing the commitment to long-term friendship, peace and harmony shared between the people of Kenya and the United States of America.

Another renowned elite carver who has over the years immensely benefitted from soapstone carving is Gerald Motondi. He was born in Tabaka, where he learned how to carve soapstone in the traditional manner at a very early age. He later earned a Diploma in Fine Art from Asumbi Technical Training College. Similar to Elkanah, Ong'esa some of the soapstone sculptures of Motondi are famous the world over, and are on display in major museums in majors cities in different parts of the world.

Motondi has also managed to represent Kenya in international art symposia, workshops and conferences including exhibitions in China, Russia, Turkey and Israel. He also has the distinction of having some of his work exhibited in the world's tallest building, the Burj Khalifa in Dubai. Gerald Motondi is justifiably proud that he has been able to contribute to the promotion of Kenyan culture around the world through his unique art work (Personal Communication).

He credits his current international recognition to his own tenacity and innovativeness. He went to China in 2002 for a competition to create a sculpture around a popular theme, "We are inseparable." His sculpture won a gold award and in addition to this, he was given an Olympic torch (See the photograph below).

Motondi receiving Olympic torch award in Beijing from Xia Sajin Vice president of OFA 2008

However, it should be noted that although Gerald Motondi is a renowned artist the world over for his unique soapstone art work, he has rarely received recognition in his own country, Kenya; his birth place. Note that Motondi has also done major works of art using other forms of material including basalt and granite.

In this regard, it should be stated that both Elkanah Ong'esa and Gerald Motondi have, over the years, been able to market soapstone products globally through their unique pieces of art that are currently on display in different countries such as the Netherlands, Britain, China and the USA. Consequently, through their unique artwork and international networking, the two Gusii elite soapstone carvers have over the years played a critical role in the globalization of soapstone industry.

From left : Mr Elkanah Ong'esa " re-known sculptor", Former U.S.A Ambassador to Kenya Michael Ranneberger and Mr. Gerald Motondi " sculptor" at the soapstone carving site.

Furthermore, it is quite interesting and yet ironic to note that outside intervention, inadvertently, they managed to promote soapstone carving and to preserve this unique Gusii heritage. This is even though other forms of external intervention (such as capitalism and colonialism) have largely been detrimental to the preservation of the Gusii culture in general.

Another factor which has also contributed to the development of the soapstone industry is that Kenyans of all walks of life now appreciate soapstone products more than ever before and so there is a large domestic market for soapstone products. According to Maranga (1985), the market for soapstone products has grown from tourists and expatriates to include local people, not only in towns and cities, but in other expansive parts of the country as well.

However, as already stated, the forms in which soapstone sculptures are produced today differ from those of the past. In this regard, according to Eisemon, et al (1988), Similar to the Inuit of Northern Canada, the current forms of soapstone carvings among the Gusii were suggested to them as unique artistic medium by people outside their cultures who purchased craft objects made of soapstone, and as a consequence encouraged local artisans to produce objects that were authentic to their indigenous cultures. In this regard, cultural intrusion has had to a certain extent positive effects.

For one, it has provided a unique opportunity for indigenous societies undergoing rapid social change and economic transformation to be innovative and improve upon traditions that might otherwise have disappeared by now. It has also had a major economic incentive to strengthen these indigenous cultures while exposing artistic talent and creativity.

In other words, although soapstone carving was practiced mostly for functional purposes by the Gusii, it was the intervention of people from the outside world that transformed the societal status of soapstone carvings to commercial items and pieces of Fine Art that are sold all over the world. In this regard, as traditional culture is relentlessly eroded by various forces of capitalism and globalization, it can be argued that, to a certain extent, soapstone carving acts as a form of cultural preservation among the Gusii people albeit in a transformed modality in the currently highly globalized world. Particularly, many soapstone sculptors have adopted cultural themes in their work such as traditional folktales, legends and symbols in order to enhance creative and innovativeness of their artwork. Therefore, the soapstone carvers act as cultural conservatory agents through their unique soapstone sculptures in the broader context of a highly globalized world.

Soapstone Sales and Marketing

As already stated currently, the Gusii soapstone carvings receive wide appreciation from buyers all over the world.

Consequently, the major markets for soapstone carvings include the USA, Britain, Italy and New Zealand. Also, in recent years, Gusii soapstone carvings have found their way into major cities in Eastern Africa such as Kampala in Uganda; Arusha, Tarime and Dar es Salaam in Tanzania and Kigali in Rwanda.

At the same time in the 1960s, Joseph Murumbi, Kenya's second Vice President and an avid arts collector, set up the African Heritage Centre in Nairobi. This centre became a major depository of Gusii soapstone carvings, and their exhibitions in Nairobi and abroad further boosted international interest in soapstone sculptures. In addition, Murumbi founded the African Soapstone Company which concentrated on the marketing of soapstone carvings in the local and international market.

As a result, Kisii soapstone carvers gained a new perspective on how they could market their products both locally and overseas. Thus, although soapstone carving is majorly a handicraft industry, the rising demand for soapstone products both internationally and locally influenced Gusii soapstone carvers to reorganize their modes of production, so that they could produce carvings in large quantities, similar to mass produced industrial goods.

Furthermore currently, soapstone carving is closely associated with the Kenyan tourism industry and has become a major foreign exchange earner. This is because tourists who visit Kenya's National Parks and Cultural Centres, often see soapstone sculptures and artifacts for sale in or near the tourist hotels or lodges in different parts of the country.

Consequently, tourists can buy soapstone products at almost any tourist destination in Kenya, and the products are also available in curio shops in major urban areas throughout the country. In this regard, due to extensive marketing network of soapstone products, soapstone carvers are able to contribute significantly towards Kenya's foreign exchange earnings. In addition, the main soapstone carving centre at Tabaka has become a major tourist destination in itself, and some tourists buy soapstone carvings directly from the region. In this regard currently, soapstone carving is a major economic activity in Gusii and indeed in the whole of Kenya.

According to Maranga (1988) in his article entitled, *Self-EmployedSoapstone Carvers in Kisii*, by 1985, there were an estimated 5,000individuals Gusii carvers who derived some income from soapstone production and marketing. At the moment, the number has increased to over 13,000 soapstone producers. It should be noted that this figure does not include direct and indirect dependants.

It should also be noted that from 1985 to early 1990s, the sales and marketing of soapstone carvings was at its peak. This was because it was the time when the Kenyan tourism industry was performing quite well. This situation particularly provided an opportunity to the local carvers and vendors to sell the products directly to the international tourists without incurring transport and export tariff expenses. The result was a high demand for the items that tourists bought either as souvenirs or as pieces of unique African art.

However, currently due to incidents of insecurity with the attendant incessant travel advisories in major tourist generating countries such as the UK and USA, the number of international visitor arrivals to Kenya has reduced. This has had a direct negative impact on the Gusii soapstone industry. However, it is expected that the situation may change for the better as the Kenyan county and national governments intensify their fight against terrorism which is a major cause of insecurity in Kenya.

The Challenge of Middlemen

The impact of middlemen has also, over the years, posed a major challenge to the production and marketing of Gusii soapstone carvings. It is common practice for middlemen to purchase soapstone products cheaply from Gusii carvers at Tabaka and then sell the same products at exorbitant prices in the national and international market and; thus exploiting the carvers who do not receive their money's worth. Consequently, although the quantity of soapstone being mined and carved is larger than ever before, the apparent "privatization" of the soapstone industry allows unscrupulous middlemen to have a field day, as they can easily manipulate the various soapstone carvers, because they lack a unified strategy on crucial business issues such as the pricing and marketing of the soapstone products.

Many carvers at Tabaka confirmed that the disintegration of co-operative societies that initially brought several soapstone producers together to jointed produce and sale the carvings and eventual creation of numerous individual companies, had negative impact on the pricing and sales of soapstone carvings (Personal Communication). In this regard, after the collapse of the co-operative societies, many soapstone carvers began moving to urban centres such as Nairobi, Mombasa and Nakuru where they sold their carvings individually to prospective buyers.

However, lacking marketing skills and the attendant bargaining power, most of these individual soapstone sellers ended up selling their carvings at rock-bottom prices to unscrupulous middlemen who are always eager to maximize their profit margin.

Furthermore, most middlemen capitalized on this situation and travelled to Tabaka in large numbers to directly purchase the soapstone carvings at knocked-down prices. As a result of these factors, the general market price for soapstone products went down drastically. Cosmas Onchomba (owner of a soapstone quarry at Tabaka and himself an avid sculptor, although aged) places most of the blame on the shoulders of the former co-operative society leadership, which he describes as corrupt and incapable of representing the common interests of the members in a democratically accepted and accountable manner (personal communication). Onchomba further asserts that the extremely poor pricing of soapstone products has led to over exploitation of the raw material without any shroud of improvement of the livelihoods of the owners of the soapstone quarries at Tabaka and other adjacent areas.

Worse yet, when the researcher met the old man for the first time, he had the following to say in the Ekegusii language '*Mbuya tore aiga, nenchara yatonyarire*', meaning "we are doing fine though we lack food."As already stated, the old man (Onchomba) owns a quarry that has over the years been massively mined and is currently almost being exhausted, yet notwithstanding this socio-economic phenomenon of soapstone mining and production all one could see around him was high levels of poverty. To a certain extent, the same can be said concerning most of the other soapstone quarry owners in the Tabaka region. Consequently, due to increasing levels of poverty and existing ignorance of the economic value of the soapstone, owners of the quarries are selling this unique stone at throwaway prices of as low as Ksh.1,000 (US$ 10) for twenty tones of soapstone. Moreover, huge amounts of these valuable stones are currently being used in the construction of access roads instead of using ordinary stones that are easily available in adjacent areas.

In this regard, most middlemen who travel to Tabaka tend to encourage unwarranted competition among soapstone producers and sellers since they stand to immensely benefit from the inordinately low prices of the carvings. Nevertheless, it should be stated that if this unfortunate trend is allowed to continue, it may bring the whole soapstone industry to eventual collapse. As one well known soapstone carver at Tabaka, Thomas Mogendi, puts it, "currently, even the middlemen are finding it harder to sell the items since they, quite often, compromise on quality as they rush to get cheaper carvings that are on offer in the local market" (Personal Communication).

Particularly, the problem of middlemen is exemplified by the experiences that were elucidated by Thomas Mogendi, a former member of the Tabaka Classic Carvers Company. Over the years, the Company had a business partner/middleman called Peter Wahome, who was the proprietor of a firm based in Nairobi called Crafts of Africa. Wahome introduced the Tabaka Classic Carvers to another proprietor of a private company known as Crafts Village based in the UK where they sold their carvings at relatively good prices. The UK firm made the payments through Wahome who later sent the money to the soapstone carvers after making huge deduction as his commission.

In the course of time, a major disagreement arose between Wahome and the UK Company over the pricing of the soapstone carvings, as the proprietor of Crafts Village felt that too much profit was going to Wahome, instead of the carvers at Tabaka.

Eventually, the UK firm wrote a letter to Tabaka Classic Carvers seeking to enter into direct agreement that will allow the firm to purchase the soapstone carvings directly from the Tabaka Classic Carvers without going through Wahome. This noble arrangement removed Wahome from the picture, as he had turned out to be just another unscrupulous middleman whose main motive was to maximize his profit margin. Thomas Mogendi says that as a result of this new arrangement, the prices for their carvings began to improve (personal communication).

In this regard, it is important to note that, in recent years, many overseas firms, particularly in Europe and North America work hand-in-hand with fair trade organizations which ensure that the original producers of goods, particularly from Third World countries such as Kenya are not inordinately exploited by middlemen, and; that the original producers of items such as soapstone carvings are able to receive value for the money, and this in the long-run contributes to sustainable development and inclusive growth. For instance, Crafts Village, UK pays the Tabaka carvers a minimum of Kshs.500 (US$ 5) per a carving. In addition, they send representatives to Tabaka to check on product quality, creativity and innovativeness.

After ascertaining the overall quality of the soapstone carvings, these overseas sales representatives purchase the products and make direct payment to the carvers, and; finally transport the carvings to the UK at their own expense. Furthermore, the copyright of Tabaka Classic Carvers is also protected under the agreement with Crafts Village, UK. Currently, the partnership is still on though it has not been revised to be in tandem with current socio-economic conditions. In this regard, it can be stated that although the adoption of formal and/or binding legal agreements between carvers and buyers is a step in the right direction for sustainable development of the soapstone industry, there is urgent need for local carvers to protect their long-term economic interests by seeking legal representation whenever they enter into formal agreement with foreign firms in the UK and other parts of the world.

Inculcating Indigenous Skills and Social Responsibility

In most instances, the soapstone carvers themselves do the mining of the stones, as they need to examine the overall quality and dexterity of the soapstone beforehand to ensure that it meets their carving requirements. Once the carvers have quarried the quantity of soapstone they need, they pay the quarry owner and take it to their carving sites. The soapstone is eventually cut into specific sizes using ordinary handsaws, as well as using double-handled saws that are operated by two people; they also use *pangas* (machetes) to cut the soapstone. Particularly, the carvers select suitable stones with good texture by inspecting them for possible cracks and other irregularities. This is done by cutting off small flakes, and hitting them with pangas to judge their hardness and overall dexterity from the sound they make.

After the stones have been selected, carvers usually make rough carvings of their intended sculptures so that they can remember their final purpose. Once this has been done, women and children, usually family members of the carvers, carry the soapstone in baskets and other forms of containers to the carvers' workplaces. The entire carving process is performed by men, while the polishing is a collaborative effort between women and the youth.

The task of polishing soapstone also helps the children to learn how to work with soapstone at a very early age. In this regard, even very young children participate in this activity, which involves soaking the soapstone sculptures in water, before being smoothened using sandpaper while they are still wet. Afterwards, the sculptures are dried in the sun, and then they are waxed with a mixture of floor and shoe polish. Despite the involvement of children in the polishing process, they are usually given items of lower value, such as animal sculptures and napkin rings, so that breakages, if any, will not have significant monetary implication.

Through polishing, children learn about the texture and fragility of soapstone, its variety of colour, how to use sandpaper, the differences in the design of different objects, the procedure that has to be followed in completing a carving, and also how to go about the process of marketing and selling the end products. Older children, usually boys, go to the quarries with their fathers, where they observe the soapstone selection process and learn the qualities of soapstone, such as soapstone with dark brown grains of iron, stones which make a full, hollow sound when hit by a panga, and soapstone of irregular colour, which cannot be used. The children also learn the value of soapstone by watching the purchasing process. Finally, they learn how to sort out the overall quality of the purchased soapstone, so that poor quality stones are used to make carvings of less monetary value.

Thus, the way in which a child is inculcated into the life of soapstone carving is through observation and imitation which is a form on indigenous apprenticeship. Once the children have an understanding of the texture of soapstone from polishing it, they begin imitating the elders by experimenting with smaller carvings. These experiments, in conjunction with the practical experience they acquire in all other aspects of carving soapstone, mean that they can become skillful soapstone carvers by the time they reach adulthood.

Another noted characteristic of soapstone processing and production is the existence of a culturally enforced division of labour system in the soapstone industry, which keeps everybody occupied. Despite this, the involvement of children may be affected by schooling and laws against child labour. In addition, the exclusion of women from the actual carving process means that they are de facto employees of their men folk. However, it is hard to ascertain whether cultural attitudes will change to enhance direct women participation in soapstone production and marketing.

Gerald Motondi, a veteran soapstone carver, states that he also learnt to carve through the procedures described above, and he is in favour of children being taught soapstone carving, but he insists that children should complete their formal education before dedicating themselves to soapstone carving (Personal Communication). The aspect of safety in the quarries is also a major concern as quarrying has led to deaths in various places. Cosmas Onchomba states that there is a quarry at Nyabigena that has killed at least six people in the recent past. However, he states that the Government mines officers have visited soapstone quarries to instruct them on how to mine the stones safely. Nevertheless, the industry still requires additional safety equipment in order to prevent more deaths in future.

Once a child is old and skilful enough to sell their first carvings, they usually buy their first carving tools, which are a carving knife and a panga. Specifically, machetes are used to shape the sculptures, while knives are used to add detail to them. Furthermore, due to their lifelong experience in the soapstone industry, the young carvers eventually master the critical skill of being able to select soapstone that has got requisite dexterity to produce quality carvings. In addition, some of the young carvers may use the income which they earn from soapstone carving to pay school fees for their studies. Consequently, through the various processes of enculturation, the youths are able to learn various skills in soapstone design, sculpturing, polishing and sales.

Cross-Cultural Exchange

The soapstone industry has also affected the residents of Tabaka in terms of exposure to the outside world, as people from different communities in Kenya and others parts of the world visit the Tabaka region either as tourists or as businessmen.

In this regard, it should be stated that not only have the Gusii soapstone carvers managed to have their unique products recognized and sold in different parts of the world, but in recent years, there has also been an increasing influx of people from other parts of Kenya and the outside world who visit Tabaka to have first-hand experience of soapstone sculpturing.

Furthermore, other people from different parts of Kenya have settled in Tabaka and are currently engaged in soapstone production. Among the people who have moved into the soapstone carving business in Tabaka and its environs are members of the Luhya and Kamba communities. For instance, the entry of the Kamba people into soapstone carving is particularly interesting because they originally have a reputation of being excellent traditional wood carvers. However, the depletion of indigenous forests, coupled with restrictions on the harvesting of certain types of wood, particularly those from indigenous trees, means that the Kamba carvers no longer have access to their traditional raw materials. In this regard, since there is no specific restriction imposed on the quarrying of soapstone, it is rational and makes economic sense for the traditional Kamba wood carvers to transfer their wood carving skills to the sculpturing of the soapstone at Tabaka. This phenomenon has led to the introduction of new knowledge and skills on soapstone sculpturing and marketing. Consequently, there has been an increase of skilled human power in the area promoting the production and marketing of quality soapstone products.

In addition, it is important to note that existing socio-economic linkage and cross-cultural interaction between the Gusii soapstone carvers and the people from the outside world has, over the years, played a critical role in the introduction and usage of information technology in the Tabaka region and its environs. For instance, soapstone carvers are using the internet in the sales and marketing of their products, thus; bypassing exploitative middlemen in order to deal directly with buyers within Kenya and the outside world. Consequently at present, most of the carvers attribute the overall improvement in international marketing of soapstone carvings to the increasing usage of the internet. The enhancement of internet connectivity is a boon to the small producers, although as indicated earlier, the proliferation of increasing numbers of individual carvers is likely to be detrimental to overall prices and sales of the soapstone products.

Furthermore, it is now possible for customers to send new and/or tailor-made designs over the internet, thus cutting down on the duration and cost of creating new designs and transporting them to Tabaka for eventual implementation and production.

In this regard, with the drop in orders caused by the recent global economic recession, carvers have tended to have more time allowing them to experiment with the new designs sent to them via the internet. Also, if the time between orders is relatively extensive, the carvers are able to experiment with their own designs, so that when orders resume, they have something new to present to their customers, thus; extending the product range and market niche.

The soapstone industry has also benefitted the people of Tabaka in other ways. For instance, formal education has been improved through the construction of learning infrastructure such as classrooms and workshops using proceeds of soapstone sales. For example, Gerald Motondi cites the construction of Tabaka Primary School, which was financed by the proceeds that were acquired from sales of unique soapstone items that were sold to a firm in New Zealand (Personal Communication). This community project culminated in the construction of ultra-modern three storey building at the school which was completed in 1994, thus; greatly enhancing the learning environment for local primary school pupils.

Another positive impact is the unifying effect of soapstone carving. Gerald Motondi enunciated that, due to soapstone carving, artists and artisans come to Tabaka from areas adjacent to Tabaka such as Bomachoge and Bosinange. This socio-economic interaction has helped reduce inter-clan rivalries among the people that are particularly aggravated during parliamentary and civic electioneering period. In addition, the presence of carvers from other Kenyan ethnic communities has helped in the process of promoting national cohesion and cross-cultural understanding.

Moreover, despite the leadership deficiencies and wrangles that affected the soapstone co-operative societies, most carvers are convinced that soapstone carving is a unifying factor in the Gusii region and beyond, as carvers from Tabaka usually go to sell soapstone carvings in Nyatike and other adjacent areas of Luo land in Southwestern Kenya.

It is, therefore, fair to state that despite apparent challenges within the soapstone co-operatives, the actual business of quarrying, shaping and marketing of soapstone products has, over the years, assisted to unite the Gusii people and neighbouring communities especially the adjacent Luo community in Migori and Homabay Counties.

With increased scarcity of land in Kisii due to recent rapid population growth, soapstone production is increasingly becoming a major source of livelihood for the people of Tabaka and the adjacent areas. Originally, soapstone carving was done in conjunction with other economic activities such as farming and animal husbandry, as people would work on their farms and tend to their livestock in the morning hours, and later on carve soapstone in the evening. However, with the recent growth of the soapstone industry, especially from the 1980s, an increasing number of people have abandoned farming in favour of fulltime soapstone carving.

Furthermore, soapstone production has also become a tool for globalization of indigenous culture since the Gusii carvers use the unique sculptures to transmit their socio-cultural values and indigenous heritage which is inherently expressed in the carving that are sold in different parts of the world such as in Europe, Asia, North America and other African countries. For example, over the years, Elkanah Ong'esa (discussed earlier in this chapter) has travelled widely, to different parts of the world promoting the community's cultural values through the unique carvings he makes.

Gerald Motondi has also managed to market the Tabaka carvings with Gusii cultural values in many countries where his unique pieces of art have been internationally appreciated and recognized by people in different parts of the world. In addition, in recent years, soapstone sculpturing has developed to status where it is being used as a form of international sport. For instance as stated earlier, Motondi is one of the Gusii sculptors who have managed to participate in international carving sport competition in different countries including China, Greece, United Arabs Emirates, South Korea and Turkey where he has successfully competed with other renowned international carvers.

Way Forward and Conclusion

In the overall, notwithstanding the various problems and challenges confronting the Gusii soapstone industry as such as leadership wrangles in the co-operative societies, exploitation by middlemen, and lack of modern marketing strategies, this study contends that the future of the soapstone industry is relatively bright. However, a number of appropriate measures and strategies are required to mitigate the challenges and enhance the level of inclusive growth and long-term sustainability of the soapstone industry.

The following are critical policy related recommendations that can assist in enhancing sustainable development and inclusive growth of the industry: Establishment of entrepreneurial centres for the training and development of soapstone industry artisans.

These centers will help train and develop the artisans on how to design, produce and market soapstone products. The centres should also provide basic skills on book-keeping and financial management techniques. These should be aimed at empowering the soapstone carvers with appropriate knowledge and skills on how to manage their income and other financial returns, and also be able to keep proper books of accounts. The dissemination of marketing skills to the local carvers will enable them identify existing market niche as well as local and international demands of their products. The training centres can also empower soapstone carvers with basic skills on internet sales and marketing and ways to use mobile phone devices to reach both the overseas and domestic markets. Furthermore, they should also be trained on skills that can enable them to use basic computer design models to produce products for specific markets.

The number of female soapstone carvers is smaller compared to that of their male counterparts. There is therefore need to sensitize and empower women financially and through capacity building initiatives so as to increase their number as carvers and marketers of soapstone products. There is also need for improved transportation and communication network in the area. Soapstone is a major foreign exchange earner for the country and a major source of livelihood for many people. There is therefore need to have such a productive area accessible to both local and international traders and tourists through the improvement of transportation infrastructure such as roads. Also, the nearby Suneka Airstrip should be improved to allow easy and efficient access to Tabaka and the adjacent region in South-Western Kenya.

There is also need for both the national and county government to support the soapstone industry. Particularly, both governments should support the producers by providing them with modern tools of work as well as a robust tertiary level education that will boost the quality of soapstone production.

For instance, as Hany Faisal a renowned fine art academician in Egypt contends, "the lack of modern equipment limits Kenyan carvers to small sized carving that generated little income. In Egypt, use of advanced technology helps artists to come up with big valuable sculptures" (nation newspaper 29/Aug/2011 Pg 19). Getting equipment may also help carvers standardize their production and hence realize mass marketing. The downside, though, is that such standardization and mass marketing may impact the artistic production of carvers' products. It is possible that current production sell for the prices they do due to the fact that the pieces are unique and hence 'special'.

Soapstone producers in Kisii should organize themselves into a strong co-operative society. The initiative has already been taken by the Kisii Soapstone Carvers Co-operative Society (KSCCS). An effort should be made to ensure that all soapstone carvers, including those who are just joining the industry become members of the co-operative. In this way, soapstone carvers will be able to negotiate better prices for their products, and eliminate the possibility of individual carvers undercutting the rest, which is detrimental to all soapstone carvers in the long run. This can also assist minimize the menace of middlemen who usually buy the soapstone products from individual carvers at throw-way prices and ended up lurking huge profits, particularly when they sell the products in overseas markets. The Kisii Soapstone Carvers Co-operative Society (KSCCS), in collaboration with the government, should make its presence felt in the international market through trade fairs and advertising. There is need for the enactment of a draft policy and legal framework to protect the soapstone carvers from blatant exploitation by unscrupulous middlemen, businessmen and investors.

This legal frame should be particularly drafted with the main aim of protecting the social and economic interests, innovativeness and creativity of the soapstone carvers. Specifically, there should be a clear legal channel to protect the copyrights and patents of the unique carvings from blatant infringement by unscrupulous businessmen.

In conclusion, this study has demonstrated that a critical feature of the soapstone industry is the local people's resilience in the development of the industry as a sustainable form of livelihood capable of withstanding internal and external challenges. Thus, the industry has over the years managed to survive and adapt to changing conditions and demands due to the uniqueness of the soapstone products and the adaptive skills and innovations of the local people that responded to changing socio-economic and cultural needs. As a consequence, unlike other forms of indigenous industries that were unable to withstand forces of colonialism and Western capitalism, the soapstone industry still flourishes and has great potential in making significant contribution in the promotion of sustainable livelihood of the local people.

Editor's Note: *As the soapstone industry grows, there should be a balance between economic gain and environment impact.*

CHAPTER THIRTEEN
CONCLUSION

Introduction

The onset of colonialism and forces of globalization in Gusii land and other parts of Africa disrupted the people's age-old and time-tested cultural, social, economic and political institutions. These forces set in motion major processes of transformation and/or external interruption and control whose impact continues to reverberate in present times. As presented in various chapters of this book, over the years, the Gusii had undergone complex processes of evolution and diverse forms of socio-economic development. These processes had perhaps taken hundreds, if not thousands of years, dating back to 3000 BC when the Bantu started evolving as a major African group. However, as also stated elsewhere in the book, due to minimal existence of verifiable historical information, most of the social, economic and cultural events that took place during this critical period of Bantu evolution are not known and/or clearly understood.

It is within this broader context of Bantu evolutionary and dispersal processes that the Gusii people emerged as a distinct Bantu subgroup, and settled in Southwestern Kenya by around 1700 AD. Here, they were surrounded and/or sandwiched by non-Bantu (and often hostile) communities such as the Luo in the West, the Kipsigis in the East and the Maasai in the South. As such, the Gusii, over the years, evolved various survival techniques in the different spheres of life including socio-political, cultural, and economic spheres. These adoptive strategies enabled the Gusii people to survive, against all odds, as a distinct ethnic community. However, with the conquest and eventual establishment of British colonial rule over the Gusii in the early nineteenth century, the people were, in most instances, coerced, even through the use of brutal force and military might, to abandon their time-tested social, cultural, economic and political systems as they were required to abruptly adopt alien Western institutions of governance and socio-economic development. Thus, in most instances indigenous cultural and economic practices were seen by the British administrators, missionaries and other agents of Western civilization as being, at best, inferior and, at the worst, barbaric to be eliminated at all cost. The following section presents a brief elucidation of some of the far-reaching impacts of western civilization over the Gusii people as is discussed in detail in the various sections of this book.

Illustration of Positive Gusii Cultural Attributes

In the recent years, indigenous socio-cultural structures and systems that governed individual and communal behaviour that were anchored on core Gusii governance principles known as *chinsoni* have been eroded and indigenous social governance structures and systems are rapidly disappearing and/or have disappeared all the same as the people adopt contemporary top-down systems of administration and modern governance structures. As is articulated elsewhere in the book, the *chinsoni* principles of governance stipulated various ways in which people belonging to different age groups and gender conducted their social behaviour, and how they related with each another in different cultural contexts and physical environment, starting from the smallest unit of Gusii governance system, the homestead extending to the village or clan level, and eventually extending to the whole Gusii community.

However, with the loosening, and eventual disappearance, of the many aspects of indigenous modes of individual and communal codes of conduct and social relations, there has been extensive cultural disorientation and increased cases of social disorder. These include disrespect of the elders by the youth, unauthorized/unsanctioned marriages, child bearing out of wedlock, young girls giving birth at a young age, abortion, rape and incest and many other vices that were rare in indigenous Gusii cultural and social settings. These are increasingly manifesting themselves with attendant, far reaching, negative consequences that are being witnessed up to this time. Further, it should be underscored that the abrupt adoption of Christianity and other forms of Western cultural values and believes did not manage to fill the void that emanated from the abrupt and sudden destruction of time-tested Gusii indigenous socio-cultural institutions of governance and social networks.

Gusii Youth Encampment

With the establishment of the contemporary centralized top-down systems of administration and law enforcement, the Gusii indigenous institution, *ebisarate*, where all able bodied young men from the same lineage or clan were supposed to live together in encampments that were situated in strategic geographical locations throughout Gusii land were/have been criminalized and forcefully disbanded. One of the cardinal duties of the youths in the encampments was to protect the community against any form of external aggression. In addition, it was in these encampments that livestock, especially cattle, belonging to different homesteads that belonged to the same kinship were kept for security reasons (i.e. to minimize theft and loss of livestock due to attacks from cattle rustlers and wild animals). The youth were supposed to keep constant vigil over the livestock, especially at night when the enemy and/or cattle rustlers were most likely to attack. They also took turns to make regular surveillance in areas adjacent to the various Gusii homesteads and were responsible for fending off any possible external aggressor and/ or enemy attack.

However, with the disbandment of *ebisarate*, this well-organized social system of keeping energetic youth in productive communal initiatives and call to duty to protect family and clan resources has disappeared overnight without any form of alternative strategy of engaging the young in productive family and communal activities. As a consequence, from this time onwards, the youth were, mostly, left on their own loitering in village pathways. Consequently, they are prone to various form of anti-social and/ or criminal behaviour. Thus, incidents of petty crime, thuggery, rape, family scuffles have started to be increasingly reported.

Moreover, it should be noted that increased forms of these anti-social and security related challenges that started during the colonial time, are increasingly being witnessed in many parts of present day rural Gusii. This is notwithstanding the fact that there exists modern national and county structures of governance and law enforcement.

In addition, it should be noted that one of the causes of the recent exponential growth of Gusii population is perhaps due to the abrupt interruption and disappearance of indigenous institutions of governance and self-regulation. For instance, with the weakening of the indigenous code of conduct that provided specific rules and regulations stipulating how people belonging to the opposite gender and different age groups were supposed to relate with one another, people started to engage in social acts and sexual relationships that were completely forbidden (i.e., perceived as taboo) in indigenous Gusii social setting and cultural environments. Specifically, as relates to sexual conduct, these anti-social activities started to manifest themselves in activities such as engagement in wantonness sex activities, especially among the youth, increased incidents of unauthorized early marriages with the attendant unplanned pregnancies and child birth. Consequently, with uncontrolled sexual interactions among the youth, starting from tender ages, there were accelerated child birth rates with most women having as many as over 10 children. This was due to the simple fact that the many Gusii women started entering the child bearing process at very early stages of life.

The attendant social and economic consequences of all these unwarranted sexual behaviour, and other forms of anti-social activities especially among the Gusii youth, were quite obvious and have had far reaching impacts. Thus, for instance, as shown elsewhere in the book, within a very short time frame (i.e., 1940 – 1980) Gusii population increased from pantry 200,000 people to over 1.5 million. Currently, the Gusii population is estimated to be over 3.5 million people. Thus in a very short time frame of less than 50 year, the Gusii population has increased more than tenfold; an unprecedented demographic trend even with respect to global trends.

Gusii Indigenous Justice System

As well, as articulated elsewhere in the book, the Gusii had a relatively well-developed indigenous system of administration of justice and law enforcement. These processes that were based on the principle of bottom-up approach, starting from the smallest Gusii socio-cultural unit, the homestead (*omochie*) extending to the village level (i.e., *etureti*) and eventually spreading to the topmost organ of indigenous jurisprudence, the indigenous Gusii Supreme Court, the *Abakumi* Court. This informal indigenous Supreme Court was responsible for the administration of justice in the whole Gusii community. The *Abakumi* Court, particularly, handled intricate and/or precedent setting cases affecting the whole Gusii community such as unresolved murder and witchcraft cases and protracted land disputes involving two or more families. Perhaps, more importantly, the Gusii indigenous legal systems were usually based on egalitarian principles of equity, consensus building, reconciliation, and natural justice. Thus, the main aim of administration of Gusii indigenous justice systems was to promote peace and social harmony in the whole of the Gusii community. Thus, the indigenous legal systems were not retributive in nature.

Perhaps more importantly, it should also be noted that there were no established forces of systematic cohesion and law enforcement as seen in modern systems of administration of justice and law enforcement such as the police force and paramilitary units. Instead, what was mainly used to maintain and promote adherence to law and order was the existing magical-religious powers that were bestowed on the Gusii elders, who administered justice at various levels. The Gusii elders had what was perceived to be presumed mystical power to invoke the use of a curse, particularly on the offending person or party. However, as was the case with other Gusii indigenous institutions, with the on-set of the contemporary system of administration and justice structures, the Gusii indigenous legal system that was mainly anchored on the principle of reconciliation and conflict resolution has almost disappeared.

Moreover, as shown in the book, with the increasing erosion and/or disappearance of Gusii indigenous supportive structure and systems, such as the conception of the principle of *chinsoni* that governed Gusii individual behaviour and social relations, the whole orientation of Gusii life has been torn asunder. In this regard, with accelerated weakening and destruction of Gusii cultural values and the indigenous social fabric and structures that held the people together and made life meaningful and worth living, several far reaching negative consequences have been set in motion; the very consequences that are being witnessed among the Gusii people today. For instance, the respect and moral authority that was bestowed on the Gusii elders as the custodians of the Gusii communal information, knowledge, skills, and competencies were eroded with the attendant negative consequences including the break-down of law and order in the whole community, family disintegration, and increased incidents of arson, theft, rape and general violence arising from the accumulation of many unresolved cases. These are the very daunting legal issues and challenges that are confronting the Gusii people and other African communities in the contemporary society.

Furthermore, with the increasing disruption of Gusii indigenous social fabric that held the people together and eventual disappearance of the indigenous legal systems that handled sensitive and sometimes emotive cases involving intricate and sometimes emotive issues (e.g. witchcraft, murder, rape and land disputes), aggrieved parties started taking the law into their own hands while attempting to settle scores and/or wrongs, whether real and/or imaged, that had been committed against them as individuals or groups.

This usually led to incidents of extreme violence with the attendant negative attitude and/or mentality that mighty and excessive use of force to subdue opponents is always the right thing to do. These are the very negative attitudes that are being witnessed in most parts of Gusii land and other parts of Kenya and indeed the whole of Africa. Consequently, with the abolition of indigenous systems of political governance and administration of justice, in recent years, regular infighting and scuffles amongst opposed parties over issues such as land disputes, especially among immediate family members have become increasingly common in rural Gusii, with the attendant negative far reaching consequences of fatalities, injuries, and wanton destruction of property.

Negative Ethnicity

Unlike what most Eurocentric historians and Western-oriented social scientists would like us to believe, during most of the pre-colonial period that lasted thousands of years, various African communities such as the

Gusii and their neighbours including the Luo, Kipsigis and Maasai were not always at variance with each other nor were they always at war with one another. In this regard, although there were occasional intra-ethnic altercations and inter-ethnic skirmishes, these were in most instances localized incidents that cannot be compared with major wars that took place in the Western world including the I and II World War. In this regard, as was the case with most other African communities in different parts of Africa, the Gusii co-existed in relative harmony with their neighbours. Thus, as presented elsewhere in the book, over the years, there existed symbiotic social, economic and cultural relationship between the Gusii and their neighbours who interestingly were predominantly non-Bantu. For instance, for hundreds of years, the Gusii conducted extensive barter trade with their neighbours, the Luo who unlike the Gusii who lived in the highland ecological zone, lived in low lying ecological zones adjacent to Lake Victoria. The Gusii sold to the Luo several farm products such as maize, sorghum, and millet; in return, the Gusii acquired natural salt, milk and meat from the Luo.

Furthermore, there were many incidents of inter-ethnic marriages and continues enculturation between the Gusii and their non-Bantu neighbours. In this regard, the Ekegusii has got very many non- Bantu words and/or names that were most likely borrowed from their neighbours, especially, the Luo and Kipsigis people; making the Ekegusii language to be one of leading Bantu language with so many non-Bantu words and idioms. Thus, it can be argued that what eventually evolved into Gusii culture is a hybrid of many cultural elements that were borrowed and/or adopted from neighbouring communities that had regular social contact and long-term cultural interactions with the Gusii; this gives credence to the long held historical fact that there is no pure African ethnic community, as many current social scientists and other researchers with a Eurocentric perspective would want us to believe.

However, it should be stated that during the period of British colonial rule over the Gusii and other African communities, in most instances, the colonial administration applied a deliberate policy of divide-and-rule as they compartmentalized various African communities such as the Gusii into distinct administrative units with clearly demarcated administrative boundaries (e.g. the initial Kisii, Kipsigis, Luo and Luhya districts in Western Kenya). These very administrative units have existed up to the present time with minor adjustments and/or creation of more administration unit depending on existing political and administrative exigencies. Thus for instance, whereas, currently, Migori and Homa

Bay County are predominantly Luo, Kisii and Nyamira County are predominantly Gusii. Similar to other parts of Africa, the same scenario where most administrative units are made of people of one ethnic community is lubricated throughout the entire Kenyan Republic.

Furthermore, the mobility of the African people moving in and out of these ethnic-based administrative enclaves was curtailed by the colonial administration. Thus, for instance, traveling from one district to another, one had to get special permission or clearance to enable him/her to travel; otherwise it was a punishable offence for an African person to enter another district other than the one he/she was domiciled without express permission from the colonial administrators. Consequently, unlike during the pre-colonial period, there was minimal cross-border economic, social and cultural interactions between various neighbouring African communities as people became permanently confined to the artificially created colonial boundaries; a situation whose effects prevails up to this time. This is notwithstanding existing current government policy of allowing free movement of people, goods and services throughout the country.

With these form of colonial segregation the various social, cultural and economic interactions that had existed, for hundreds and perhaps thousands of years among different African communities, were curtailed as people remained cocooned in their controlled tribal enclaves and/ or colonial administrative units. As a consequence, due to this forms of prolonged political and economic isolation, people in each of these ethnic-based administrative enclaves started perceiving themselves as belonging to distinct tribal or social affiliations, and different cultural orientations that were, in most instances, diametrically opposed to one another. In this regard, it can be argued that the current problems of negative ethnicity that are rampart in Kenya and other African countries with the attendant severe and far reaching negative consequences such as increasing social and economic strive and large scale political instability can be traced to the period of the establishment of British colonial rule in the African continent.

Editor's Note: *The promulgation of the Kenya Constitution 2010 ushered the county's government structure whose boundaries invariably coincide with ethnic boundaries.*

Conclusion

As elucidated in the book, it had taken hundreds, if not thousands, of years for the Gusii people and other African communities to evolve various social, economic, cultural and political institutions that allowed them to manage their affairs in a relatively sustainable manner. These homegrown institutions were based on indigenous philosophical orientations, cultural values and indigenous holistic understanding of their world and their overall destiny as a people. Similarly, the colonial institutions of governance that were imposed on the Gusii and other African communities were anchored on Western philosophies and socio-cultural values that were best suited for the Western world. It can therefore be argued that as much as these Western models of governance and economic systems worked relatively well in Western societies, they did not fit relatively well in the African social and economic milieu.

Consequently, it can be stated, without any fear of contradiction, that these colonial and/or postcolonial institutions of governance that are still being applied in modern day Kenya and other African counties are the root cause of most of the current political, economic and cultural challenges and problems that are bedeviling the African people such as the Gusii. Based on the forgoing, it should be stated that it is not a coincidence that most societies or countries that have managed to progressively move forward in the right path of human development and overall socio-economic advancement such as Japan, China, Indonesia and Taiwan, the common denominator is the fact that as much as these countries have adopted various aspects of Western models of political governance and technological skills and knowledge, most people in these Oriental and/or Indo-Chinese societies have remained anchored in their indigenous social and cultural systems and religious values.

In this regard, in one way or the other, most people in these countries have managed to keep their indigenous social, political and cultural values intact while at the same time adopting key technological and scientific knowledge and skills from the Western world, especially as relates to material wellbeing and overall technological advancement. As a consequence, most people in these Oriental countries promote and enhance their homegrown social, cultural and religious institutions and indigenous values as they continue to cope with the ever increasing forces of modernity and new emerging intricacies of globalization as humanity moves towards what is called a global village in the postmodern period. Thus, it is hereby concluded that there is no society that can sustain itself, in the long run, if people in that society abruptly abandon their time tested social and cultural value and are advertently or inadvertently coerced to adopt alien social, cultural and political institutions of governance and socio-economic models of development as is currently happening in most parts of Africa.

CHAPTER FOURTEEN
EPILOGUE
OVERVIEW OF THE SOCIAL, ECONOMIC, CULTURAL AND POLITICAL DILEMMA

Introduction

This book, provides a critical analysis of the political, socio-economic, cultural and judicial aspects of the Gusii of Kenya. The movement and settlement of the Gusii in their present homeland has been a reality dictated largely by the interaction with the neighbouring ethnic groups, especially the warrior-like Kipsigis, Maasai and also the Luo. However, it is important to note that these neighbouring communities were non-Bantu societies whose lifestyles and other forms of socio-economic orientations were, in many instances, dissimilar to that of the Gusii. A number of observations can be made regarding how these historical circumstances impact the political, socio-economic, cultural and judicial activities of the Gusii up to the contemporary period. Consequently, on close purview, some of the pertinent issues covered in the book continue to have influence on the lives of the Gusii today.

Within the broad social, economic, political and cultural perspectives, the following are critical salient features concerning the nature of the Gusii heritage and an overall projection on the current Gusii development dilemma and possible way forward.

The Gusii Homestead

Throughout this book, it is evident that, the Gusii rarely came together as a nation, state, homogenous entity; and/or, united social, economic and political entity. In particular, the Gusii lacked central authority around which they could rally in pursuit of a cause or tradition.

As presented in the text, the Gusii homestead formed the basis of the overall Gusii economic well-being and social welfare. The homestead was under the control of a family patriarch referred to in Ekegusii as *omogaka bw'omochie*. In this regard, the homestead formed a distinct and independent social, judicial, economic and political entity. Indeed, to a large extent the homestead was almost self-reliant under the family patriarch, *omogaka bw'omochie*.

In particular, a typical Gusii homestead consisted of the family patriarch and his wives (i.e., in a polygamous arrangement), married sons and their wives, and other unmarried children of the homestead. The head of the

homestead was highly venerated and was largely the final authority in all
matters pertaining to the homestead. In effect, the family patriarch was a mini-
king in his homestead and commanded absolute authority over the family.
In this regard, all the members of the homestead were supposed to strictly
abide by orders stemming from the family patriarch who administered
all spheres of the daily life of the homestead, including in the judicial,
economic, social and political aspects.

Considering the patriarchal nature of the Gusii society, within a given
village or clan, each homestead was referred to as *so and so*'s homestead. It
had clearly demarcated territoriality and/or spatial location. Consequently,
in their daily social milieu, people in a given village or clan would always
say (referring to the homestead), *aaria o'nyarebe. (e.g., aariabw'Orina,
bw'Otwori, bw'Orango, bw'Akama, bw'Omorabi, o'Kemoni, bw'Ondieki,
o'Bundusi, o'Manua, o'Gichana, bw'Okemwa, o'Barare, bw'Ongeri,
o'Mokoro, bw'Anunda,* etc.) By word of illustration, all theserefer to typical
patriarch names in Gusii.

With the patriarchal nature of the society, it was taboo to refer to a
Gusii homestead as belonging to a female entity even if the patriarch of
the family is not alive (i.e. *o'Moraa, o'Mokeira, o'Nyanchera, o'Kemunto*
and *o'Nyakerario).*By word of illustration using some typical Gusii female
names. This is a critical aspect that is clearly demonstrative of the little
powers, if any, Gusii women possessed in the society at large.

Furthermore, in the Gusii social and cultural milieu, women were
barred from using their real names especially when appearing in the
public. Instead, quite often, married women were referred to (in literal
sense) as 'cooks' for the family patriarch, *omorugi o'nyarebe* (*so and so*'s
cook).

Polygamy was common and taken as a norm in the society. In fact, a
patriarch with many wives had a high social standing and received great
societal admiration. In part this was because such a man's wellbeing was
based on the number of wives and children he had. Not only did he have
many hands to work the fields, but also got respect because of his ability
to keep so many people under control. For this reason, such a person was
highly venerated and was perceived as a person of great authority and/ or
power. In particular, this was more so where the man had several sons as
well. In this regard, not only would the sons protect the homestead from
any form of aggression, but they also assured a large number of progeny
capable of perpetuating the patriarch's lineage into the future. Consequently,
whenever they convened in their social settings, for example in village or clan
gatherings, such elders were treated with utter respect.

Furthermore, when the men gathered in any social event, such as partaking of the traditional brew, wedding ceremonies and/or any form of social gathering, the sitting arrangement depicted their status in the community. In such social gatherings, men with one wife would be ridiculed particularly by their age mates who would refer to them, derogatorily, as a man with 'one eye', *omosacha bw'eriso erimo*. In particular, men with one wife were not supposed to sit near the drinking pot, but were directed to sit near the entrance away from the pot. On the other hand men with several wives and sons sat in the inner space of the living room, close to the pot where they could sip the traditional brew at easy.

A specific reason advanced with respect to this sitting arrangement is that a man with one wife was perceived as a miserable person who could easily run and trample on the drinking pot if he was informed that something bad had happened in his homestead, e.g. his only wife or son had fallen sick. On the other hand, a man with several wives (or sons) would most likely continue drinking on receiving the information that there was a problem in his homestead, and, after having his fill, he would calmly inquire from the person who brought the bad news which particular wife or son was afflicted. Eventually, after composing himself, he would then walk away without making unnecessary or uncalled for commotion. With such a person, there was no possibility of trampling on the drinking pot and spoiling the party for others.

Furthermore, the Gusii informal justice system and its administration was anchored in inherent authority of the family patriarch. In this regard, the head of the homestead was responsible in settling all family disputes and any form of transgression in the homestead. Consequently, the patriarch commanded absolute power and veneration from his wives and children, and any orders involving the social, economic, political, economic and religious well being of the family were strictly adhered to. In this regard, these orders were taken as absolute commands and/or law. They could not be challenged in whatever the circumstances.

Additionally, in the unlikely event, if one disobeyed the patriarch of the homestead, then one could receive various forms of socio-economic and religious sanctions. This magico-religious position gave the patriarch even greater authority within the homestead as he was perceived to be closer to the family's departed ancestors and/or ancestral spirits that the rest of the family relied upon for their overall wellbeing. As such, he had the authority to intercede and offer sacrifices to the ancestors on behalf of other members of the homestead. Furthermore, he had powers to curse any offender in his home stead. Such reverence and fear of eternal punishment (a curse) kept those in the homestead in check and obedient.

The patriarch would also apply a number of economic sanctions or could publicly reprimand his wives and son(s) in case of any form of defiance and/or offence. Additionally, the family patriarch used his authority and applied sanctions to deter conflicts and quarrels among his wives, children and to assert his power over them.

The Lack of Central Authority and its Implications on the Gusii

A critical political and socio-economic phenomenon covered in the book is the overall tendency of extreme individualism and/or lack of coherent communal unity among the Gusii. Even at present, it is common to hear a Gusii person retorting that *tari bwoo imenyete*, which literally translates to 'I do not stay in your home' nor 'do you in any way feed me', *tindikoragera bwoo*. This underlines the fundamental Gusii characteristic of extreme individualistic tendencies and lack of solidarity among the Gusii people. In part, one can aver with great likelihood that it is due to the Gusii homestead conception and the immense powers of the patriarch in the management of all the affairs of the homestead which made it, particularly, difficult to bring together these difficult governance units to form one united governance system for encompassing the whole Gusii community. As such, it can be argued that a person who utters such adages has the mindset of a Gusii patriarch of yore who had a completely independent mind in the management of the affairs of his homestead.

The lack of central authority among the Gusii had a major impact on their survival and; this resonates to date. It can also be argued that if the Gusii had a tradition of centralized authority and governance, they would not have suffered the many losses they did in the hands of neighbouring groups. The situation was worsened by the fact that these groups happen to be more warrior-like than the Gusii. Therefore, if they had a central authority even as they wandered and faced conflict, it is possible that they would have had a different destiny from one they have today. They would have been better placed to face the enemy in the many encounters they had, as a united entity.

For instance, it is probable that a central authority would have enabled the Gusii develop better military strategies. In addition, it would have enabled them to prepare better to protect their lot against any form of external aggression coming from warlike communities such as the Maasai and the Kipsigis. More significantly, a central authority would have assured a sense of common destiny that would have provided the necessary emotional rallying point for collective survival as a community

A case in point where lack of communal unity and centralized authority led to disastrous and far reaching negative consequences for the Gusii was the encounter with the Kipsigis at Kabianga. The Gusii had settled in the place and were contented with growing of subsistence crops such as finger millet, sorghum, pumpkins and the spider plant. Consequently, after a full working day in the farm and the accompanying tiredness, they had little inclination towards waging fights with their neighbours. This is despite their suffering occasioned by crop failure and death of livestock. Indeed, the name Kabianga literary means 'things have refused to be'; 'the place where crops and livestock were destroyed *en mass*' or 'a place where the Gusii people faced a lot of calamities of unprecedented monstrosity'.) Here, the divided Gusii were attacked by Kipsigis warriors who were advancing from the North East, Sigsis Hill. They were massively defeated. The misfortunes challenged the Gusii people to the very core of their existence.

In particular, similar to other African pastoral communities such as the Maasai, Somali and Turkana, the Kipsigis were a war-like people who fought their neighbours with abandon, using relatively advanced military skills and weaponry (light spears, shields, bows and arrows) compared to the cumbersome heavy spears and shields of the Gusii and other non-pastoral communities.

In this regard, the war-like Kipsigis were able to overrun the sedentary Gusii community. In the years that followed, the belligerent Kipsigis warriors kept waging constant wars to capture the priced Gusii livestock with substantial success. Similar to other pastoral communities, to the belligerent Kipsigis warriors, the art of cattle rustling was perceived as a noble age-old tradition of going to bring back their God given birth-right (i.e. cattle that was owned by the other communities); particularly from the non-pastoral communities.

Eventually, in the epic war that emerged between the Gusii and Kipsigis at Kabianga, the Gusii people were ruthlessly attacked and uprooted by the marauding Kipsigis warriors targeting the priced Gusii cattle.

Further, conditions were to worsen for the Gusii. Thus, soon after they lost their livestock to the Kipsigis, an epidemic cattle disease (rinderpest) wiped out what remained of Gusii livestock. Consequently, it was now a matter of life and death for the besieged Gusii.

Staring at probable death, elements of some Gusii sub-clans switched language and culture and were eventually assimilated into the Kipsigis community. For example, members of various Gusii clans and sub-clans such as *Abasweta* became Boswetek; those of *Abatabori* became *Tobol*; those of *Ababasi* became *Bassy;* and those of *Abagisero* became *Boguserek.* The the original names, as used among the Gusii, were derived from the Bantus vortex (i.e., *abanto*), meaning people. With the switch to a completely new language that was based on the Nilotic vortex, the intonation and/or pronunciation of the original Gusii names changed to be in tandem with the Kipsigis intonation.

A peculiar phenomenon which emerged thereafter lives to this day. The Gusii clansmen who switched over and became absorbed into the Kipsigis, developed near mortal hatred and great enmity towards the Gusii. They derogatorily referred to the Gusii as *Gosobideth* meaning 'displaced people' or 'people who are always on the run'. Based on this hatred, the adopted members of the Kipsigis community, over time, would be instrumental to prosecuting continued war against the Gusii, their former kin. They were particularly effective in these attacks considering they understood the weak defensesystems of the Gusii. In typical attacks, these (now Kipsigis) warriors could raid at night, taking the Gusii by surprise. They would then proceed to torch entire Gusii homesteads, wantonly killing any person in sight, and raping any women they came across. In the emerging confusion, they would drive away all the Gusii cattle they could capture and make off as fast as they came.

It is in this context that the Gusii composed the following sorrowful song that portrays the hopelessness of the situation where people lost herds of cattle almost at will.

mbweri are eee	the cattle rustler is inside the cattle shed	
mbweri are eee	the cattle rustler in inside the cattle shed)	
Mbweri omorumbwa Arap Chuma	the cattle rustler Arap Chuma from	
	Rumbwa1	
Chiachire eee	The cows have been taken away	
Chiachire chiombe chiomogesi	The cows belong to a senior bachelor	
	meant for his dowry have been stolen	
Kura mono eee Kura mono Moraa	Make the distress call Moraa to awaken	
Kura mono	the warriors	
Kura mono Moraa kura mono!	Make the distress call Moraa to awaken	
	the warriors	
Beng beng titi, beng beng waya	Rhythmical sound imitating	Gusii
	traditional musical instrument	called a
	lyre (*obokano*)	

In such environment of constant warring, the Gusii were unable to concentrate on the routines of life like tilling the land and rearing cattle as they were constantly under attack. Consequently, there was massive outbreak of famine and starvation and breakdown of the Gusii as a distinct culture

Eventually, remnants of fragmented Gusii sub-clans such as the *Abatabori, Abasweta, Ababasi* and *Abagisero,* unable to bear the pain anylonger, decided to make a tactical retreat. They retraced their way back to where they had moved from in the present Gusii Highland region in South Western Kenya. This region was/is characterized by steep hills and mountain ranges such as *Manga, Sameta, Gesere* and Iberia Hills in Central and Southern Gusii. In addition, since this region receives extremely high amounts of rainfall throughout the year, it had dense vegetation cover. This was ideal for hiding from marauding Kipsigis and Maasai warriors.

****

A fundamental question which can be asked is whether all this suffering would have happened had the Gusii developed a modicum of unity (centralised governance system) and a common sense of purpose. Clearly, lack of a central authority and common purpose aggravated their suffering and near decimation. Perhaps what happened years after Kabianga gives an indication of what could have taken place had the Gusii united as a community.

During the rare historical occasion when the Gusii managed to face the enemy as a united front in the renowned Osaosao Battle (also, referred to as the Mogori War by the Kipsigis) the outcome was astounding by any stand. Here, after a certain period of time, the Kipsigis warriors had managed to track the Gusii into their homeland in the South Western Highland region; a place where they had retreated to after being vanquished and forced to more from Kabianga. Realizing that they were, once more, staring total annihilation in the hands of the marauding Kigsigis warriors, the various Gusii clans came together and took an oath (*emuma*) swearing to fight the enemy as a united front. Sure enough, with this unity of purpose, the Gusii repulsed the enemy and almost wiped out the entire generation of Kipsigis young men,

****

Interestingly, these inter-tribal skirmishes, mainly centred on cattle rustling, have persisted to the present. They are particularly intense in the border region of Bomet and Kisii County. Many a time, the Kipsigis cattle rustlers stealthily enter Gusii homesteads at night and take away Gusii livestock. By the time the sleepy Gusii realize that something has gone wrong, the livestock would have been driven into the swampy and impenetrable Chebalungu forest where it is difficult for the Gusii and/or security agents to enter and recover the stolen livestock.

In this connection, while addressing a fundraising gathering for the Catholic Church at Nyabururu Parish in Kisii County on 22nd October, 2016, an exasperated and visibly angry Deputy President, William Samoei Ruto retorted that, *'sasa ninawezaje kuwa* Deputy President *wa wezi wa mifugo? Hata nikienda ng`ambo nachekelewana wenzangu kutoka nchi zingine'* (how can I be a Deputy President of people engaging in the barbaric and outdated practice of cattle rustling? Whenever, I meet with colleagues from other countries, they sarcastically say that 'this is the Deputy President who comes from a country where people engage in cattle rustling (Personal Communication, October, 2016). This clearly demonstrated the intensity and/or severalty of the cattle rustling menace.

Ironically, the Deputy President is himself a Kalenjin of Gusii descent (i.e, it is said that his paternal grandmother was Gusii).

Furthermore, Bomet County is perceived to be the region where most cattle rustlers come from. Consequently, with the recent increase of poverty and unemployment particularly among the youth, the practice of cattle rustling along the border has become more intense and frequent, notwithstanding the many Government police officers and other security personally who are currently deployed along the Gusii-Kipsigis border.

Also, it is worth noting that a large number of the Kipsigis people in Bomet County are of Gusii origin, most of who have moved and settled in the county from the neighbouring Kericho County in recent years. Moreover, it can be postulated that the name 'Bomet' is of the Gusii origin, meaning 'people who do not smear their houses', *mbaometi,* a common practice of pastoral communities; a practice that goes back to hundreds and probably thousands of years.

When the Gusii first encountered members of the Kipsigis pastoral community, they were astonished to find that Kipsigis did not smear their houses. As a majorly pastoral community, the Kipsigis were always on the move in search of pasture and water for their livestock. As such, to them, there was no need for long-lasting houses or homesteads. Instead, their huts were made of sticks, twigs and leaves for convenience as the shelters were temporary.

****

In the long run, it is important to note that the existing implicit rivalry and social divisions among the Gusii continue to manifest themselves to the community's detriment as it has done over years. Quite often, whenever one Gusii clan and/or sub-clan was attacked by an external

1. Personal Communication[1]

aggressor such as the Kipsigis or Maasai, the various Gusii clans did not face the aggressor as a community. The social divisions and petty clan rivalry resulted in a situation where members of clans, other than the one under attack, could just watch and/or be indifferent as their fellow kinsmen are attacked by marauding Kipsigis and Maasai cattle rustlers. In this regard, instead of rallying to help the clan under attack, members of the other clans that were not under attack, would derogatorily say 'let the in-laws be taught a lesson'.

As such the character of fragmentation we see among the Gusii people even today has roots in days long gone. Clearly, this social behaviour never served the Gusii interests in the past nor does it do so today. However, we should not lose track of the fact the Gusii are now part of the larger community of Kenya, and in ideal circumstances should see themselves as Kenyan first and Gusii second.

****

There are others who believe that the Gusii are cursed[1] and hence their lack of unity. The tale goes back to the last days of the mother (Nyakomogendi) of the Gusii children (now clans). It is said to have happened in Kisumu following their sojourn migrating down from Nyimbo area in Siaya and selling in the current Kisumu region. The father (Osogo/Onsongo) had died and was buried Nyimbo. In Kisumu (which is also a Gusii word meaning kraal – *egesumua*) the mother of the Gusii children is said to have fallen terribly ill. Unable to continue with the journey, the children are said to have coldly resolved to leave her behind. She would die "soon" anyway they reasoned, according to oral claims. Noticing that she had been abandoned, Nyakomogendi, is said to have uttered an eternal curse on them, pronouncing that they will neither find unity nor peace among themselves. It is, thus, said that she pronounced a curse of fragmentation where no one would come to the help of the other when faced with an external aggressor.

As so, believers in the Gusii curse, claim this to be the source of the Gusii fragmentation and implications on their development thereof.

Gusii Fragmentation in today's Perspective

Last, but not least, there is yet another point of observation with respect to the fragmentation of yore and the impact on the Gusii population today. As we saw previously, the Gusii split almost four-fold: with Gusii clans among the Kuria, Luo as well as among the Kipsigis with the remainder retreating to their present homeland in the South Western Kenya highland region.

The pertinent question is: what would have been the current size of the Gusii population today were the community to stick together against all odds and avoid the said fragmentation? It is possible that Gusii population would be in the range of over 7 million people (as opposed to the current 3 million people) with potential consequences of playing a major role in shaping Kenya's current political landscape.

1. Rumbwa is a forested area in Bomet where most of the stolen cattle is hidden.[1]

APPENDICES

APPENDIX 1 – PICTORIAL PRESENTATION OF SOME GUSII CULTURAL ARTEFACTS

Gusii Traditional Prophet, Sakagwa Ng'iti, in the mid 19th Century

A soapstone sculpture, which is an impression of *omobani Sakagwa*, the famous Gusii traditional prophet. He lived in the mid 19th century, probably between 1870 and 1918. The prophet foretold the coming of *omo-sota (rirabuso)*, the colonial white man, to Gusii land. He also predicted the emergence of Getembe town, currently Kisii Town. The two proph-ecies were hard to unravel at that time due to his usage of a metaphorical language. For instance, he stated thus: *"Kaa rirabuso ndiche Getembe! Timomorwania kiagera nyuma ing'a agende* (There will come to our land clay-like man; he will carry fire; do not fight him, but rather live with him in peace). 'Clay-like' here refers to the white man, and 'fire' symbolizes his rifle. In his second prophecy, he said: *"Kaa amandegere n'ame Getembe, ko bono oyore n'abamura n'ere orayae* (mushrooms would sprout in Getembe and only those with strong youths would harvest them). The 'sprouting of the mushroom' here represents the buildings, offices, bustling busi-nesses, wealth and prosperity that were to comprise the development of Getembe/Kisii town. 'Strong youth' symbolizes those locals who would acquire the education and enter into businesses and other forms of economic initiations. The two prophecies came to pass as per Gusii folk history. The white man came as foretold and Getembe sprung up to become a bustling town. Nevertheless, just like his prophetic utterances, Sakagwa's death remains a mystery. According to Gusii folk history, he is said to have vanished without trace. His grave is unmarked and its location is unknown.

Otenyo Nyamaterere (Early 20th Century)

Otenyo Nyamaterere is a Gusii legend. He courageously led a contingent of six hundred (600) Gusii warriors in resisting colonial incursion into Gusii land in the beginning of the 20th Century. He organized the warriors and attacked the KAR (Kings African Rifle) soldiers at the pres-ent day Mosocho area of Bogetutu (current Kitutu Chache South). This was in 1908. Otenyo motivated and encouraged Gusii warriors by making a claim that the skin of *abasota* (white people) were "as soft as children" and therefore could easily be maimed. With this proclamation, coupled with their fighting prowess, the warriors were filled with hope and were able to repulse the KAR contingent. This came as a surprise to many, including the KAR soldiers themselves.

Otenyo later presented himself (in true warrior tradition) to the colonial administration as demanded, as one of the pre-conditions for the surrender of the Gusii to colonial rule. He was shot by the colonial officers and eventually succumbed to his injuries. It is said that he was then decapitated and his head taken to England. The Gusii elders and the Abagusii people are presently agitating for the return of his head for formal burial in his ancestral land.

A picture of a middle-aged Gusii warrior proudly displaying *ritimo,* (a spear) and *enguba* (a shield). He is adorned in traditional ceremonial regalia worn by Abagusii warriors during war/battle with their enemies. He has head-gear known as *ekiore* decorated with *chisonoi* (beads). Around his legs are *ebitinge*(ankle-rings). This outfit was regarded as befitting a true warrior within the Gusii community. The Gusii people were surrounded by hostile Nilotic communities, such as the Maasai, Kipsigis and the Luo. There was almost constant warring to fend off aggression from these groups. The Gusii warrior was charged with noble responsibility of protecting the lives of people and their property especially their livestock. The warriors were highly regarded and their respect grew with successful defence of the community. Songs were composed in praise of the warriors who successfully retrieved stolen livestock from the neighbors as were those that successfully raided and returned home with livestock to replenish their stocks. The initial Gusii, given their small numbers, would have been wiped out of existence had it not been for the acts of such brave warriors.

This is a Gusii traditional musician playing *obokano,* the Abagusii lyre. The musical instrument has eight strings made from cattle tendons with the "drum" section fashioned out of animal skin. The *obokano* took a special skill to master and was featured in most traditional ceremonies as the musical instrument of choice. A typical player was usually an elderly man adorned in *egobia (*a traditional head gear),*engobo* (clothes made from animal skin), and *chinchigiri* (metals that produced sound like a bell) worn round the ankle. *Obokano* was especially played during happy occasions, such as *ekeria-boko* (pre-weddings), *enyangi* (weddings) and *bware* (circumcision) ceremonies. The Gusii revered traditional musicas an art that was unique and respected the musicians who mastered the art. Consequently, these musicians held a special position in the society due to their entertainment gift.

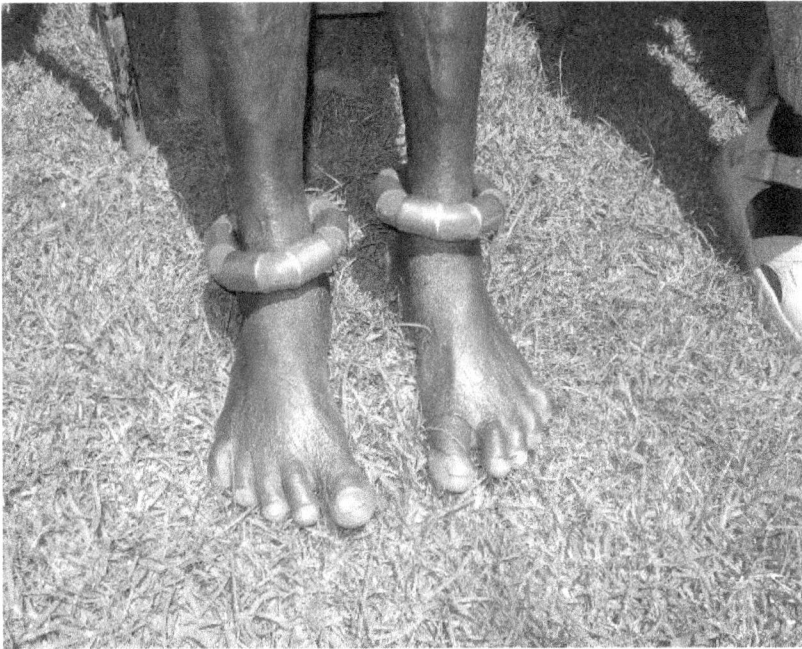

Egetinge (plural, *ebitinge*) was an ankle ring won by married Gusiiwomen. It symbolized a lifelong bond for the woman to the man to whom she was married. The woman would not leave her matrimonial home even when her husband died. The *ebitinge* were made of rings (*chintere*) that were filled with animal skin to give them the ring shape. Typically, there were six rings per *egetinge,* except for cases of big women who needed seven rings. The rings were made from smelted iron (i.e, the Gusii were smelting iron from red soil. The iron was then used to make metallic artefacts,such as spears, arrows, knives, jembes, pangas and musical instruments).

Ribina (Rain Dance):

Ribina (plural. *amabina*) was held on special occasions and was ritualistic in nature. It was specifically performed when there had been a long dry spell and the community needed to specifically dance and pray for rainfall. On such occasions, the women dressed in a special manner; typically they wore *chingobo* (traditional costumes) and *amandere* (necklaces) performed this ritualistic dance to appease the ancestors and the Gusii Supreme Being (i.e. *engoro*).

(Abagaaka ba Gusii) *Gusii Elders*

These are elders relaxing as they take traditional beer (amarwa) from a pot (enyongo) using traditional straws (chinkore; sing. orokore). The elders are sitting on traditional stools called (ebiteni or ebitumbe). These stools were carved from mature tree pieces. Omotao (a special calabash) was used to get boiling water from fire to pour into the pot containing alcohol. While pouring the hot water, women had to kneel because they wore chingobo (animal skins) which were very short. The kneeling was deemed to be a sign of respect. Gusii traditional beer was made from finger millet (obori/ wimbi) or millet (amaemba). Wimbi that had freshly sprouted was dried, ground and used as yeast to enhance the fermentation process.

Omogaka (old man)

This is an old man enjoying his traditional beer (amarwa) using orokore while the old mother (omong'ina) is giving him company.

In the background, is a gourd (ekerandi) and a basket (egetonga). The old man is also holding a spear (ritimo) in his left hand. The spear was the main weapon of choice for the Gusii and was fashioned from traditionally smelted iron. It was used for the protection of the family and property against enemies such as cattle rustlers. However, it was unusual for somebody to drink beer alone.

As noted elsewhere in the book, as much as the spear was the Gusii's weapon of choice it was effective in close combat. As such it proved inferior to the bows and arrows used by warrior groups such as the Kipsigis. Over time, the Gusii had to learn to fashion bows and arrows to counter the enemies. The two weapons proved complimentary

These Gusii women are wearing costumes called chingobo (clothes made out of animal hide/skin). From left to right, the women (abang'ina) are carrying the following tools:

a. **Ekerandi (gourd):** This gourd was and is still used to ferment milk, carry/store porridge.
b. **Egetega/enyang'eni/ Ensiongo(pot):** enyang'eni (pot) was used for cooking traditional vegetables such as chinsaga (spider flower); ensiongo (pot) was a special pot for brewing /storing traditional liquor (ebusa).
c. **Egesanda (Calabash):** This was made by carefully splitting a gourd into two equal pieces. The calabash was used for drawing water from a river, drinking milk, porridge, and water/fresh blood from animals.
d. **The basket.** It was used for carrying maize, millet, sorghum, sweet potatoes, and vegetables among other things.

Chinsonoi/Amandere/Amameka

These items were worn by women (abang'ina) for adornment and beauty. At hand is egetita (basket). The basket is for carrying cereals or vegetables.

Engobo – This is a garment worn around the waist. Unseen are chinsonoi (woven beads), worn as an inner garment also for beauty.

Amameka - This is a necklace worn to enhance beauty.

Ekonu no'omosuago (Mortar & Pestle)

Young ladies refining millet to remove husks (omoiruro) using mortars (chikonu; sing ekonu). In doing this, they use pestles (emesuago; sing omosuago) for crushing millet in the mortar to remove chaff.

Chikonu (sing. Ekonu) (mortars)

These are the Abagusii traditional mortars (chikonu). Ekonu singular for mortar was used to pound wimbi, cassava and herbal medicine to the required state and taste by way of using a pestle, omoswago. Every married woman in a Kisii homestead was expected to own a mortar and a pestle for household use

Chinyomba (huts)

These are traditional African huts. The walls were made of mud/earth and a grass-thatched roof. The bigger hut is a family house as the other one was used by the sons of the family (esaiga).

Enyomba n'ekiage (A Hut and Granary)

This is a traditional grass-thatched hut/house. The roof is made of grass called ekenyoru. The granary (ekiage) under construction is used for storing grain (maize or millet) immediately after harvesting.

Ekee (The Gusii Bowl)

This is an old lady (omong'ina) making (weaving) the gusii bowl known as ekee used for serving traditional foods including ugali made from millet/maize flour. Ekee could also be used to serve traditional beer (amarwa).

This is a complete wooven Gusii Bowl (ekee) for use. It was used to serve brown ugali (obokima bw'obori) for special occasions like marriage ceremonies, a visit from the in-laws (chikorera). Food in this vessel would remain warm for some time. Reknown ladies in fine art handcrafted the Gusii Bowl using dried finger-millet stocks after the harvest.

Gourds (ebirandi; sing. ekerandi)

These were mainly used to ferment milk, store porridge and any other liquid foods. Ebirandi were classified such that there was a special guard for the head of the family (ekerandi ki'omogaka) and for other members of the family. These containers were not only used by the Abagusii community alone but also by the Kipsigis, Maasai, and Turkana among other communities in Kenya and Africa.

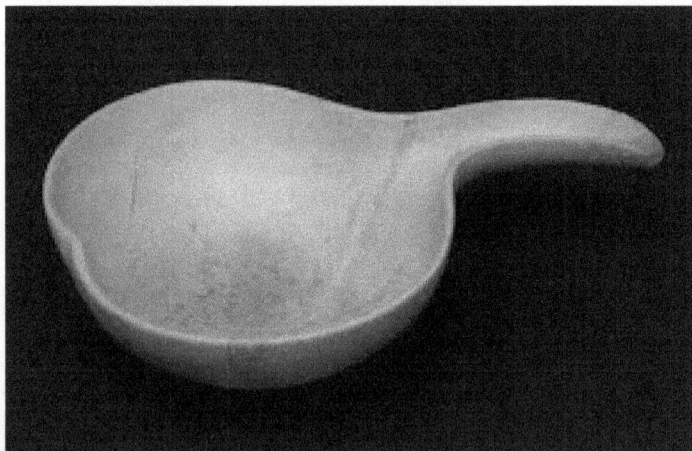

Egesanda (pl. ebisanda) (Calabash)

The calabash was made by cutting the gourd (ekerandi) in two halves. The gourd was cut into two equal parts to make a calabash. It was used for drawing water, drinking porridge or as a plate for serving food.

Chinyongo *(Water pots) balanced on a ring* (Engata)

Water Pot (chinyongo) balances on a ring (engata)
On the engata (ring) is where a pot rests i.e. for balancing purposes. The ring is made out of banana husks.

***A rock* (egetare; pl. ebitare)**

A huge rock over-looking a typical Gusii village.

Cave (**rikuruma**)

This is a subterranean chamber that remains after a mining activity or erosion of rocks and soil over a long period of time. Caves and caverns are very common in a limestone region because this rock easily dissolves in water. These features form major tourist attraction sites in Kenya and other parts of the world.

Forest (**rinani**)

This is a man-made forest of mostly eucalyptus trees. Surrounding it are human settlements and people's farms.

(NB: rinani can also be used to refer to giant or ogre.

Rigena ri'egware (Soapstone Rock)

This is a quarrying site where carvers obtain stones for their carvings. The quarry is made of a very huge rock which is cut into sizeable pieces for easy carrying and carving too

Chintuga (termites)

These insects were and are still being eaten. They can be eaten raw or fried. No cooking oil is needed because they contain 80% fat. Termites are rich in protein. They are mainly eaten by women and children. These edible termites are very popular in the Western and South-Western regions of Kenya, particularly, among the Abagusii, Luo and Abaluhya communities.

Ribururu (Pl. amabururu) (Grasshopper)

The insect/locust is eatern as food by children (and in some cases by adults). The grasshopper is rich in protein. During their peak season, they are dried for future use as food.

Obokima bw'obori (Kisii Traditional Ugali Dish made from wimbi)

This is ugali made out of millet or sorghum. The food is served in modern plates (chisani). Millet ugali was and still is served to visitors who are highly regarded among the Abagusii. No celebration is complete without (obokima bw'obori).

At the background, are chapatis (a product of wheat) served with tea; beans or beef stew.

Gusii land is generally hilly but most of it can still be used for agricultural production. The altitude is above 2000M above sea level, with annual rainfall amounting to between 2000 mm to 2500 mm per an-num, making it suitable for food crops and cash crops, such as maize, bananas, sorghum, beans, tea, coffee and pyrethrum. These factors have encouraged rapid growth of human population which has exerted much pressure on the available land. These phenomena have led to serious land fragmentation, so much that mechanization of agriculture is impossible in most parts of Gusiiland. The settlement in the above photo is clustered and the objective is to leave some space for agricultural activities in order to support the ever increasing human population. The cluster also reflects the social-cultural aspect of Abagusii preferring to stay together for pur-poses of easy facilitation and access to sharing of issues and resources.

.

This photo shows one of the most densely populated places in Kisii County. The settlement is evenly distributed across the landscape and the pressure on land is pretty obvious based on land subdivisions witnessed in this photo.

The fertility rate of women in Gusii is one of the highest in Kenya with most women having a longer lifespan due to improved medical care. This translates to many babies being born per woman. However, demographically, Kisii community is one of the medium sized tribes in Kenya. What makes them look many is the small area per Sq. Km that they occupy. The community was once surrounded by hostile Nilotic communities (i.e. Kipsigis, Maasai and Luo). For this reason, the Abagusii community could not expand outwards. This historical phenomena is responsible for the present pressure being exerted on land in Gusii land today. Consequently, there has been land degradation due to deforestation, and soil erosion that has resulted from over-cultivation and lack of modern farming techniques. However, it should also be noted that the resilience of the Gusii people have seen them overcome many challenges. The environment is, to a large extent, well conserved, enough food is produced and the surplus sold to neighbouring communities.

Omobeno (Pl. emebeno) (tree/herb):

This is a tree known as *omobeno* in Ekegusii. The tree has some medicinal value among the native population. It was used as a pain-killer.

Emesobosobo (Wild berries plant):

This is the plant that bears *chinsobosobo (*Sing. *ensobosobo*) (the berries). The *omosobosobo* was and still is used as a medicinal herb to treat intestinal complications that cause stomach upsets.

Chinsobosobo (Wild berries):

These are ripe wild berries. They grow in forested areas and woodlands. However, some farmers have domesticated these berries. They provide Vitamin C to the body as they belong to the family of fruits. However, due to the rapid growth of human population, forests have been encroached upon and these berries are rarely found. Currently they are grown for nutritional and commercial purposes.

Risosa (Pumpkin leaves):

This is a popular vegetable plant among the Gusii community. The plant is grown for its leaves and fruit (*omuongo* the pumpkin). The leaves have medicinal value especially for patients with diabetes and high blood pressure. The leaves are highly recommended for such patients. The pumpkin leaves, as a traditional dish, was mixed with *enderema* (African spinach) and served hot with *ugali*. This vegetable is rich in vitamin A. The pumpkin fruit is also rich in zinc and other minerals. There-fore, it is highly recommended for people between ages of 30 – 70 who wish to enhance their general body fitness. To grow this crop, one only needs several well dried seeds from its fruit (*omuongo*).

Chinsaga (Spider plant also known as Cleome Gynandra):

Chinsaga is the most popular vegetable among the Abagusii people. The vegetable has over several which makes it a highly benefi-cial plant. Firstly, immediately after a woman has given birth, she is given well-prepared *chinsaga* to enable her produce more milk for the baby and replenish any lost blood. Secondly, the vegetable is rich in iron which increases the haemoglobin levels in the body. The soup from the vegetable is believed to have medicinal value as well and rich in vitamins and other micronutrients. Traditionally, the vegetable was mixed with animal blood or cream to enhance its taste since no fats and/or oils were used in its preparation.

Enderema (African/Gusii spinach):

This vegetable is important and is regarded highly among the Aba-gusii people for its nutritional and medicinal value. It is thus recommended for people with diabetes, high blood pressure and stomach ulcers. Tra-ditionally, it was used to stop the growth of false teeth in children. It is said to be rich in vitamin C. It would be mixed with *chinsaga* (spider flower or amaranthus) to give it a more favourable taste. *Enderema* is also believed to have medicinal value of treating constipation. To plant this, you cut off the twigs and then plant them near a hedge or some trees where they can hang onto.

Emboga (Pigweed – Amaranthus Hybrids; also called Callaloo in the Carribean):

This vegetable was traditionally prepared and served while hot with *ugali* made from *wimbi* flour. The seeds could also be ground into powder and used to make porridge to boost the immunity of children and other sick people. A mixture of leaves from *emboga* and *ekemogamogia* (black jack) would be applied where someone had a sprain or dislocation. This vegetable was typically mixed with other vegetables (especially the bitter ones) to soften their taste. A good example is *rinagu* (the black night shed - solonum nigrum). In India, they cultivate the plant as a cereal named *Keerai.*Various sources state that this plant's extensive medicinal properties as used in other parts of the world.

Rinagu (Black Night Shed/Solanium Nigrum):

Rinagu is a popular African traditional vegetable that is consumedextensively by the Gusii. There are many other communities who consume this plant. It has a bitter taste if not well cooked. *Rinagu* can grow in the wild and/or is cultivated by farmers. It is planted by broadcasting seeds on a seedbed, then transplanting them to the main field. The vegetable is rich in vitamin C. Traditionally, cream from milk was added to it so as to sweeten it.It was served while hot with *Ugali* from maize or millet flour. Currently, *rinagu* is a common vegetable stew served in high class hotels and is grown for commercial purposes.

REFERENCES

Abagusii of Western Kenya 1909 to 1963", Ph.D. Thesis, Nairobi: University of Nairobi. Abraham, W. E. 1962. *The Mind of Africa.* Chicago: University of Chicago Press.

Abuor, C. Ojwando. 1971. *White Highlands No More.* Nairobi: Pan African Researchers. Adamson, H. 1958. *The nature of Culture.* Chicago: University of Chicago Press.

Ainsworth's Report. John Ainsworth, Report by the P. C. Kisumu to H. E. the Governor on the Recent Kisii Revolt and Its Suppression, 1908, C. O. 533/42, London: Public Record Office.

Anker, R., Knowles C. 1982. *Fertility Determinants in Developing Countries: A Case Study of Kenya.* Liege: Ordina Editions.

Ampofo, O. and Johnson-Romauld, J. D. 1987. Traditional Medicine and Its Role in the Development of Health Services in Africa. Background paper for the Technical Discussions of the 25th, 26th and 27th Sessions of the Regional Committee for Africa. Brazzaville: WHO.

Barnett, H. G. 1953: *The Basis of Cultural Change.* New York; McGraw-Hill Company Inc.

Bernard, F. 1982. "Rural Population Pressure and Redistribution in Kenya" in *Redistribution of Population in Africa.* Edited by Clarke, J. and Kosinski, L. London: Heinemann: 150-156.

Bogonko, S. 1977. "Christian Missionary Education and Its Impact on the Caldwell, S. 1976. "Towards a Restatement of Demographic Transition Theory", *Population and Development Review 2 (4):* 321-365. Caldwell, S. 1976. "Towards a Restatement of Demographic Transition Theory", Population *and Development Review 13 (2): 209 -243.*

Eisemon, Thomas Owen; Hart, Lynn M.; and Ong'esa, Elkana. *Stories in Stone: Soapstone Sculptures from Northern Quebec and Kenya.* La Federation des Co-operatives du Nouveau-Quebec and The Canadian Museum of Civilization, 1988.

Executive Council, Minutes of the Executive Council, 15 January 1908. C.O. 544/1. London: Public Record Office.

Fearn, Hugh. 1961. *An African Economy.* London: Oxford University Press. Foran, W. R., 1936. *A Cuckoo in Kenya.*London: Hutchinson.

Frank, O., McNicoll, G. 1987. "An Interpretation of Fertility and Population *Policy in Kenya", Population and Development Review* 13 (2): 209-243.

Freire, P. 1973. *Education for Critical Consciousness.*London: Sheed and Ward.

Great Britain. 1934. *Kenya Land Commission Evidence and Memoranda.* Vol. 3. London: His Majesty's Stationery Office.

History of Kisii, 1907. History of Kisii District. DC/KSI/3/4. Nairobi: Kenya National Archives. Hobley, C. W. 1902. *Eastern Uganda: An Ethnological Survey.* London: Anthropological Institute of Great Britain and Ireland.

History of the WaKisii or Abagusii, 24 May 1916, DC/KSI/3/2. Nairobi: Kenya National Archives. Intelligence Report, 1905. Intelligence Report, 3rd Kings African Rifles for 19 September, 1905, C.O. 534/1, London: Public Record Office.

Hodder, Ian. Symbols in Action: Ethnoarchaeological Studies of Material Culture Cambridge, 1992.

Jenkins 1905. E. V. Jenkins, *General Report on the Kisii Patrol,* December 1905, C.O. 534/1, London: Public Record Office.

King, Kenneth, The *African Artisan.* Heinemann, London, 1977.

Maranga, J. S. "Self-employed soapstone Carvers in Kisii," *Bureau of Educational Research,* Kenyatta   University

Ochieng, William Robert, 1974. *A Pre-colonial History of the Gusii of Western Kenya* C.A.D. 1500- 1914. Nairobi: East Africa Literature Bureau.

Ogutu, Mathias A. & Kenyanchui, Simon S. *An Introduction of African History.* Nairobi University Press. 1997

Rodney, Walter. *How Europe Undeveloped Africa.* Washington D.C. Howard University Press, 1982

Kenani, B. 1986. "Politics and Law" in Kisii District Socio-cultural Profile, Edited by Were, G. and Nyamwaya. Nairobi: Government Printer

Kenya, Government. 1989. *Kisii District Development Plan, 1989-1993.* Nairobi: Ministry of Planning. Kenya, Government. 1991. *Economic Survey 1991.* Nairobi: Central Bureau of LeVine, R. A. et.al. 1996. *Child Care and Culture:* Lessons from Africa. London: Cambridge University Press.

Kenya, Government, 2013, Nyamira County Development Profile, Nairobi Government Printer. LeVine, R. et.al. 1996. *Child Care and Culture: Lessons from Africa.* London: Cambridge University Press. LeVine, Robert A. and Barbara B. LeVine. 1966. *Nyansongo: A Gusii Community in Kenya.* New York: John Wiley & Sons.

Lonsdale, J. M. 1977. "The Politics of Conquest: The British in Western Kenya, 1894-1908", *the Historical Journal,* XX: 841 -70.

Mackay's Report. Report on Operations against the Rebellious Sections of the Kisii tribe, 1 April 1908, C.O. 533/43, London: Public Record Office.

Manning 1905.Minute by Manning, 30 September 1905, on Stewart to Lyttleton, 8 June 1905, C.O. 533/2.

Matson, A. T. 1958. "Uganda's old Eastern Province and East Africa's Federal Capital", *Uganda Journal* 20: 43-53.

Maxon, Robert M. 2003. *Going Their Separate Ways: Agrarian Transformation in Kenya*. London: Associated University Presses.

Maxon, Robert M. *Conflict and Accommodation in Western Kenya, the Gusii and the British, 1905-1963.*London: Associated Universities Press.

Mayer, P. 1950. "Privileged Obstructions of Marriage Rites Among the Gusii", *Journal of the International African Institute* 20: 113-120.

Mayer, P. 1950. *Gusii Bride wealth Law and Custom*. London: Oxford University Press.

Mayer, P. 1951. *Two Studies in Applied Anthropology in Kenya*. London: His Majesty's Stationery Office. Mungeam, G. H. 1966. *British Rule in Kenya, 1895-1912*. London: Oxford University Press.

Munro, J. F. 1975. *Colonial Rule and the Kamba*. London: Oxford University Press.

Njoroge, R. J., Bennars, G. A. 1986. *Philosophy and Education in Africa*. Nairobi. Trans Africa Press. Northcote. G. A. S. 1909. The Kisii, KNA: DC/KSI/3/2.

Northcote's Diary. Diary of G. A. S. Northcote, 1907-08. DC/KSI/4/1. Nairobi: Kenya National Archives. Nyamwaya, D. 1986. "Health and Medicine" in *Kisii District Socio-Cultural Profile* edited by Were, G. S. and Nyamwaya, D. Nairobi: Ministry of Planning and National Development, 100-111.

Nyamwaya, D. 1992. *African Indigenous Medicine: An Anthropological* Nyanza Report, 190506. Report of the Province of Kisumu for the year 1905-06, PC/NZA/1/1. Nairobi: Kenya National Archives.

Nyang'era, N. K. 2014. *The Making of Man and Woman under Abagusii Customary Laws*, Kisii, Kenya. (Self-published by author.)

Nyanza Special Report. Nyanza Province Special Report, 31 December 1909. PC/NZA/1/4. Nairobi: Kenya National Archives.

Nyanza Special Report, 1905-1906. Report of the Province of Kisumu for the year 1905-06, PC/NZA/1/4. Nairobi: Kenya National Archives.

Ochieng' W., 1974.*A Pre-colonial History of the Gusii of Western Kenya from 1500 to* 1914. Nairobi: East Africa Literature Bureau.

Ojany, F. F. and Ogendo, R. B. 1988. Kenya: *A study in Physical and Human Geography.* Nairobi: Longman.

Omwenga, P. 1969. Field Interview in Gusii region by Robert Maxon, 25 May 1969. Ongaro, Mzee. 1969. Field Interview in Gusii region by Robert Maxon, 25 May 1969.

Orvis, Stephen. 1997. *The Agrarian Question in Kenya.* Gainesville: University of Florida Press. Partington, H. B. 1905. "Some notes on the Kisii people", *East Africa Quarterly,Perspective for Policy Makers and Primary Health Care Managers.* Nairobi: AMREF.

Peters, R. S., 1966 Anker, R., Knowles C. 1982.*Fertility Determinants in Developing Countries: A Case Study of Kenya.* Liege: Ordina Editions.

Sindiga, I. 1995. *Traditional Medicine in Africa.*Nairobi: East African Educational Publishers.

Schoenbron, David Lee. 1998. A Green Place, A Good Place: Agrarian Change, Gender and Social Identity in the Great Lakes Region to the 15th Century. Nairobi: East African Educational Publishers. Thairu, K. 1975. *The African Civilization.* Nairobi: East African Literature Bureau.

Tosh, John. 1980. "The Cash-Crop Revolution in Tropical Africa: An Agricultural Reappraisal" *African Affairs,* 79, 79-94.

Uchendu, Victor - C. and Kenneth R. M. Anthony. 1975. *Agricultural Change in Kisii District, Kenya.*Nairobi: East African Literature Bureau.

Uchendu, V. C. and K.R. M. Anthony. 1975. *Agricultural Change in Kisii District, Kenya.* Nairobi: East African Literature Bureau.

Vansina, Jan 1990. *Paths in the Rainforests, Towards a History of Political Tradition in Equatorial Africa.* Madison: University of Wisconsin Press.

Were, G. S. and D. Nyamwaya eds. (1986). *Kisii District Socio-Cultural Profile.*Nairobi: Government Printer.

Wisner, B. 1976. "Health and the Geography of Wholeness." In *Contemporary Africa. Geography and Change,* edited by C. G. Knight and J. L. Newman. Englewood Cliffs: Prentice Hall, pp 81-100.

Woodward, E. M. 1902. *Précis of Information Concerning Uganda Protectorate* London: His Majesty's Stationery Office.

BIBLIOGRAPHY[1]
PRIMARY SOURCES

Kenya National Archives, Nairobi
Kisii District Annual Reports DC/KSI/1/4, DC/KSI/I/6-7
Kisii Political Records DC/KSI/3/7.
The Kisii, DC/KSI/3/2.
History of Kisii District, DC/KSI/3/4.
Diary of G.A.S. Northcote, DC/KSI/4/1.
South Nyanza District Team, Record of Meetings *PC/NZA/2/1/200.*

Public Record Office, London Colonial Office Records
Official Correspondence C.O. 533/2; 533/41-43; C.O. 533/60.
King's African Rifles C.O. 534/1.

Oral Interviews
Geteri, N. Kambini, West Kitutu Location, 1995.
Marita, S. Nyatieko, West Kitutu Location, 1995.
Mogeni, B. G. Ogembo, Bomachoge Location, 1996.
Motondi, Gerald, Bomware, Tabaka Location, 2010.
Onchomba, Cosmas, Bomware, Tabaka Location, 2010
Omwega, J. Ogembo, Bomachoge Location, 1995.
Omwenga, Peter, West Kitutu Location, 1969.
Ongaro, Mzee. West Kitutu Location, 1969.
Ngoge, N. Nyamonyo, Bomachoge Location, 1995.
Ngoge, S. O. Nyamonyo, Bomachoge Location, 1995.
Ondigi, Mama, Bomosambi, Bomachoge Location, 1996.
Ong'esa Elkanah, Bomware, Tabaka Location, 2010
Onyinkwa, Mama. Bomosambi, Momachoge Location, 1996.

---

1. The data included in this section are based on interviews with 46 traditional
   healers in Suneka Division, Bonchari, Kisii District, during 1989.

Published Primary Sources

Kenya Government. *The Constitution of Kenya, 2010.*Nairobi. Government Printer, 2010

Kenya Government. *National Atlas: Survey of Kenya.* Nairobi: Government Printer, 1991. Kenya Government. *Economic Survey* 1991. Nairobi: Government Printer,

1991. *Kisii District Development Plan,* 1989-1993. Nairobi: Ministry of Planning, 1989.

Kisii District Development Plan, 1997-2001. Nairobi: Government Printer, 1997.

Nyamira District Development Plan, 1997-2001. Nairobi: Government Printer, 1997.

*Kenya Population Census.*1962.3. Nairobi: Ministry of Planning and Economic Development, 1966. . *Kenya Population Census.*1969. 1 & 2. Nairobi: Ministry of Finance and Economic Development, 1970.

Secondary Sources Dissertations/Theses

Bogonko, S. "Christian Missionary Education and Its Impact on the Abagusii of Western Kenya, 1909 to 1963". Ph.D. Thesis, Nairobi University, 1977.

Kiagayu, N. N. "Property Ownership Structure among the Kikuyus: Its Impact on the Status of Women". M.A. Thesis, Nairobi University, 1979.

Maxon, R. M. "British Rule in Gusiiland, 1907-1963". Ph.D. Dissertation, Syracuse, 1972.

Mbori, Bob J. O. "A Study of Noun Phrase Errors among *Ekegusii* Speaking Standard Seven Pupils in Kisii District". M. Phil. Thesis, Moi University, 1994.

Monyenye, Solomon. "The Indigenous Education of the Abagusii People".M.A. Thesis, Nairobi University, 1977.

Mucai, V. W. "Matrimonial Property in Kenya: A Study in Proprietary Rights of Women". M.A. Thesis, Nairobi University, 1976.

Nyanchoka, J. "The Law of Succession Act and Gusii Customary Law of Inheritance". M. A. Thesis, Nairobi University, 1984.

Ogechi, N. O. "Trilingual Codes-witching in Kenya-Evidence from *Ekegusii, Kiswahili,* English and *Sheng'*.Ph.D. Thesis, University of Hamburg, 2002.

Ondimu, K. I. "Planning for Cultural Ecotourism in Kenya: An Assessment of Potential in the Kisii Region". Ph.D. Dissertation, Moi University, 2002.

Rajwani, F. A. " The Interaction between the Indian Traders and the Gusii in Kisii Township, 1908- 1945". B. A. Dissertation, Nairobi University, 1971.

Books

Abraham, W. E. *The Mind of Africa.*Chicago: University of Chicago Press, 1962.

Abuor, C. Ojwando. *White Highlands No More.* Nairobi: Pan African Researchers, 1971. Adamson, H.*The Nature of Culture.* Chicago: University of Chicago Press, 1958.

Anker, R, and C. Knowles. *Fertility Determinants* in *Developing Countries: A Case Study of Kenya.* Leige: Ordina Editions, 1982.

Barnett, H. G. *The Basis of Cultural Change.* New York: McGraw-Hili and Company, 1953.

Baron, R. and N. Spitzer. *Public Folklore* Washington and London: Smithsonian Institution Press, 1992. Bhatt, D. N. S. *The Prominence of Tense, Aspect and Mood* Amsterdam: John Benjamins, 1999.

Brunvand, J. H. *The Study of American Folklore: An Introduction.* New York: New York Folklore Society, 1968.

Bunting, H. ed. *Change in Agriculture.* London: Gerald Duckworth, 1969. Cammenga, Jelle. *Gusii Phonology and Morphology.* Koln: Kuper Verlag, 2002.

Clarke, J. and L. Kosinski.Eds. *Redistribution of Population in Africa.* London: Heinemann, 1982. Eliade, M. *Rites and Symbols of Initiation* New York: Harper and Row, 1965.

Fearn, Hugh. *An African Economy* London: Oxford University Press, 1961. Foran, W. R. *A Cuckoo in Kenya* London: Hutchinson, 1936.

Friere, P. *Education for Critical Consciousness.* London: Sheed and Ward, 1973. Guthrie, Malcolm. *Comparative Bantu.* Farnborough, Hants.: Gregg, 1971.

Hakansson, T. *Bride wealth Women and Land: Social Change among the Gusii of Kenya.* Uppsala: Amquiest and Wilsell lntemational, 1988.

Heyer, J. et. al. eds. *Agricultural Development in Kenya.* Nairobi: Oxford University Press, 1976.

Hobley, C. W. *Eastern Uganda: An Ethnological Survey.* London: Anthropological Institute of Great Britain and Ireland, 1902.

Hufford, J. R. *Grammar: A Student's Guide.* Cambridge: Cambridge University Press, 1997.

Hufford, M. *American Folklore: A Commonwealth of Cultures.* Washington: Library of Congress, American Folklore Center, 1991.

Kudadjie, N. *Ga and Dangme Proverbs for Preaching and Teaching.* Accra: Asempa Publishing, 1996. Letsoale, E. *Land Reform* in *South Africa: A Black Perspective.* Johannesburg: Skotaville, 1987.

LeVine, Robert A. et. al. *Child Care and Culture: Lessons From Africa.* Cambridge: Cambridge University Press, 1996.

Levine, Robert A. and Barbara B. LeVine. *Nyansiongo: A Gusii Community in Kenya.* New York: Wiley, 1966.

LeVine, Sarah. *Mothers and Wives:* Gusii *Women of East Africa.* Chicago: University of Chicago Press, 1979.

Leys, Colin. *Under-development in Kenya.* London: Heinemann, 1977.

Mair, Lucy. *Native Policies in Africa.* Edinburgh: Edinburgh University Press, 1936.

Maxon, Robert M. *Conflict and Accommodation in Western Kenya: The* Gusii *and the British, 1907-1963.*

London: Associated University Presses, 1989.

Going Their Separate Ways: Agrarian Transformation in *Kenya, 1930-1950.*London: Associated University Presses, 2003.

Mayer, P. Gusii *Bride wealth Law and Custom.* London: Oxford University Press, 1950.

The Lineage Principle in Gusii Society. London: International African Institute, 1949.

Two Studies in Applied Anthropology in Kenya. London: His Majesty's Stationery Office, 1951. Mungeam, G. H *British Rule in Kenya,* 1895-1912. London: Oxford University Press, 1966. Mbiti, J. S. *African Religions and Philosophy.* London: Heinemann, 1969.

Njoroge, R. J. and G. A. Bennars. *Philosophy and Education in Africa.* Nairobi: Trans Africa Press, 1986. Nyamwaya, D. *African Indigenous Medicine: An Anthropological Perspective for Policy Makers and Primary Health Care Managers.* Nairobi: AMREF,· 1992.

Ochieng', W. R. *Kenya's Peoples: Peoples of the South West Highlands, the Gusii.* Nairobi: Evans Brothers, 1986.

A *Pre-Colonial History of the Gusii of Western Kenya* c. *1500 to 1914.* Nairobi: East African Literature Bureau, 1974.

Ochieng', W. R. and R. M. Maxon eds. *An Economic History of Kenya.* Nairobi: East African Educational Publishers, 1992.

Ojany, F. F. and R. B. Ogendo. *Kenya: A Study in Physical and Human Geography.* Nairobi: Longman, 1988.

Okin, Sarah Moller. *Women in Western Political Thought.* Princeton: Princeton University Press, 1979.

Omosa, M. *Re-conceptualisation Food Security: Interlocking Strategies, Unfolding Choices and Rural Livelihood in Kisii District.* Hague: Service Centrum Vans Gils BV, 1998.

Oring, E. ed. *Folk groups and Folklore Genres: An Introduction.* Logan, UT.: Utah State University Press, 1986.

Orvis, Stephen. *The Agrarian Question in Kenya.* Gainesville: University of Florida Press, 1997. Payne, T. E. *Describing Morophosyntax: A Guide to Field Linguistics.* Cambridge: Cambridge University Press, 1997.

Peters, R. S. *Ethics and Education.* London: George Allan and Irvin, 1966.

Schoenbron, David Lee. A *Green Place,* A *Good Place: Agrarian Change, Gender and Social Identity in the Great Lakes Region" Century.* Nairobi: East African Educational Publishers, 1998.

Senoga-Zake, G. *Folk Music of Kenya.*Nairobi: Uzima Press, 1990. Shorthose, W. T. *Sport and Adventure in Africa.* Philadelphia: Lippincott, 1926.

Sindiga, Isaac. *Traditional Medicine in Africa.* Nairobi: East African Literature Bureau, 1995.

Suter, John ed. *Working with Folk Materials in New York State: A Manual for Folklorists and Archivists.* Ithaca: New York Folklore Society, 1994.

Thairu, K. *The African Civilization.* Nairobi: East African Literature Bureau, 1975.

Toelken, B. *The Dynamics of Folklore.* Boston: Houghton Mifflin, 1979. Tylor, E. B. *Primitive Culture.* New York: Brenteon's Press, 1924.

Uchendu, Victor and R. M. A. Anthony. *Agricultural Change in Kisii District, Kenya.* Nairobi: East African Literature Bureau, 1975.

Vansina, Jan. *Paths in the Rainforests: Towards* a *History of Political Tradition in Equatorial Africa.* Madison: University of Wisconsin Press, 1990.

Webb. V and Kembo-Sure eds. *African Voices: An Introduction to the Languages and Linguistics of Africa.,*Capetown: Oxford University Press 2000.

Were, G. S. and D. Nyamwaya. *Kisii District Socio-cultural Profile.* Nairobi: Government Printer, 1986. Whiteley, W. H. *The Tense System of Gusii.* London: King & Jarrett Ltd., 1960.

A Practical Introduction to Gusii. Nairobi: East African Literature Bureau, 1965.

Woodward, E. A. *Precis of Information Concerning Uganda Protectorate*. London: His Majesty's Stationery Office, 1902.

Yudelman, M. *African on the Land*. Cambridge: Harvard University Press, 1964.

Zeitlin, S.*A Celebration of American Family Folklore*. Cambridge, M. A.: Yellow Moon Press, 1982.

Articles

Amide, A. A. "What is a Class? A Study of *Kiswahili*". *SOAS Working Papers In Linguistics* 22 (1994): 75- 105.

Ben-Amos, D. "Toward a Definition of Folklore in Context". *Journal of American Folklore* 84 (1971): 3-5. Caldwell, S. "Towards a Restatement of Demographic Transition Theory". *Population and Development Review* 2, 4 (1976): 321-65.

Davy, J. 1. M. and Derek Nurse. "Syntactic Versions of Dahl's Law: the Multiple Applications of a Phonological Dissimilation Rule". *Journal of African Languages and Linguistics* 4 (1982): 157-95.

Frank, 0 and G. McNichol."An Interpretation of Fertility and Population Policy in Kenya". *Population and Development Review* 13,2 (1987): 209-43

Harbeson, John. "Land Reform and Politics in Kenya, 1954-1970". *Journal of Modem African Studies* 9 (1971): 231-51.

Lonsdale, 1. M. "The Politics of Conquest: The British in Western Kenya, 1894- *1908*". *The Historical Journal* 20 (1977): 841-70.

Kingston, 1."The Expansion of the Gusii Tense System". *Current Approaches to African Languages* 2 (1983): 31-56.

Matson, A. T. "Uganda's Old Eastern Province and East Africa's Federal Capital". Uganda Journal 20 (1958): 43-53.

Mayer, Philip. "Gusii Initiation Ceremonies". *Journal of the Royal Anthropological Institute* 83 (1953): 9-36.

"Privileged Obstructions of Marriage Rites Among the Gusii", *Journal of the International African Institute* 20 (1950): 113-20.

Partington, H. B. "Some Notes on the Kisii People". *East Africa Quarterly* 2 (1905): 328-29. Stephens, R. "A Study of Swahili-English Code switching in England". *SOAS Working Papers in Linguistics* 10 (2000): 333-54.

Tosh, John. "The Cash-Crop Revolution in Tropical Africa: An Agricultural Appraisal", *African Affairs,* 79 (1980): 79-94.

Internet Sources

Dorson, R. What is Folklore? http//www.nyfolklore.orglresource/what. html Georges, M. Sound Archives: A Guide to Their Establishment and Development. http//www.nyfolklore.orglresource/what.html

Unpublished Secondary Sources

Ampofo, O. and J. D. Johnson-Romauld, *Traditional Medicine and Its Role in the Development of Health Services in Africa.* Background Paper for the Technical Discussions of the 25th, 26th, and 27th Sessions of the Regional Committee for Africa. Brazzaville: WHO.

Hakansson, T. Landless Gusii Women: A Result of Customary Land Law and Modem Marriage Patterns. Working Papers in African Studies Programs, Department of Anthropology, University of Uppsala.

Koning, A. M. *Preliminary Notes on Chindwaki of North Mugirango.*

GLOSSARY

Abagaka be'egesaku	lineage elders
Abagaka	elders
Abako	the in-laws
Abakungu bateneine	infertile women
Abamenyi	individuals incorporated overtime into the homestead
Abamoreki	autopsies, punctures part of the body to release pressure
Abanto baminto	Our people
Abanyaisaga	members of the village effort (work) groups
Abanyamosira/abanyanabi	sorcerers
Abare	circumcised boys or girls
Amabuko	twig from a ritualistic plant
Amarwa	traditional brew/beer
Amarwaire	diseases
Amasangia	punishment given to anyone committing adultery or extra-marital affairs
Arwane bobisa	to fight the enemy
Arwane Irianyi	to fight to the West
Arwane Maasai	to fight Maasai
Arwane sigisi	to fight Kipsigis
Arwane Sugusu	to fight to the East
Aye okwanigwe na moeti na mogendi	you will be greeted by passersby and travellers
Chieni	Luo elder
Chinsaga	Spider Flower
Chinsoni	Abagusii Code of Conduct
Chinyanduri	stinging nettle
Chisaiga	huts for the unmarried sons
Chisokoro	ancestors
Ebarimo	a mad person
Ebibiriria	evil eyes
Ebintere	a young blacksmith man

Ebisara	false teeth/abnormal development of milk teeth
Ebisarate	Military encampments
Ebisimba biairire engoko	the wild cats have taken the chicken
Ebisimba	indigenous wild cats
Ebitinge	specially designed ankle rings
Ebitoro	gifts
Eburu	defence systems
Echorwa	bride's consent to get married
Echorwa	the second day of the wedding ceremony
Ee mwana one borania chiombe na abanto	yes my child have the blessings of having a lot of cattle and children
Ee sanyera abanto	Unite all the Gusii Warriors
Ee sanyera	yes, unite
Ee tiga areme mboremo bwamoborire	Yes let her dig because, she does not have where to dig
Ee twanchire	yes we have agreed
Eeri y'egesicho	the apron bull
Eeri ya egekobo	the bull of returning the bride
Eeri ya enyangi	the bull for the wedding
Eeri yomoyega	the bull of celebration
Egechabero	decorating the bride
Egesagane	uncircumcised girl
Egesaku/Ebisaku	the smallest socio-political unit
Egesanda	calabash
Egesieri kia bweri	the door facing the cattle kraal
Egesieri kia bweri	door leading to the mother's house
Egesieri ki'egesaku	breached door
Egesingero	love cup
Egetaorio	the first day of the wedding ceremony
Egetono	small pot
Egoree	billy goat
Ekeera/egekuba egeku	asthma
Ekeore	a special head dress
Ekerecha/ebirecha	evil spirits
Ekerende egekungu	the female stick
Ekerende egetwani	the male stick
Ekeriboko	celebration (eating) at the bride's home

Embori ya amaseko	the laughter goat
Embori ya enyangi	wedding goat
Embori ya magokoro	grandmother's goat
Embori ya omosubati	goat of the sister
Emebiara	the suckling cow's offspring
Emeino	traditional male songs
Emingichi	ram
Emuma	a supernatural oath
Enchage	Zebra
Enda y'enchogu	the stomach of an elephant
Endurume	epilepsy
Endwari ya inda	splenomegaly
Engo/Abagirango	Leopard
Engoge	Baboon
Engoro	supreme Being
Enguba	shield
Engubo	Hippopotamus
Enkuri	one who cried during circumcision
Enyabububu	mysterious
Enyaini/endonge	liver cirrhosis
Enyamosono/enyamorero	gonorrhoea
Enyangi	wedding
Enyimbo ya obogambi	stick/staff of rulership
Esabarianyi	a ritualistic song sang by boys accompanying the circumcised
Esamusamu	boils
Esigani	a go-between
Esimbore	Abagusii circumcision song
Esosera	malaria
Esuguta	traditional ritualistic grass
Esumati	a jacket
Esumu	poison
Etureti	clan council,
Eturet	Gusii indigenous judicial structure
Etwon	cockerel
Inguba emo yana koira ngombe roche	one shield cannot take cows to the river (meaning "Unity is Strength".)

Kabianga	place where nothing flourished
Karwe isiko riaito	leave our front-yard
Makomoke oremire nchera igoro	my aunt has dug on the road
Masaba	Ecological zone in the East
Misiri	Egypt
Monchari omache chindiba chiobokendu	the people who originated from the deep sea
Moteoitimo	herbs
Mwana one onywe mache maya na ase ogotacha obonyasi boseboke	my child drink good water and may the grass on the ground you step on sprout
Mwanchire twensi tochake esegi na ababisa baito Abagusii	have you all agreed that we declare war against Kipsigis
Ngararo	epic battle fought by Gusii & Maasai people in Transmara
Obogomba	women infertility
Ogoita kwamosiabano	manslaughter
Ogokama eng'iti enene yarure roche	the mysterious beast from the lake
Ogokonwa	bewitched
Ogosonia	arousing sexual desire
Ogosonsorana	cleansing ceremony
Okoira chiombe oboko	delivering dowry to the in-law's home
Okomana chiombe	dowry negotiations
Okoosia	protective ritual
Okorigia omoiseke	identification of a suitable girl
Okoromia omware eng'iti	letting the snake bite the initiate
Okorora omoiseke	a visit to see the girl
Omobani/ababani	prophet/prophets
Omobari/ababari	traditional surgeon(s)
Omochie	homestead
Omoebia	healer dealing with love charms
Omogaka bwo'omochie	The family/homestead patriarch
Omogaka	Gusii elder
Omogere	a luo person
Omogomba/abagomba	barren/infertile woman/women
Omoimari	best maid to the bride
Omoiseke	a young circumcised girl

Omoisia omoke ateta ngina	a young man to copulate with his mother
Omoisia omoke mbororo bwamorire	the young boy is in pain
Omoisia	uncircumcised boy
Omokireki	one who uses medicine to prevent diseases and misfortunes
Omokumi/abakumi / abanguru	member of council of 'judges'
Omokundekane	pastor/priest/priestess
Omokururo/ekenyamoguku	used when measles appears in children
Omomoreki	one who performs localized blood letting to relieve pain
Omomura	a young circumcised boy
Omomura	young man
Omongwansi	best man to the bridegroom
Omonyamete	herbalist
Omonyibi	rain maker
Omorabi/abarabi	traditional birth attendant(s)
Omoragori	diviner
Omoriori	witch smeller
Omorogi/abarogi	witch(es)
Omosari	the initiator/circumciser
Omosari/abasari	initiator/circumciser
Omosegi	sponsor as referred to matters of circumcision
Omosichi	assistant sponsor
Omotang'ani	a girl from the bridegroom's home/place
Omotembe	Nandi Flame
Ororeria	generation
Orosao rwa abana	infantile diarrhoea
Orosao	diarrhoea
Orotuba	specially designed crib: manger
Orwaki	Forts
Osaosao	the battle between the Abagusii and the Kipsigis

Oyo otarochi tigache kwerorera	whoever has not seen let him come to see
Riburu	ritualistic bed for the initiate/ circumcised
Rikwege/amakwege	chronic wound
Risaga/amasaga	a temporal effort group of co-operative neighbours
Ritana/amatana	the juicy meat between the forelimbs
Riuga/amauga	bone marrow
Tata na baba boraniango	Dad and Mum 'consult' each other

www.ingramcontent.com/pod-product-compliance
Lightning Source LLC
Chambersburg PA
CBHW030401270326
41926CB00009B/1212